50 Camels and She's Yours

Tales from FIVE WOMEN across FIVE CONTINENTS

Stephanie Green

Françoise Hivernel

Sally Haiselden

Seeta Siriwardena

Jane Wilson-Howarth

Cover design: studiomarc.co.uk marc@studiomarc.co.uk

50 Camels and She's Yours
Tales from FIVE WOMEN across FIVE CONTINENTS

Introduction

For more than 13 years, five well-travelled women have been meeting to discuss their writing. Being travellers, gathering has been intermittent but we have tried to meet once a month to share food and views about current events then read aloud our pieces of writing, discuss them and encourage one another.

Between us we have lived and worked in and visited a large part of all five continents. Two of us have come to live in Britain so bring a new perspective to their adoptive motherland. We pause, we look, we listen, we chat and compare and aspire to gain an understanding of our destinations. Between us we speak Amharic, Arabic, Bahasa Indonesia, French, German, Japanese, Nepali, Sinhalese, Swahili and a smattering of Acholi, Urdu and Waray. We are unashamed eaves-droppers and people-watchers; we have written about more than 30 countries.

Although we are very different characters, ages and professions and our styles of writing contrast one with another, we are kindred spirits – inquisitive and in need of new challenges – women who take professional risks and strike out to explore new cultures, and novel regions. We have all travelled alone. Some tales hark back 40 years while others – like Jane's medical work with Syrian refugees last autumn – are bang up to date.

Stephanie and Sally's warm self-deprecating writing closely observes the bewildering array of situations they find themselves in.

Françoise' lyrical prose focuses on the inner dimension of her actual journeys while evoking the atmosphere of the desert and home fires.

1

Seeta writes wisely about racism and how India looks to a Sri Lankan and as Jane travels to wild and remote places she discusses patients, family and other wildlife.

This anthology is aimed at travellers of all styles: armchair, wishful thinkers and adventurers alike. It is particularly aimed at women who think, 'Oh, I wish I could do that!' Come with us and be inspired by the extraordinary journeys of five ordinary women: two medical doctors, a teacher, an accountant and a psychoanalyst.

You Don't Have to Go Far to Travel (but it helps)
Sally Haiselden

In fact you only need to go as far as the end of your street to enter a new world, see a new culture. St Philip's on Mill Road on a Saturday evening during winter. Liam arrived before me with his large, black holdall and had staked his claim to a corner of the floor. I was busy rolling out mats, sleeping bags and liners for the other guests. Liam may have chosen a quiet corner but it did not help him get to sleep. I kept him company until 2 a.m. He could not lie down because his stomach hurt too much so we sat up and shared easy silences, me talking of my travels, he sometimes commenting whilst he sandpapered the yellow nicotine stains off his fingertips. After a while he reached into the pocket of his blue anorak and brought out a tin. Taking the lid off revealed an orderly grooming set. He exchanged his sandpaper for a finer grade. By the end of my shift he had finished both hands.

Liam was not there the following week. It seems he asked someone to call him a taxi very early on the Sunday morning to take him to A and E because of his stomach but no one had seen or heard from him since in the other temporary shelters set up for homeless males during the winter. I met Pedro again though. He was not as reticent as Liam. He was Angolan by way of Portugal and had been over here for 16 years. I ate with him and as we tucked into the sausages, mash and gravy he started to talk about his mum's cooking back home. I let him talk and allow it all out of him and to wash over me in warm waves of African sunlit images of an uncomplicated life lived in nature. After a while he excused himself and went out for a cigarette. Whilst he was gone the team leader Carol came over and said, 'We nearly lost him this week you know.' The confusion was clear on my face. 'Attempted suicide. We're giving him a lot of support.' Suddenly the images in my mind were splattered in

3

blood from gunfire and the Angolan civil war came to a church in Cambridge.

For both Liam and Pedro all I could do was listen and empathise. Or is that sympathise? I know in the right-on culture of Britain at the moment (in fact I guess we cannot even call it 'Britain' for too much longer) it seems the word I might use to describe my attempt at trying to understand someone else's life experiences is incorrect. All I do know is that it is a thin line between them and me. A lost job, a failed relationship, a politician's careless word sending a country into turmoil, a soldier's finger on a trigger and stability and security are shattered. And in our homes of snug wood burners, luxury marshmallow hot chocolate, Sunday Times travel supplements and smug Danish '*hygge*', we do not always let ourselves acknowledge the world inhabited by others at the end of the street.

Then Serena turned up. I had heard her come in whilst I was chatting to Pedro. 'It's your turn now to keep her company. She's mad. She shouldn't be here. She's got issues with immigration you know and the police want to speak to her. She can't stay here as it's all male. We're trying to find alternative accommodation. And she keeps asking me to do things for her,' Carol reported. Serena was not mad. This time it helped that I had travelled far. Looking at her wearing a red, boldly patterned dress and a white feathered hat on top of a wig, holding her bible, I was met by all the matriarchal African mamas I had ever known holding court in the shade of their verandas. 'You look the age of my daughter. Come sit,' she said. 'I was looking at this verse in John. Look, I underlined it before because it spoke to me and is again today.' She read it aloud and explained to me what it meant to her. 'Can you get me some water to drink?' and this dutiful daughter did so. Like Pedro she wanted to talk and I let

4

her. I let the mellow African intonation, smile and gestures wrap me in comforting nostalgia and I understood her.

Later I explained to Carol. Many Africans are very knowledgeable about the bible because it is the only book that is easy to get hold of. Many are regular churchgoers and use the book to help them. She is old and in her culture her sons' wives and their daughters would wait on her and take instructions from her. She is used to being listened to. I know this I said because I have seen and listened to, befriended and served myself ladies like Serena. Don't judge her.

And she is tough. It seems Serena, now 70, was invited to the UK a number of years ago, by her nephew and English wife to look after their Down's syndrome baby daughter whilst they went out to work. The wife's family sponsored her for her visa from Zimbabwe, so leaving sons and nephews in her own home, Serena booked her ticket. However, as she landed at Heathrow the baby died and Serena was no longer needed. She moved to Sheffield where there was a Zimbabwean community and worked as a cleaner and carer. After an issue in her rented accommodation she packed up, put her suitcase and herself on a National Express bus to Cambridge because she wanted to, 'explore this fine university town'. She arrived but her suitcase with all her documentation in did not. To cut a long story short, or to listen to a shrewd lady who has had to survive by her wits for most of her life and was practising a narrative which would explain her predicament to immigration officers, that is how she ended up homeless in the foyer of St Philip's church talking to me and me to her. 'I have to go to the police station on Monday morning,' she said. 'Which church is open tomorrow so I can sleep well to prepare myself?' 'The night shelters for women won't take her tonight,' Carol told me, 'because she's here illegally,' she added. 'She can stay here.' Together we arranged some screens in the foyer into a private space and Carol escorted her to the toilet whilst at her request I arranged her things. Then with dignity this lady bade us goodnight and we could hear her rummaging in plastic bags and shifting to get comfortable on her mat. In the morning after I had served her tea and toast she left the same dignified manner, pushing her shopping trolley out into the foggy darkness and then vanishing.

A few days later I was in London with my bike standing in line at Liverpool Street station so I could find out the rules about bikes on trains in rush hour. Expecting the worst, I wheeled my bike up to the desk manned by Hassan as his badge announced. 'What type of ticket do you have ma'am?' I told him. 'In that case you can travel at any time.' This was not the answer I had expected. 'Are you sure? With a bike?' The start of his answer started to get my back up, that familiar reaction to the sense that people working in customer service find all customers stupid or an inconvenience. 'Ma'am, I cycle a lot myself and…' It was the way he said it, the smile spreading on his face. 'Are you from Uganda?' I blurted out. He beamed more broadly. 'How did you guess?' I just knew. 'I spent two years living in Kitgum,' I explained. We continued. 'Where are you from?' 'Do you like my country?' 'Why are you here?' The warmth and connection were real and genuine. We joked. We laughed. We asked after each other's families. I asked him his thoughts on the English weather. The queue behind was not important, neither was the fact that he was at work. He was working, Uganda style, in a friendly manner at a relaxed pace and I eventually wheeled my bike away made happy by this chance encounter where having travelled far had come home to roost.

AFRICA

Fifty Camels and She's Yours
Seeta Siriwardena

Just after sitting her A-levels, my eighteen-year-old daughter
announced she wanted to visit Egypt. As she had never travelled
abroad on her own, I thought the safest solution was for me to
travel with her, as I too had always wanted to go there.

Almost everybody we spoke to advised us that Egypt is
not a country for females to visit on their own. 'It is perilous', 'it
is risky', 'it is foolish,' was all that we heard.

The trip we booked included a cruise to Luxor. We flew
into Cairo and had a wonderful few days seeing the sights,
including the camel ride which left me so sore that I preferred to
stand and not sit down for a few hours after.

Next was the cruise from Cairo slowly down to Luxor.
After a couple of stops I noticed a handsome young man trying
to attract my attention. He wore the garb of a prince with heavily
decorative gold jewellery hanging from his neck. A man held a
large parasol over him all the time and there was a retinue of
three or four men always around him. He proved to be a Nubian
prince.

At one of the stops he spoke to me saying he wanted my
daughter. He offered five camels for her. I ignored him. At each
subsequent stop he would come to the quayside and, on seeing
me, call out, 'Mama, mama!' and proceed to increase his offer of
the number of camels until finally it reached fifty. Can you
imagine how I would bring fifty camels back to England?

A middle aged English couple who were on board the
cruise ship had noted all this, and they suggested that we should
join the two of them. I readily accepted the offer. We were very
glad to have met such nice people. From then onwards we
always formed a foursome when we got down from the boat to
visit any tourist sites. We didn't see the Nubian prince again.

How to get Yourself onto a Camel
Françoise Hivernel

I have never known these beasts as being friendly to humans.
The amount of varying noise a camel makes is quite
extraordinary and very difficult to make sense of. Happy,
unhappy, tired, hungry, cross, who will know... their almost
prehistoric shape, angular, is not one which is easily readable.
Well, once all is said, how do you mount one of these beasts? It
must be made to sit properly on its haunches with its folded four
legs. That in itself is already a tour de force and better left to its
handler. Then you try to climb on the folded leg by pulling and
holding onto the various bits hanging down from the sitting part
higher up on top of the camel and from there, haul yourself into
the saddle. Well it sounds quite easy and it is after you have done
it a few times, but for a youngster, who had never been on one of
these beasts before, it is not so. Greg my 10-year-old son had
successfully encountered horses many a time before, but never a
camel. In the process of climbing the beast, his light weight
enrolled itself, with his arms firmly gripping around the camel's
long neck, it then raised its back legs and then its front ones
leaving Greg dangling until a camel herder slung him back onto
the saddle with one big palm on his small bottom. Good scoring
man! Trying to embrace the camel from an angle it obviously
didn't like was a mistake. Once on it, comfortably settled at the
top, it was bliss, and we travelled along the Jordanian Wadi Rum
desert, in relative silence once all our camels had settled
themselves into the measured rhythm of the walk.

Mass Murder before Breakfast
Sally Haiselden

There are lots of unidentified sounds after dark in a house in the Ugandan bush. Just before dawn I was woken by a new sound – a metallic clonking, which made me think the hot water tank was about to boil over again. I checked that I had indeed turned the heater off before going to bed. The noise persisted so I looked out of the window to see the vocalist – a distressed, handsome black, white and tan bird, sat on a rock with a mouse in its bill. It was a harassed warning cry and I saw why when a small bird of prey with almost luminous slate blue plumage fluttered down to intimidate the mouse out of the beak of the agitated bird. The former with the strength panic can give you, managed to push its way through the fence into the dense undergrowth beyond. The mouse was oblivious to its value in death.

Other night voices are variously owned by geckos, frogs, owls, cicadas and the bats which roost under my metal roof. There are scrapings and scratchings inside too which I have my suspicions about but would rather not identify just yet. However, the murdered population were silent, dogged and relentless.

I walked towards my kitchen area to prepare morning coffee to find ants had invaded. It was a double flanked attack. One group were streaming in from a hole in the wooden window frame – three parallel columns heading purposefully down the wall and around the sink. A smaller commando platoon was entering through a crack in the tiles in the shower and finding a route through the wall to the kitchen taps. We think ants are always after sugar or jam but this army were not or I had ambushed them early enough. If you observe columns of ants, it is often difficult to understand as a human the point of their movement or their destination. I'm sure it must make sense to an ant.

10

There were thousands of them, five-millimetre-long automatons, advancing. I could not leave them, as I could not predict where they would end up. The dining table? Bookshelves? Bed?! Once established would I ever oust them?

I did have my reservations about stopping them and I did apologise as I raised the can of Mortein Doom and prepared to kill. My food preparation area and sink were doused in chemicals with the capability of 'Kills Instantly' as claimed in big letters on the can. Below were nine pictures of species of crawling and flying victims. I used to crawl once – I did wonder what the long term effects on me of spraying might be as on the back I read under 'First Aid and Toxicological Information: antidote - none.'

The massacre was over in seconds. The floor below the sink was black with bodies. The off-white shower tray now had a dark black rim round it. The house smelt of danger – the aroma of nerve paralysing gas. I drank my coffee outside.

I recounted the dawn raid to colleagues in the staffroom. 'Yes, and I committed mass murder before breakfast!' The irony was not lost on them in this country of Idi Amin and Kony and his child-abducting Lord's Resistance Army.

Kennedy, the science teacher advised, 'You need to get some paraffin Sally and a little cloth and rub it around the windows and doors. Then it will keep them out. It's good against snakes too.' I am not sure I am ready for reptilian, potentially venomous, invaders yet, at least not before breakfast.

Botswana in a Nut Shell
Françoise Hivernel

It was time again to go and visit Christophe, my eldest son, who was doing Community Development Work, at Majakathata, near Gaborone, which is the capital of Botswana.

However, things are never quite straight forward when one travels in Africa, and I soon discovered that I couldn't fly directly to Gaborone from Europe but had to go via Johannesburg and then double back onto Botswana. Of all the possible ways to do it, this appeared the simplest, the quickest and the cheapest of all.

After discussing this problem with Chris via his temperamental mobile telephone, we agreed that he'd come and pick me up at the airport and that we would take a leisurely drive back together, north through South Africa to reach Botswana. So this was the plan when I booked my ticket and started the journey.

In the early hours of the morning of the said journey, I elbowed my fellow passenger into awareness and got him to raise the window blind so that I could see what was outside after that long night flight. I knew that we had just crossed into Botswana from the computer map charting the progress of the plane and lo and behold I just had time to see the huge expanses of the salt flats near the Okavango Delta before we hit the clouds again. In Johannesburg airport, having arrived three hours behind schedule, my yearning mother's heart searched for her elusive son. As I couldn't see him anywhere, I went to the bank get some coins to telephone him and tried desperately to get the said coin-fed telephones available in the airport to work. The last one I tried swallowed my remaining coins, but still refused to work, and I sat forlorn wondering what to do. In the meantime, slim young man started picking money from 'my' telephone box

12

with a hair pin... Without a thought, I sprang up and grabbed his black arm spluttering: 'But...this is My Money and I need it to call my son!' He looked at me in disbelief, then laughed and said, 'Come on mother, I'll help you.' He then dialled Chris's number correctly and I got through … I gave the man a huge smile and he left giggling!

'Where are you Chris?' I wailed.

'In Gabs, Mum.'

'But you were supposed to come and fetch me in Johannesburg...' Then I heard something slurred which I did not understand...and then the affirmation that he was still in Gaborone dawned…

'But... how am I going to reach you?' I whined.

'Oh stop being silly Mum. Catch a bus. There is a direct one from Jo'burg to here, it only takes about a day... or fly and I'll pick you up from the airport.'

As one having flown all the night to see my 'darling' son, the beast of burden, lugging her huge old blue backpack, a suitcase and other bits of luggage for her renegade offspring, mumbled, 'I'll catch a plane.' I could not even think of a long bus trip. A few hours later, Gabs came into sight – I saw some mountains on the way and encountered biltong in the cabin. In case you do not know about biltong, it is a sort of dried meat made out of beef, a specialty of South Africa. I rushed out of the airport expecting at long last to meet him, but still he wasn't there. I borrowed forcefully the mobile phone of an airport employee using my status as an elder and the excuse that I needed to call my son. Chris finally arrived half an hour later with good excuses as he always has, so I had to grudgingly pardon him. It was a good initiation to Botswana life where nothing ever runs according to plan and timetables are immaterial.

13

The other mind-numbing discovery was about the flatness of Botswana. It is an immense plain with the odd and spurious cliff rising here and there. Perhaps the absence of any natural obstacle of any size helped shape the lack of boundaries of the people there too!

My memories of these two weeks are getting blurred already, a haze of heat, sweat and hard work at the craft shop, where Christophe officiated. I came to appreciate the challenge these young kids with minimum attention span had but enjoyed seeing their delight at witnessing their artistic abilities emerging and their curiosity at exploring new avenues. I also loved creating my own brand of bush jewellery using nuts, feathers and recycled bits and Christmas cards of home-made batik. But over everything else by far my biggest pleasure was of seeing Christophe living every minute to the full. My motherly pride glowed at seeing all the things Chris had achieved. He had raised money for the handicapped, as well as money for the bee keeping project. He had established markets for the craft shop and had computers given to the project coming together with solar panels. He helped the junior football team as well as too many other projects which I cannot remember. On another level I also admired his dancing skills at first hand, during a party launched in my honour in the compound of the Botswana family he was lodging with. His ability to drink gallons had not abated either! He was a good match in every way for the local lads and the many girls after him...

One morning we had a hilarious battle with cockroaches descending like black treacle from the corrugated iron roof of my shack. They came down the wall, probably dislodged by the racket that the man repairing that very roof was making. We developed a technique resembling cricket to cope with them. I would brush them down with a broom and Chris would bat

14

them out of the room as soon as they hit the floor with another broom in one well-coordinated hit and the cat in the courtyard would finish them off. We had such a laugh.

We had great times in the bush too, where one day we went to bring water to the bush clearing team in the Mokolodi Reserve and arrived at a ghost camp. Shining leather boots were at the ready by the tents, but not a soul was to be seen, so we went to track them down. After two hours of arduous walking, up and down mountain sides we found no trace of them and returned sweaty and caked in powdery yellow soil which had turned into compacted mud. We were sunburnt and parched. The huge containers of water on our pick-up truck called to us and with the help of a hose pipe we stripped to wash ourselves and our clothes and hung them to dry on the thorn bush fence around the tents. Then we set about transferring the water in our barrels into the camp's own containers. If anyone had arrived, they would have wondered what these two white, barely clothed people were doing in the middle of nowhere. We hoped that we were only been watched by ostriches and kudus (gazelles). Once the water was safely into the camp's barrels, we got into our cleanish dried clothes and left. The mystery of the missing bootless crew still remains!

The only purposefully organised sightseeing which I did was on the Sunday, where we walked into the bush for about 10 miles, to go and see some bushman rock paintings. It had just rained and the bush was miraculously covered with all sorts of refreshed and strong smelling flowers. It was almost as if we could see them coming up and opening as we stared. We eventually prised ourselves from the mesmerising vegetation and arrived in the small village of Manayana. And there by trial and error we found the site at the very base of the Kolobeng Hill. We managed to locate some depicting antelopes and giraffes. The paintings were not easy to see but those that we found were good and were created around 2,000 years ago probably by the San people. We retraced our steps lost in a thoughtful dream-like state induced by the blazing heat.

The last night I spent in Botswana was magical. We had a sumptuous meal at the restaurant in the Mokolodi reserve and I drove the truck back on an empty road under African stars. Thanks Chris for that and I won't tell anyone about the cognac or about the paralytic state you were in!! I'd like to think that it was because I was going back home the next day and you were soooo sorry to see me go. Hmmm...!

For the return journey, I got a bus ticket in Gabs and had the amazing pleasure of getting two discounts. The first one was because I was over 60 years old and the other discount was for having a YHA card! The cost of the journey down to Jo'burg was reduced to very little and took about six very worthwhile hours to savour my Botswana adventure. Then in no time at all, I was boarding the plane for London, already dreaming of the next chance to go back.

Bugs in the Butter and Other Places
Sally Haiselden

The good thing is the bugs here in Uganda are seasonal. The bad thing is that there is always one species in season. At the moment it is tiny black flies, small enough to come in through the mosquito mesh. They then sizzle on the lights, crawl between the buttons of the keyboard, drop into your butter, water, always extra protein for dinner. They don't bite but are everywhere at night. More annoyingly they get up your nose and into your ears. You start to cough them, see them and itch. By morning, except for a scattering of black corpses on the tablecloth, they have all gone. Where to? Some into the geckos that look particularly plump at the moment. Outside is also full of bugs. There are huge spiders' webs dangling from the mango trees at head height. I can't see the spiders but they must be around. The ground is littered with glued together leaves; small nests made by wasps. Carpenter wasps, black, leggy things inhabit the shelter where the chicken feed is kept. Sinister and quiet, they take you unawares with stings that have your hand swollen and itchy for days. There are also creatures, the same colour as the sand that scuttle across the compound in front of you. I haven't been able to move fast enough to follow one of these small whirlwinds to see the camel spider within. And then there is the perpetual hazard of bugs and your underwear. The putsi fly likes to lay eggs in your drying underwear and when the eggs come in contact with human skin they hatch and burrow into some quite private places and become itchy boils.....

Luckily I am not squeamish and don't mind getting bitten or dive-bombed. I see it as part of being a VSO volunteer to be stoic about such occupational hazards. There is one potential hazard though which I really must take seriously with the approaching dry season and that is snakebite. Last week I finally

17

felt like a true expat in Africa when I had my first snake experience. A long lime green snake undulated across the road in front of the truck. It was moving really quickly so I instantly decided because of that and its colour it had to be a green mamba. Raymond, my Ugandan driver and Expert in All Things commented, 'Yes, it is poisonous,' so that helped. I had read that snakes can get flipped up onto running boards or under bonnets to emerge really pissed off when the vehicle stops. The Expert was sure he had seen this one in the rear view mirror but I reminded myself to be like a true African explorer and check the wing mirror before exiting the truck. When we stopped though I forget and so did the snake if it was around. Seriously though, last night unusually we drove home in the dark and spotted two puff adders on the road. 'You wait,' said Raymond, 'You will hear lots of stories about snakebite.' Upon our return, Bosco the guard proudly came to report that he had killed a Very Poisonous Snake (they all are here, apparently) which had been eyeing up Diana the guard dog and her new pups. The Finnish family's children have not been so visible charging around the compound of late. Miko the dad had seen two large black cobras in broad daylight near their house. Their mum Henni is going to buy some anti-venom in Kampala and store it in Kitgum. An over-reacting mum, or wise insurance policy?

Why Mauritania?
Françoise Hivernel

And why not I could reply? A question of chance... After all, I
could just as well have found myself in Paris, Cambridge or
Timbuktu to celebrate the opening of the new Millennium. But
it's a long time since I stopped believing in chance. What does
Chance mean? It is a word that tells anything which one could
wish, a word to plug a hole with, a word used when one cannot
find an explanation. 'Chance', 'Luck' (good or bad of course) is
an excuse for not looking deeper at what is going on, for not
staring into the glaucous depth of the unconscious. That depth
terrifies me because I am afraid of what may be hidden there.
Just as Helen of Troyes in 'La Guerre de Troyes n'aura pas lieu' (a
play written by Jean Giraudoux in 1935) said 'I only see what I
love, the rest I do not'. Vertigo is taking hold of me, am I going to
fall? Be swallowed up by this vortex. All explanations, all
meaning is hidden there, therefore I have no further choice than
to let myself slide into these dark waters and dive into the grey
space. What a powerful metaphor to describe my fear of
engaging deeper into psychoanalysis, mine and that of the
patients I am seeing. How can I be a guide when there is no
obvious direction, no ground marked paths? But what has soul
searching and Mauritania got to do with each other you could
ask, what pushed me to go there. What threads of my destiny,
were being weaved?

It is the end of November and time to discuss and then
plan the end of the year traditional celebrations. My oldest son
Christophe has decided to go skiing with his girlfriend and a
group of friends and to celebrate New Year in Austria. My
younger son Gregoire has a broken heart after the sudden
deportation by the Home Office of his girlfriend and has decided
to stay in Cambridge with his friends. This year I have no desire

19

to organise Christmas or New Year's Eve celebrations as I have done in the past at my house. Several friends have invited me to different parties but none of these kind offers fully appeal to me. I am yearning for something different. Then towards the beginning of December, as I am tidying up papers, a copy of a magazine called 'Terre du Ciel' (Earth of the Sky) draws my attention. I probably got it at a congress on Ghandi held in Montpellier, France, in 1999. This magazine has a very appealing photograph of the sand dunes of Chinguetti in Mauritania and I have used it for my Seasons Greetings cards, so I must have already been there by some strange premonition?

I stop and spread all the papers on the floor of the study, a little further around me and start day-dreaming! Several trips are on offer but the program of the camel trek or meharee is the one which catches my attention and to which I keep coming back and back during the next few days... How can I transform this day-dream into a reality? I am skint. My psychoanalyst to whom I am telling this story, becomes the devil's advocate and states: so what is the use of credit cards then in your opinion? Terror seizes me, that of the one who doesn't want to owe anything to anyone or take financial risks. It is, also perhaps a French attitude so different in this domain from the English one. The very next day I fax the company offering the trip thinking that it is too late anyway and that there won't be any spaces left. To my pleasurable horror, I receive very rapidly a mail stating that some places are still available. I am not sure about the logic of what happened next but it is enough to say that several emails later, I have registered and the holiday is paid for, thanks to the credit card. Now the panic that is still haunting me, needs to find another object to fix upon. How on earth am I going to be able to be in Charles De Gaulle Airport in Paris to meet the group on 31st December at 5.30 in the morning, coming from Cambridge?

But I do find a ticket to get me to Paris on the 30th and some Parisian friends lend me a room for the night and I order a taxi for 4.15 am. It most certainly wouldn't have been wise to rely on public transport at this time of day, coming up to the Millennium New Year's Eve celebratory preparations.

Saturday 31st December 1999 (Day 1)

At 4.00 that morning I leave the little room I have been staying in right under the eaves of this old Parisian block of flats seven storeys high and no lift, to wait for my taxi. How strange to see Paris in the early hours of the morning, the police already at work, cordoning almost non-existent traffic off most of the main streets in the centre of Paris, in preparation for the merry making of the usual New Year celebration, topped and magnified by the extravaganza of the coming New Millennium.

At the airport I found 'Point Afrique' a meeting point for chartered travel to various destinations in Africa and discover that several groups are due to travel together – but who belongs to whom? Where are my future travelling companions? Maitie is the first one whom I met (we notice that each others' luggage is adorned by the same colourful tags) and decide to have a coffee together whilst waiting. There is something quite magical about being in transit: to leave something or someone behind and to be going towards something else. Towards what? One doesn't yet know, old fears, new hopes, a moment suspended in time. That's it: travel is for me to be suspended in time, to belong nowhere. The smell and noises of airports anaesthetize and make me sink into a passive waiting. A muffled and joyful space, the languishing of a desire for Africa which has gone on for too long, because the last time I set foot there it was in 1985, over 15 years ago. In my heart I talked to it as to a lover. What an infidelity to have waited that long. You, where I excavated and travelled every year between 1966 and 1977. The smell of your soil always so present in my memory, the images of all the criss-crossing I have done over your plateaux, valleys and mountains, the memory of your noises and your colours. But so far I only know your northern part and your eastern side and a little of your south, I haven't been to meet you on your western side yet. In fact, I have had to wait until my downing sun to visit you there.

Our charter plane touches down briefly in Marseille and takes on board another load of travellers (in fact all the rest of our group is with them). I recognise with pleasure the surroundings of the airport, and then I am transported by a playful imagination to the old harbour and the fish market, to my brother who also lives in Marseille and to the fact that it is the doorway to Africa.

The flight goes by almost unnoticed as Maite and myself speak non-stop. Landing at Atar airport is easy and what I have been expecting, longing for, is there, I am not deceived. As soon as the door of the aircraft is flung open a deep heat welcomes us, it hits me full on and I drink of it greedily. The plane squeezes out its passengers from the front exit whilst the luggage is being spewed out of the hold without any delay or ceremonies, onto the runaway there and then. There is no terminal building as such and passport control is under the shade of a tree. Once I have got back my blue backpack, I sit in the dust of the track, along the runway, leaning against my old companion, the accomplice of all my escapades waiting for my turn. Everything is there from the past, the flies, a very different rhythm of life, everything speaks to me and I understand it and it feels right as it should be. There is only one official at a wooden table, carefully writing every name down on a ruled copybook in black pencil before stamping the passports. For those who need visas they are issued there and then, but we have been told that holders of French passports don't need one. Once this lengthy formality is done, we can walk out to the truck waiting for us. It has rows of uncomfortable looking seats, some which do not look as if they are safely bolted to the floor and are covered with a sort of canvas material. The canvas on the sides of the truck is like blinds which can be lifted or lowered down. This truck is to carry us all the way from Atar to Chinguetti.

I have no idea how long we wait for or what for. Are there any additional passengers, goods to be taken up the escarpment? Anyway, the idea of the existence of time has gone and I have fun talking in French with the children surrounding the truck, exchanging addresses, touching and stroking each other with curious and fond gazes, speaking with our hands. All along, distractedly, I try to remember fragments of long unused Arabic vocabulary, but it is when one realises that communication between humans is truly 80% non-verbal, that one can finally give up and start enjoying life. 'The conference of the birds' a play written by Peter Brook in 1972 based on an ancient Persian poem is a play without words, just sounds and gestures and was taken across North Africa and the Sahara and played in front of villages audiences. It demonstrated amongst many other things that a large percentage of the emotions and the non-verbal narrative were understood by the audience. And here in Atar, the children anyway learnt French (of a sort) at school.

At some point and out of time, we are asked to go to the truck and once it has been decided that everything and everyone who needs to be on board is, the truck leaves with a cranking of gears. Almost immediately we are back on the sandy, dusty tracks I have taken in many other parts of Africa and I can say that for parts of the drive, I am not in the truck but at the driving wheel of my old Land Rover. The truck cannot be driven at the speed necessary for a smooth gliding over the corrugated tracks, as it probably wouldn't have been able to control the ensuing skidding, so and with that came a rather uncomfortable rapport with our metal seats. I think of it as training for getting our posteriors prepared for spending hours on our camel saddles. The other inconvenience is that the dust generated by the truck' wheels very often is blown back inside through the open sides and we quickly have to let the canvas down, and that of course makes the inside very hot and rather dark, but as I am on the si I quite happily peek out of the blinds from time to time. Soon th track becomes very steep. One side of it is cut into 'rotten' granite, and there is a vertiginous fall on the other side. Graders are in the process of building that track, huge machines from China entirely operated by Chinese men too, I notice in amazement. After several stops due to mechanical problems, soon resolved thanks to ingenuity and … a screwdriver… we reach Chinguetti roughly three hours after leaving Atar. Africar cleverness is without limits as far as repairing cars, trucks or anything on wheels, as long as there are no electronic circuits involved, but what fool would want to bring such fragile and complicated vehicle systems in the bush. This ingenuity is the example of a skill born out of need, that to learn how to make d with what you have and make it continue to serve your needs fe as long as it possibly can.

At the entrance to Chinguetti we bypassed a large building whose façade has been riddled with bullets and morta shots. My uneasy impression is confirmed later on, yes I am tol this is an example of the Polisario work, testimony of the guerrilla war which took place between 1975 and 1991, when Morocco and Mauritania were fighting. In fact, this war ended less than 10 years ago, and prudently I stop asking questions. W arrive at the place where we are going to spend the night and celebrate the New Year, a hardly believable endeavour as we ar

24

so far away from all the hype of the western world! Two groups will be accommodated in this caravanserai-like place, so probably around 50 people. One of the groups is going into the desert for a shorter time and has with them a girl in a wheel chair. Our group will be there for longer and we will all be travelling on foot and also on camels. I think that there are a few other people there too, not belonging to either group. The girl in the wheelchair arrived by taxi with two friends and we all help push the chair in the sand to our caravanserai. She is an amazing plucky young woman who became partly paralysed after a motorbike crash. I share a room with three other girls, and we put our sleeping mats on the thin mattresses which are in direct contact with the concrete floor. Although it has been swept from the windblown sand, it will cover it and us again in a few hours and we repair into the courtyard.

I found that evening in Chinguetti difficult, there are too many people. Our two groups intermingle trying to find out who belongs to whom, searching for one's future travelling companions. Most of the travellers are French or French speaking and some feel the need to embark on loud songs, whereas I would prefer silence or low key conversation. Have I already become that much estranged from my original culture? I do not like either the spotlights illuminating the courtyard where we eat nor the noise of the generating plant. I would prefer the obscurity in which my eyes can get accustomed to the light of the stars and the delicious couscous which we are eating could have an even better taste. To accommodate to a different way of seeing is part of what I want from this trip; it is exciting and requires letting go of a lot of western presuppositions. I leave the gathering early and crash into my sleeping bag, despite the rowdy revellers bent on celebrating the New Year. I dive suddenly into a very deep sleep, something that I had not achieved in a long time.

Sunday 1st January 2000 (Day 2)

      Woken up by the early morning noises coming from the courtyard onto which our doorless bedroom opens, I join other shadows in the cold and as yet unlit morning and make my way to the washing basins and loos. No showers here: water is too rare a commodity for wasting it in that way, so it is just a quick cat wash and brushing of teeth using bottled water. The various trips organisers are already at work gathering together the mountain of equipment needed to spend a week in the desert: cooking pots, the big communal tent for those who will not want to sleep in the open air, the food, the water and so on. I eventually find out that our group consists of 15 European adults and one seven-year-old girl. I cannot remember what I had for breakfast, probably strong coffee and bread and jam and I then go in search of the semi mythical figure of Paule Valette. She is our hostess, a French woman who as one of her book covers said shares her time between her house made of stones in the Ardeche (France) and her other house made of sand in Mauritania. She apparently came to Mauritania in 1991 (once her children were grown up and didn't need her anymore). She is one of these extraordinary multitalented women who never stop creating, and appeal to the imagination and dreams of lesser mortals. Amongst many other things: she bred a flock of pure race Bizet sheep in the Ardeche; she created a humanitarian association to help the children of Chinguetti in 1996, providing help with education, nutrition and medical services. She is an author who has published over 10 books of fiction and travel. She is what I would call a grande dame... someone who instinctively inspires respect. Her roots are in the Ardeche (a poor department in southern France), where some of my ancestors also originated. I wanted to hear her story. How did she end up here in Chinguetti? But there is no time; too many people also want her attention. I nevertheless manage to buy two of her books and get her to dedicate them, and it is significant of the type of person she is, that she took time to ask me questions and write something appropriate. As I did not want to add any extra weight to what I was taking on our desert trip, Paule Valette offered to store the books for me in a cardboard box under the sink in the kitchen. They were still there on my return!

The gear I have used for the night has been repacked and I bring my backpack to where the luggage of those going onto the week-long trek and camel trip is assembling and drop it there on the pile. I am then free to go and explore life outside our compound and to follow the guidance of my nose and ears. But by leaving the caravanserai I leave a protected space where hawkers are not admitted and all of a sudden make myself available to all the trinkets sellers, food sellers and the like who descend on me like a cloud of locusts. One thing I have to buy is a 'chechia' the traditional male head cover which I deem essential for camel riding and travelling in the desert. Of course I could have gone for the more garish female head scarves, but I find the deep indigo blue of the male's one irresistible, much more attractive and romantic. It consists of a length of at least five meters of deep blue light cotton cloth about a metre wide, which I am soon taught by the local crowd of children how to wrap around my head. This I do at the beginning in a less than artistic way, but soon learn as the days go by. I also realise that I have to leave a longish loop of the scarf dangling which I can then stretch across the face to protect my nose and eyes, in the event of a sand storm or plague of midges. It is incredibly comfortable and light, not at all hot and perfectly adapted for desert life. I playfully bargain with the people selling the cloths and as I am already dressed like a European male, and have short hair, no one tries to convince me to buy a more appropriate female one. My nose then draws me to investigate a very pungent smell of decay coming from around the corner of the street (don't imagine tarmac as there is none, just sand) and I suddenly find myself on the edge of the village, outside the clay walls and I arrive to an unexpected vision. Sand and dwarf acacias stretch away and, amongst windblown rubbish, is a place where fresh camel hides are stretched, pegged in the sand to dry, having barely finished bleeding. I am on my own, no one has followed me there and I start to study the area as if it is an old prehistoric site. The hair from the skins has been shaved, but with what I wonder? In Ethiopia I saw hides being shaved and detached from carcasses with very sharp obsidian stone scrapers. Could they be using these here too, or are they using iron implements? I am looking onto a vast processing site, rubbish of all sorts, bones which I assume where camels', bits of sinews, old blood patches dried up by the sun, millions of flies. After a while a feeling of sickness creeps over me and I can't stand the nauseating smell any longer. The lesson here is that I have been away from Africa for too long and will need to toughen up again. I retrace my steps following in my ears a cacophony of sound which lead to a place where the protesting dromedaries are slowly being assembled. The bleating these animals make is not one of cooperation or pleasure but of sheer annoyance! A wooden platform with a seat fastened on and a kind of shelter has been constructed for the young paraplegic and a group of young people are lifting platform and girl onto the back of a complaining camel and tying it in place. What an amazing sight. But it will probably take another few hours before they are finally ready to leave and I wondered how the girl is going to cope with the demands of her body. Will she have to be unloaded each time? These questions remain unasked and unanswered as I slowly go back to the caravanserai to check what is happening with our group. People are still milling around, some looking a little lost, still trying to come to terms with this unknown environment, the strangeness of it, a slight fear of what could happen in the emptiness of the desert. What if our adventure went wrong and disaster struck? Some people are feeling rather queasy. Waiting is never a good idea and we have to get used to the fact that we have to depend entirely for our survival on our guide and beasts and their handlers. Let's have faith... if we can, seems to be what some people are thinking!

Convection currents finally separate our two groups and the 15 of us are taken to where our respective beasts of burden are gathered. There are 26 camels for our whole party, which will be led by 11 staff all of which will follow later, by another route and meet up with us for the evening. The camels will carry all our belongings, a communal tent and all of the food and the water that we will need for our seven-day trip. The din is unbelievable; the camels are protesting loudly at being loaded. The men are shouting to be heard, there is a strong smell of camel shit in the air and myriads of flies are surrounding us. I can vividly imagine the old camel trains preparing to cross the desert, how much bigger and more packed they would have been! This cacophony is soon left behind and the only thing which we are taking with us is a packed lunch. We leave Chinguetti by walking up a dry waterbed known in Arabic as an Oued. The floor of it is easier under the feet than walking on the un-compacted sand, which lies on its sides.

This is an acclimatisation walk and our pace is gentle. We need to find our desert feet, if there is such a thing, and as we carry nothing apart from our individual water bottles and lunches in our small backpacks, the going is easy. We are still in the early stages of tribe building, our personal history mostly unknown to each other. Although we all have in common an interest in non-violent action and spiritual issues, this intellectual commonality is not enough to knit a group together. We slowly move from one person to the other, 'sniffing them' almost as animals do to each other, trying to work out on an instinctual level 'friend or enemy'. Group dynamics are fascinating, every person projecting unconsciously where and what they want to be: leader or follower, rebel or disciple, clown or dour face, self-centred or giving, and the rivalries which ensue. Little groups will form into which one might feel more at ease and will possibly try to plot against the perceived hierarchy, then the alliances will change again. But for the moment all is quiet and Wad Dadi is our recognised leader. He is a tall and handsome Mauritanian man, wearing flowing robes and a blue turban and our survival will depend on him and his helpers. It is difficult to give him an age; he possibly is in his late 30's early 40's. He has natural and calm authority and speaks very good French. We walk behind him. Maurice, the eldest man in our group, a tall silver headed gentleman soon catches up with Wad Dadi and their mutual appreciation becomes quickly apparent. Monique, Maurice's wife remains behind them, not wanting to interfere into this budding male friendship. Age and its perceived wisdom is revered in Mauritania as it is in many other traditional societies. I walk with Monique and Maite and we speak of this and that easily and I soon walk away so that I can enjoy the landscape and silence. I am wearied of people who talk all the time, as often happens in walking groups, leaving no time to think and look.

We pass by an ancient well (a noria), where a donkey goes round and round tied up to a wooden arm which gets the wheel turning which brings the water to the surface. There are a few gardens around, surviving despite the encroaching sand under the shade of acacia trees, and a few palm trees are managing to survive not far from this well. The last children wh had followed us as we left Chinguetti have now gone and we meet just a couple of people with donkeys. Two hours must have gone since we left and Wad Dadi declares that it is lunch time and our stomachs loudly agree. We settle under a few acacia trees and eat our packed lunch. I am not sure if I remember well, but my memory tells me that we have Bedouin bread, one hard-boiled egg, a tomato and some dates. None of us are going to get fat on this, although the bread is delicious; it is thin unleavened bread cooked on a hot stone and will acquire more and more sand and grit in its daily baking as we go along in the desert. Perhaps this is not so good for the teeth! The temperature has risen and I take off my fleece and have a quick lie down to replenish energy before we are off again. The cover offered by acacia trees soon recedes behind us and we emerge at the head of the dry river bed into the desert that is sand dune after sand dune. The animated conversation between people slowly dies down as the sand crunches under our feet, slowing down our progress and getting the perspiration going. It is swiftly dried up by the incessant desert wind, not a strong wind as it can be from time to time, but a gentle one wiping our foreheads. Walking on sand is taxing on the ankles and feet. Although soft it offers no grip and when your heel hits it, your foot has to work hard, sinking into this element and stretching all the way to the tip of your toes before being able to rise out of the shallow hole created in the sand and start another step. We probably walk for another couple of hours and our hamstrings become taught and painful, our ankles stress, so when Wad Dadi says that we are very near our camping site for the night, there is a general sigh of relief. However, where our camping site will be is everyone's guess, as the sand dunes stretch as far as our eyes can see. At some point we reach the top of a certain sand dune, one amongst all the other similar looking ones... how Wad Dadi knows where he is

31

going baffles all of us... and there down in the hollow are camels and a big round tent with a group of people busying themselves around a camp fire. A few acacias are growing out of the sand as well as a few palm trees, but nothing else and no habitation of any sort. We have arrived at our first nomadic home, the traditional bivouac of all those who travel in deserts and it is strangely liberating to be there, with the minimum needed and a group of men whom we have to trust for our wellbeing and security.

Tea is being readied over the wood fire and we gratefully gulped the three traditional small cups. Partaking in an ageless ritual, we drink the first cup which is said to be bitter as life is, the second as sweet as love is and the third one as exquisite as death. What a mind-liberating philosophy that tradition is!

The hot tea relaxed our strained muscles a little, but the night is approaching and the temperature is dropping and the need for warm clothing is becoming urgent. We are given the choice for the night to sleep under the round communal tent or if we prefer in the open air. Most of us pitch for an open air night and we all go to recover our backpacks and start looking around for a spot which seems comfortable to sleep in. I find my spot in a slight hollow not far from the dune slope and dig a shallow grave into which I lay my sleeping bag. All around me the others are also finding their sleeping place of choice. I have borrowed my son Christophe's extra warm sleeping bag, knowing that in the desert temperatures at night can easily plummet down to zero and below. I carefully put into the bag in preparation for the night, my extra warm pyjamas, a woolly hat and gloves, add an extra jumper under my fleece, before coming back for a dinner summoned by cooking smells that make my mouth water. The family has wisely decided that the tent would be their first choice for their first night with their little girl, whilst their grown up

32

sons are asserting their independence. Claudine, the artist, has already told us that you Dolma, had met the Little Prince during a previous journey and you have been elected with no possibility of refusing, to be our spiritual adoptive mother during this trip. Which future paintings are taking shape in you during that trip? Pitou, you are the adored father of Dolma and she never lets you go out of her field of vision, which inspiration do you get from the desert for your future radio and TV programmes? And finally Dolma, soon labelled by Wad Dadi and our camel guides as 'The Little Princess', the best saddles and camels will always be reserved for you. Your energy, your daringness and your love of life will be used to paint a smile back at the end of the day on the faces of even the most exhausted of us.

We all speedily gather for diner and I don't remember having been that hungry for a long time. We sit cross-legged on carpets, under the stars in a circle and tuck into the delicious vegetarian couscous. Right hand only please we are in a Muslim culture where the left hand is considered dirty. Carefully making a small ball of couscous and pressing it to give it some firmness, we dip it into the mixture of chickpeas, carrots, apricots and other vegetables and in the spicy hot sauce called Harissa. With time we become better at this form of feeding, dropping less on the carpet or onto ourselves. Some of us cheat a bit, using some of the Bedu bread as a scoop! It is all amazingly filling and after a long drink of water we each have an orange and all we wish to do on our first evening is go and rest in our duvets. I notice that the camels have been let loose for the night and Wad Dadi explains that they will find food for themselves and be gathered in the morning. It is so exhilarating to be sleeping under the stars, and half looking up and tumbling down in the process, we undress to get into our bags piling extra layers of clothing on top of the pyjamas. And then it is perfect bliss looking up into infinity. I don't know at which point I fall asleep or have been teleported into the Milky Way, but I wake up several times in the night each time gazing at a different sky as the stars have moved and my points of bearing are gone. The sand is incredibly comfortable and I don't feel the cold in the hooded duvet.

Monday 2nd January 2000 (Day 3)

The morning first light wakes me up and I am finally brought back from the fog of sleep into a silent, fresh-smelling and magically new environment of semi-darkened sand dunes. Where on earth am I, I wonder for a moment? But the odour of the fire's smoke is tantalizingly floating over us and when I look up, yes the fire is blazing and our helpers are already at work preparing breakfast.

But it is cold and the prospect of leaving the sooooo warm cocoon of the sleeping bag even for breakfast is not very appealing. From the depth of my slow functioning brain an accusatory voice says, 'you can't be lazy on your first day in the wilderness. Get up!' The process of dressing inside and then extricating one's body from a sarcophagus-like sleeping bag, with wrigglings and writhings begins. At the end of the process I am fully clothed and no longer cold!

Someone's harsh cough brings back the reality. The name of Maite comes back straight into my mind; I had forgotten her in this immensity and her cough has been plaguing her for a very long time! In the plane she was not feeling well, but now her chest is ablaze with a spluttering which is tearing her apart. Despite this she is determined to carry on and will start taking antibiotics which she brought with her just in case. Her night was not good and her face is rather haggard. I give her some vitamin C from my stash to take at breakfast to try and ease her exhaustion. During the day, Wad Dadi will kindly but firmly suggest that she should be riding a camel instead of walking and

34

it is where she will stay for the rest of the trip, too weak to walk. We pack up our sleeping bags as instructed to do yesterday evening and return our big backpacks to the camel herders who will load them onto the beasts and take them to our next night stop. And then we are allowed to go and have breakfast!

I ravenously eat whatever is spread onto our table on the sand. It consists of a piece of Bedouin bread and an aluminium packed slice of a cheese called La Vache qui Rit (Laughing Cow) which reignites memories of my childhood. A bowl of burning-hot tea for some and one of boiling-hot coffee for me. It all taste extravagantly delicious in its ordinariness when drunk in the still fresh and pure air of the desert under a slanting morning light. We are all a bit stiff after that first night and also because of having to sit at ground level, only Dolma jumps up and down with all the agility of her seven years. Our bottled water is of course rationed as it has to last for the whole trip and we are each allowed the use of a cupful every morning and evening to wash teeth and face and hands after breakfast and dinner. This will be our ritual wash for the duration of the trip. I must say a quick word about going to the toilet in the desert, which can at first be quite disconcerting. We discover that if we walk purposefully some way away from the camp, no one is going to look! It is a sign that we need privacy. Loo paper is not allowed on the trip and we also learn to use sand as a very effective cleaning product as well as for covering what we have left behind. We adopt our hosts' traditions in which the left hand is the utilitarian one and the right one reserved for eating! All the morning routines accomplished, we wrap up our chechias around our heads (this will become easier with time) and we are ready to go, not raring to go I should say, but ready in a mindful way, before this word became fashionable.

Today is a hard slog as we walk across a vast desertic plateau of hardened sand littered with basalt stones. I trip on a stone and fall flat on the ground just averting my face in time to avoid smacking it on the ground too, but winding myself totally. My rib cage is hurting, but luckily nothing has been broken. I'll have to look at where I put my feet instead of day dreaming. It is becoming more and more obvious to me that I didn't undertake this trip just from the touristic interest. I discover that I desperately need space and solitude to think through and feel things thoroughly and then hopefully some decisions will be reached, when the yeast of the unconscious will have had time to do its work.

Our caravan group is spacing itself out, small bunches of people fluidly turning to a single file, each one of us retreating into our inner world dwarfed by the immensity of our surroundings. Some individuals get further and further away from the main group (including me) as we delve deeper into ourselves and the contemplation of the emptiness of the desert. remember at some point being seized by fear as the traces of camels and humans which I had been following had disappeared, obliterated by the desert wind. Luckily my nomad homing instinct brought me back in the right direction and I saw in the distance the floating blue dress of Wad Dadi.

Our days become like the beads of a prayer string each the same although different in our desert pilgrimage. Wad Dadi blue robe is our only firm anchor in the ever changing landscape of the fluid desert dunes. Our aristocratic and unruffled guide, elegant albatross of the desert, your flowing blue or white jelabi float from one dune to the other, a beacon of faith for all of us in this immense and endless desert. You manage this feat of logistics which consists in giving each of us the freedom of movement as much as we wish. Each of us doing as we pleased whilst keeping an eye on the blue flag and him doing the same for his free spirited charge! It is a freeing, a rejection of all that is not essential to life, a trusting into our guide and none of us get lost, all gathering in the end back at the resting places.

Somewhere in the dunes I find the iron-blue carapace of a dung beetle, filled with sand. I stop and pick it up, filled with wonder that such beauty can be found in the middle of this emptiness and with a great deal of tenderness and care, I carry it with me during the many hours of the walk. Then all of a sudden it appears so very obvious that what I am carrying with me is the symbol of this ancient love which died a long time ago but of which I am still a prisoner. I gently drop the little iron blue carapace. It is still beautiful but it is empty and meaningless. This is such a simple gesture, but I feel such an intense liberation that tears silently flow from my eyes.

Eternities of sand follow on eternities of sand, interrupted from time to time by features which are uncannily familiar or expected, despite the fact that I have never before set foot in Mauritania. These are large depressions which I had spotted from a distance and in which sediments darker than the surrounding sand dunes have accumulated making it obvious that these were ancient lakes or swamps known as Sebkhas (in geological language). The darker sediments are the decayed remains of past vegetation which once grew on its edges. Am I going to find some prehistoric sites of ancient fishermen around the dried up shores? Sure enough, here they are, as we then discover, with their meticulously shaped minuscule arrowheads, such refinement is hardly believable. What beautiful jewellery would they make if they were mounted on silver. Pottery fragments are also present, broken grinding stones and ostrich eggshells, some perforated and ground in the shape of beads. Fabian, young Harrison Ford with a fiery soul, asks me to guide him and his brother Jeremy into understanding this past which is so present here for all of us to see and with his little sister Dolma they soon become experts at spotting prehistoric sites and arrowheads, and me the experienced one, now not finding what lies under my nose! I have to thank you Fabian for pointing me to my first arrowhead. I found two more and I stopped (one for each of my sons and one for myself). These will be the pointing signs of our lives. I still wanted to find a grinding stone (a whole one if possible) not to take it home but for the joy of the discovery and all of a sudden it appeared, very beautiful, very large made of granite. I admired it, photographed it and left it where it had been standing for centuries, could I possibly hazard since around 3,500 BC, or am I totally wrong? A question without an answer! Two much older sites, from a time period called the Acheulean complete my treasure hunt. I have renewed acquaintance with my archaeological past, savoured it and I can now let it go and move onto my life's next stage. I withdraw once again in the contemplation of the desert and its sumptuous architecture.

How possible is it to have such perfect curves with such pure lines, looking as if drawn for infinity but made of... sand, sculpted by the wind? The little wind furrows are almost the perfect mirror image of those left by the pulses of the sea in the sand of the estuaries and on the beaches.

Tuesday 3rd January (Day 4)

After our meal around the fire, trying to keep warm, we went in search of our respective 'bedrooms' under the stars as we called them and I fell asleep listening to the debate between Maurice and Georges about where the Big Plough was and the Southern Cross, and the trick played by the southern hemisphere on the westerner's eye. Maurice, is a man of few words, from the Auvergne, who always want to know everything on the stars and planets and all alternative sciences, he has the soul of a child and marvels at everything. I will not tell your age, it is irrelevant as none could beat your energy and enthusiasm when you danced with so much determination around the fire in the evenings.

Of course stars are important for navigation, especially in a desert. Our survival depends on Wad Dadi's knowledge of them, that is if we had walked at night which we didn't, but whatever landmarks he uses during the day they are still positioned in reference to stars and sun. My mother taught astronomy beside maths and she dutifully tried to impart her knowledge to her daughter when I was in her class, but my unruly spirit chose not to remember much of what she was trying to teach me and I regret it very much during this trip. Whatever little I knew seemed useless.

It is funny how people regrouped after a few days of common life for night time purpose. Some of the family of Claudine, Pitou, Dolma and Fabian found a common 'bedroom', somewhere over there. Jeremy, the other brother, and Sabine, his girlfriend find somewhere more private and sheltered. The three young women Agnes, Yolanta and Pernette regrouped for the night. They had stayed late around the camp fire talking and joking with Wad Dadi, Ismene, Sidi and some of the camel guides. But us solitaries (Geo, Jacques and myself), we were never far from each other and generally chose a bit of dune, asserting our need for space but not total isolation. Maite has long retreated under the tent under orders from Wad Dadi and is being nurtured back to health with traditional medicine, unfortunately I realise now that I never asked what it consisted of.

During the day, I discovered in each of you my travelling companions, extraordinary richness and talents, and I have often wondered how much more remained hidden to me, for lack of time, or an insufficient openness to the others.

I discovered that Sidi Ahmed, one of our cooks, humble and shy has a Master in Law and a mind-boggling knowledge of philosophy. We spent many hours discussing Descartes, Khafka, Camus and poetry after diner. I am savouring the very essence of Arabic culture – the erudition coupled with the simplicity of life of a people living in the desert. Nomadic cultures seem to free the spirit. There is limitless time to think during these journeys on endless dunes. I must try to find again the poetry written by 'Dassine' also called The Sultana of Love, a Touareg musician and poetess who wrote beautifully haunting poems at the turn of last century. I read her poetry a very long time ago and although I have forgotten the words, its beauty and music are still with me. I cannot resist quoting an example of her poetry found on the internet and translated by me:

'You write what you see and what you hear using such small crammed letters, huddled together like ants and which go from left to right, from your heart to your right of honour. The Arabs, they have letters which lie down and wriggle, kneel or stand up erect like spears: it's a form of writing which wraps itself up and unfolds like a mirage. It is learned as time is and is proud in combat. Their writing goes from their right of honour in order to reach their left, because everything ends there: in the heart. Our own writing in the Hoggar, is a writing of nomads because it is all in sticks, which are the legs that all the herds have: legs of men, legs of camels, of zebu cows, of gazelles, all of whom that roam the desert. And then there are crosses which indicate that you are going left or right and the dots – you see there are so many of them – those are the stars which guide us at night. For us people of the Sahara Desert, the only road which we know is that which has the sun and the stars for guides. And we

40

go from our heart and we turn round around it in ever increasing circles in order to embrace the other hearts in a circle of life, just as the horizon does around your herd and you'.

This Dassine poem comes from Maguy Vautier 'La Femme Bleue' 1991.

Another amazing young Mauritanian in our group is Yislm who has a 'mission' for his life, he is a guiding star. He tells me with great fervour what he is trying to achieve when he is not working with expeditions such as ours. He and his friends are actors and have an itinerant theatre. Their aim is to teach young people about ways of protecting themselves from AIDS. His love of the desert is as intense as his mission in life and he fights incessantly against those who pollute the environment. The desert is a clean place, but humans are not... we produce so much rubbish!

Wednesday 4th January (Day 5)

Opening my eyes in the morning has always been a challenge, but here more so than ever as it means accepting that I will have to emerge from my warm cocoon into the outside world, and this morning there is a frost on my sleeping bag! Despite the excitement of the trip, we are now on Day 5 and I am beginning to feel really tired and all my joints are complaining. But I cannot resist for very long the knowledge of the amazing prize awaiting me; that of emerging in this perfectly clean and clear primeval morning light which etches so precisely the crest of the dunes above us. The sun has not yet fully reached us; it is teasingly playing, trying to decide whether or not to melt the small ice crystals away. A quick glance at the immediate surroundings will reveal which visitors I had during the night, as the sharply defined foot prints are engraved in the still moist sand writing in beautiful calligraphy the curiosity of the little creatures, or sometimes bigger ones which came to sniff at us.

This morning there is the trail of a lizard or snake or creepy crawly of some sort, but I forgot to ask our guides and my night visitor will remain forever anonymous.

I dilly-dally a little longer reminiscing about all the ancient human cultures that we have encountered so far, as the wind of the desert incessantly whips the dunes, covering and uncovering ceaselessly just as the marine tide does, the strange remains of human history. And the history of humanity in the Mauritanian desert goes back almost to the dawn of time and the landscape which we are now experiencing has not been like that always. The image of Theodore Monod in whose footsteps we are walking invades my mind. This extraordinary ascetic French man last dismounted from a camel aged 91 after 60 years spent exploring the desert. He was a scientist (a member of the French Academy of Sciences who founded the IFAN, Institut Française d'Afrique du Nord in Dakar) devoted to the study of the culture language and environmental science of the West African French colonies. He was above all a profound humanist, pacifist and strict vegetarian. After his initial work on Monk Seals on Cap Blanc, on the Mauritanian shores, he was soon lured by the love of the desert and his search for meteorites is responsible for his discovery of many prehistoric remains, as well as of rock art site

The first human cultures in the part of Mauritania which we are exploring probably date from around 700,000 years ago. 'From around' – what a strange expression to use, but in saying so I am relying on what is called scientific dating methods which can have as a margin of error +/- 100,000 years. However this period of time is not well known in this area and is very difficult to date because of the poverty of the dating remains. The acidity of these ancient soils has destroyed very early bones and organic matter. The tools of this time period are made of stone so how can you date this material? If there were implements made out bones or other material they would have been eroded out and destroyed by now. My fellow Anglo-Saxon archaeologists call this period the 'Pebble Culture' because the implements used are made of pebbles.

During this time period the humans smashed and shaped pebbles and used them either as hammers to break bones (so they could eat the marrow) or as knives to cut meat and sinews. The bones used, probably came from scavenged dead animals as the early humans were not particularly gifted as hunters; they probably did not have the experience yet nor the necessary weapons either. These rough tools may point towards a diet which relied more on gathering of plants or insects than meat.

The Acheulean time period comes next and Monod discovered several locations including the famous El Beyyed site not far from Chinguetti. The stone tools of that period were mainly hand-axes and bifaces. Do you remember the bifaces found earlier on our trip? There were hundreds of them spread on this hammada, sharing this rocky plateau with a few recent funerary Touaregs monuments (tombs). How old was the Acheulean in this part of the world? Perhaps around 100,000 years.

After the Acheulean there are various other stone tool industries, but we did not encounter them, as we seem to jump straight into the Epipaleolithic. The Epipaleolithic gently leads us towards the Neolithic around the 7th Millennium BC. The Mauritanian Neolithic represents the transition between an economy of predation to that of production. It sees the domestication of some animals (bovids, sheep and goats). It seems as if the caprines (goats) were domesticated around 7,000 BC as well as some grains (millet - Pennisetum). The prehistoric sites yielded amongst other things grinding material (portable

43

grinders) for grinding cereals, some pottery which appears around 5th millennium and later on polished stone axes as well as ostrich egg shell beads and other stone bead pendants.

Do you remember these marvellous arrow-heads which I mentioned earlier on and which could also have been used for fishing? If you remember, these sites were found in the vicinity or on the edges of ancient lake depressions with diatom deposits. The geologists and paleobotanists tell us that there were two extended and intense rainy phases in the region with large isolated lakes that reached 15m in depth during the first episode around 24,000BP and then lakes of 30m deep around 9,000-8,000BP, before beginning to disappear around 5,000BP.

The fauna which lived during these wetter times was varied, and typical of lake margins. There were flamingos, fish, reptiles, hippopotamus, crocodiles and tortoises amongst others. It was dated to the 4th millennium in one of the prehistoric sites of the area. But further away from the lakes edges a fauna typical of a savannah prevailed with species such as gazelles, ostriches, rhinoceros, goats and sheep. The vegetation as a whole never was that of a jungle, but how can we know all this, you may ask?

Firstly because bone remains have been found in the lake deposits or in the prehistoric excavations but also through rock art which depicts ostriches and hippos amongst others. Unfortunately, we did not see any in our trekking area, although Monod described some not far from Atar as well as in many other places further away.

The sun has by now risen enough to tempt me out of my day dreaming. I say a temporary goodbye to Monod (who was to die aged 98 in November that very year 2000) and I slowly make my way to breakfast. We have a long day ahead today but the promise of reaching an oasis tomorrow, should keep us going, beyond the stage of deep tiredness, eyes strained on the horizon which seems bent on revealing dune after dune and nothing else.

I just spoke of dunes after dunes, didn't I, but I didn't anticipate what we were going to see. At lunch time Wad Dadi started talking about the 'Grande dune mugissante', translated into English it becomes quite alarmingly 'the huge bellowing dune' or again 'the big mooing dune' as only cattle or the wind and sea 'mugissent' in French! I later discover that these dunes can also be called Dunes musicantes. The word 'musicante' means to make music, to sing. In many ways I would prefer that dune to be singing rather than bellowing, but it would mean losing the frightening eerie mooing of the unexpected. As humans we seem to have the need to explain everything in order to tame the unexplainable, in order to possibly make it less daunting? The nomads in the olden days believed that the noise coming from the dune was in fact made by the djinns who inhabit it and which are spirits prowling through the desert, fond of stalking and tricking humans to an early death. Apparently this is recounted in the 1882 novel: 'La Peur' ('Fear') by Guy de Maupassant. This story also reminds me of the singing sirens in Homer's Odysseus luring the sailors to their death. But this time the sailors were on their camels also known as 'ships of the desert' and I have never heard of djinns portrayed as beautiful women. None of us had any idea about what Wad Dadi was talking about, but we respected him too much to wonder if the Saharan sun had affected his senses. As he would say no more, so as not to spoil the pleasure of the impending discovery, we continued to follow him doggedly. Our rollercoaster progression led us into a sandy valley and a mammoth dune came into focus, or perhaps our sense of perspective had become distorted? Wad Dadi led us to the bottom of that huge creature and declared that we had reached the amazing singing, bellowing, mooing

curiosity the 'Grande Dune Mugissante'. We waited awestruck....
but nothing happened.

Wad Dadi said that, like with everything else on this trip,
we had to work hard to earn our experiences. To hear the dune
perform, we needed first to climb it and slide down its side. Soon
a challenge was issued as to who would reach the top first and of
course Monique, our little mountain goat, had almost reached the
summit by the time I slowly started at the bottom. Then she let
herself slid down with a shriek of joy like a small child, little
expecting the very audible bellowing sound which followed her
most of the way down. It was electrifying. She raced to the top
again to slide down again, yet again triggering this melancholic
but perfectly tuneful sound.

Monique, Maurice's wife, you are a diminutive agile little
goat, always dancing like a will-o'-the-wisp. Affectionately called
by Maurice 'the little morcel', you managed to climb the Great
Dune four or five times when we lesser mortals had to stop every
10 seconds to catch up our breath – I will not tell your age either.
Your voice left its imprint on the grains of sand, as you spoke or
sang faster than the wind could move them!

No need to say that most of us only made the dunes sing
once. Climbing a dune as steep as this one is exhausting. It is one
step forward, then slide back down just as with the snakes and
ladders game. What was the cause of the sound? We had to wait
our return to civilisation to find a scientific explanation. The
ubiquitous internet provided the following information: it is a
very rare phenomenon and only about 30 dunes in the all world
have earned the name of dunes mugissantes or dunes
musicantes, which are also called singing sand, whistling sand or
barking sand.

The sound emission may be caused by wind passing
over dunes or by walking on the sand. It certainly was our

experience that we had to climb and slide down to produce the noise. But our displacing movements would not, on their own, have made the ordinary sand sing; other conditions are required. The sand grains have to be round and between 0.1 and 0.5 mm in diameter. The sand has to contain silica (quartz). The sand needs to be at a particular humidity. The noise may be generated by friction between the grains or by the compression of air between them. It's a bit like an avalanche which creates this acoustic phenomenon. The sound frequency appears to be controlled by the rubbing of one layer of sand upon another, with one layer acting as an amplifier membrane. The frequency of the vibration is related to the thickness of the dry surface layer of sand and the sound waves bouncing back and forth between the surface of the dune and the surface of the moist layer, creating a resonance that increases the volume. The sound produced is very different from that of littoral dunes which is just a crunching noise and determined by different mineral compositions.

The singing dunes only occur in arid deserts and the dune has to be at least 200m high. That's a good explanation for my breathlessness I thought a posteriori.

I want to thank Mr Internet search engines...but before I close the matter one last reference which is that Marco Polo mentions the subject in his writings in a much more appealing way that any of the scientific theories will ever be able to achieve. 'The singing sands sometimes fill the air with the sounds of all sorts of musical instruments as well as that of drums or again the clash of armours'.

After fooling around for a while we wearily rejoined our usual and thankfully smaller and quieter dunes, and were soon looking for a place to camp. The camels were unloaded and then let loose to fend for themselves as they were every evening. We would look for them in the morning, and they never went too far.

It is a little mysterious to imagine how they could find anything to eat in this desert, but the occasional lonely and gnarled acacia tree seemed to delight them. Geo, the man of the stars and of the pedometer, with a riotous beard you chose the freedom of not belonging either to the sky or to the earth. You were the barometer of how our disparate group fused together. When we had to leave you behind in Chinguetti – you had decided to spend an extra week alone in the desert – most of us cried and a spontaneous song sprang from our lips as well as tears from our eyes. (Ce n'est qu'un au revoir mon frere....).

We were all dead tired after the long day's walk and the exercise on the bellowing dune and soon collapsed after diner, or at least I did, hardly glancing at the stars. I was just happy and relieved to stretch out on the soft sand.

Thursday 5th January (Day 6)

The promise of an oasis today got our stiff bodies out of their resting places. The accumulation of tiredness and lack of washing facilities meant that hair and scalp felt like sand paper, itching and sweaty under the chechia (head dress). The rest of my body had become separated from my mind, like a foreign entity, better ignored, clothed in dirt and sweat. Whatever skin exposed to the elements had dried out in the sun and wind and was flaking off!

Once on my feet, I joined – as usual – the early morning camel gathering crew. The scanning of the horizon and the spotting of things seemed to come naturally to me just as it does to a nomad, and this was confirmed to me by Wad Dadi. I could also happily ride in the saddle for hours after hours, never sick nor bored. If I believed in past lives and reincarnation, I would immediately reach the obvious conclusion that I must have, in one of these former lives, been born in the desert to a nomadic family.

48

All camels brought back to their duties, we started again walking into this infinity of sand, peering down the sides of the dunes for the always foiled hope of the dark patch of an oasis. From time to time the prevailing wind caught up the edge of a dune and whipped up its already wind-carved concave side into spectacular orangey shapes, djins or clouds. For hours we went up like this and isn't it always when you give up the hope that what you desired so much could come, that it finally appears? But there was a dark patch, still a long way away in the hollow of a dune. Camels and humans' steps lengthened, drawn by an irresistible force, that of water... and of course vegetation and other humans!

Several hours later we arrived, so stiff and parched and disoriented. It was difficult to take in the reality of the oasis: in a sense it was too much. Our helpers were laying mats on the sand in the shade of palm trees and were already preparing some tea. Some of us went for a quick incursion into the palm-grove discovering with delight an open-well and small irrigated gardens. Unfortunately, I cannot remember what they grew. But after a while we felt embarrassed to explore the oasis without having had a formal invitation by the local people to do so and we went back to our invigorating tea. A few women joined us and a few words were exchanged in French but mainly via Wad Dadi acting as a translator.

I suddenly had a craving to wash my hair, having removed the chechia and tentatively asked Wad Dadi, if there was somewhere women could go for a private bath. The women present laughed and got back to their feet and signalled us to follow. And then I had the most pleasurable experience of women complicity in the ordinariness of daily life I had ever experienced. They took us to another open-well, quite deep into the oasis, and to a private area enclosed by pieces of linen and

49

signalled that we could strip there and shower ourselves. It was easy to draw buckets of water from the well and there was an old tin to scoop it out. Maitie who couldn't face cold water as her chest was still not healed, offered her services and brought us the water needed. After the unexpected cold shock, how can I describe the extraordinary feeling of clean water running on my head and body? I shivered at first but soon every pore of my body seemed to lap it. I felt revived, a sort of a rebirth. We were very conscious of using as little water as possible, so as not to deplete our hosts supply, but it was like manna. I can truly say that I enjoyed every drop of it. I have always thought that the essentials of life are water and friendship and this certainly reinforced my belief.

Pernette, the mysterious, always wrapped in your veils and leaving on the sand the star shaped imprints of the ski poles you walked with. You drew half hidden and refused to show anyone the products of your charcoals. We didn't dare pry, but there you were with us all under the cleansing water! Agnes with the generous smile, a trading woman, so close to your African sisters and tied up in the same cloth-selling business. Yolantha, blonde, pure and hard, another business woman with a company producing classical records. I wondered which melodies the desert evoked for you. Sabine the so very soft, always smiling, always ready to help. You and Jeremy lost in the dream of your love for each other.

And we emerged as new, cleaned and gleaming beings at the edge of the oasis, to discover that the men had done the same as us in another part of the grounds and that we were all converging towards a wood fire and the smell of roasting meat! A goat had been killed and we celebrated the evening with our hosts, with music, songs and dances. Out came the anzad a monochord violin and the tende, a small tambour/drum covered

50

with goat skin. The oasis was home to an extended family of about 20 people in all including children. That evening was very much enjoyed, knowing that we had nearly arrived at the end of our desert trek and that tomorrow we would again be at Chinguetti, in what had become the idea of a civilised environment. Our last true night in the desert, made even more special by the luxury of the shower, the mechoui, the music and songs.

Friday 6th January (Day 7)

A strange and sad feeling hovered above most of us all that day. We were in between two worlds, still in the desert but with the idea looming in our minds and with every step becoming more of a reality that we would be back in Chinguetti that evening. This was a space in-between, a space of ambivalence and incertitude, slowly moving from one dream state to another. The geographical stage is still the same, but the story is changing. We are still in the same country but with each step taken towards Chinguetti, we are disentangling ourselves from the wind tentacles and the haunting spell of the desert.

Our 'tribe' is in the process of creating a global memory of our trip added to the accumulated body memories of its physical aspects of the trip. Feelings triggered in us in response to past memories, each in our own ways of course, adds to this interesting mix. All the six past days experience are gelling into that common background. But how do we let go of these past days and willingly move towards something new, in this 'in between zone'? The love and longing of the nearly ending experiences in the desert, the struggles of our daily life, the lure of better bodily comfort, where will all that take us, as a group and individually!

It is easy to imagine how ancient men and women found solace with each other in ever larger tribes. Protection and pooling resources so that one's daily life is less hard through sharing with the others. There is the increased comfort and share of the children, and also the mind opening possibilities of discussing ideas with others. Inventions would have crept in, knowledge accumulated, and it was towards one such small village, which I cannot call a town that we were heading.

So I was heavily plodding from the unwritten culture of the previous occupants of the desert towards the written words of the following generations.

Our game with the big dunes changed inexorably during the day to another with the flattish desert of plateaux and then the dusty greenery of the gardens surrounding the wells and towards the end of the afternoon we entered Chinguetti. Poor, humble Chinguetti still fighting for survival against the encroachment of the desert, a former 7th century settlement having been swallowed whole by the desert and awaiting an enthusiastic archaeologist to excavate it.

Once upon a time, Chinguetti was a rich and populous town at a crossroad of caravan routes. Some say that in the 13th century it had some 20,000 people living there and was a centre of learning, both religious and scientific. It is also known in West Africa as the 7th sacred town of Islam. To top it all it bears the name of the Sorbonne of the Desert.

I am not making all this up...this is not the product of a hallucinating mind affected by her trip into the desert. UNESCO classed it as a Cultural Heritage of Mankind site as early as 1989 and it achieved the status of World Heritage Centre in 2000, in fact sometime after we had visited. So what sort of riches did this poor, much reduced and humble little village have, to earn such a prestigious title? The answer is a wealth of ancient manuscripts, belonging to the local families who have been jealously guarding them. Our old friend Theodore Monod discovered these libraries in the 1930's. An inventory done in 1996 recognised 3,450 volumes. That's quite hard to believe, isn't it?

So after this load of information was thrown upon us we became pensive, in a way different to that which had happened to us previously. Paper against abrasive sand. I cannot even start to remember what our meal was tonight, or what our first night back in a town with all the civilisation that one's ancient unacknowledged desires yeaned for.

Truly, one by one, we drifted into a sleep which inexorably led us to the day where we were going to re-enter a 'civilised state' by coming out of our deep emotional withdrawal. Withdrawal from what you could ask? After all, we had been gone only for seven days! Nevertheless it felt as if we had disappeared for a very very long time.

Saturday 7th January (Day 8)

So at waking up time, with no freezing cold weather, disoriented by the roofs which had appeared over us and the unnatural number of bodies around, we got up, trying to re-invent our story with that of the people we had left behind some time ago. But perhaps more importantly to reassure ourselves that we were still, or at least partly whom we were before, after our trip in the desert. A hearty breakfast helped us plunge back into the new awe of our surroundings. These coming mysteries had so much swollen my mind yesterday that I wondered what to expect in reality today.

We hovered on a narrow and convoluted path which had taken us away from our earlier abode experienced previously only for one night, our arrival night, and had left the next day. There were very few people around and I only now wonder why. Where were they hiding? What were they doing? How could they keep their innate curiosity towards us foreigners so much in check? Anyway we halted in a narrow alley facing a sizeable house with its front door half opened. It was a two storey house severe behind its yellow stone building but somewhat bedraggled. The door was not very high and if I recall well we had to bend to negotiate an entrance into a courtyard and then it was obvious that the buildings themselves were not as small as had first thought them. The next chicane to negotiate was to bend yet again and enter a rather smallish room which I would now call a Library, having been shown its precious contents. This room was properly plastered and niches organised at regular intervals on the walls with cubicles full of what we amazingly found to be parchment. The ancient guardian who showed us around, was impressive and full of respect towards all these treasures and he handed them one by one into our hands. It felt like if it was the birth of some strange experience and it was such a good thing that we had been in the desert for six days before coming here. We had shed away from ourselves so much of what we knew and we were coming back to civilisation with a new perspective, that of 'unknowningness'. Each of these manuscript was made on what? Sheep skin? Camel skin? Or something else? They looked nearly pristine despite their age, which we had no idea about. And when a date of 8th Century was given to us, I felt a deep silence inside me, a reverie which abstracted me from where I was and flung me into an ageless space.

Chinguetti, the 'Sorbonne of the Desert', is also the 7th sacred town of Islam, I feel like repeating this fact again, in an amazed voice. Chinguetti counts six libraries now after having had 20! The library I am in now, manned by this very old and very dignified soul, contains the oldest manuscript in the whole of Mauritania. It is gathered in gazelle's skin. Poetry works, jurisconsul work, mathematical books and so on, engaging us on a poetical withdrawal which kept us going for a very long time. At some point we noticed that this library had ventilation holes in the ceiling and buckets containing water in the corners of the room to maintain a necessary level of hydration. All the manuscripts have been catalogued and this house called a public library has been restored. Each family will eventually get storage space in it.

What a marvellously lengthy amorous day that was! I admired endlessly these treasures, drawn by venerable human hands and brought before our eyes from the dark into the semi light. It was a mystical moment for us as bearers of the past. Had I not sketched for some of the members of our travelling group a little about the culture of the past 2 or 3,000 years, arrow heads and so on? Now we had to envisage something much younger, which spoke to us in the way the arrow heads had not. It was a huge jump in imagination from the hard matter of stone to the lightness of paper! Paper or parchment, thin, cleaned and written on with dark burnt coal eliciting for us the mysteries of mathematics at that time! To see this amazing knowledge humbly shared by this elderly man brought a wave of emotions in me. I touched gently, respectfully, each of these ancient pages, imagining the men who drew these cabalistic signs of Arabic from right to left with the incredible elegance of the movement between fingers and wrist.

Later on, on my return home to England, my brother sent me an article published in France in September 1999. The UNESCO classified these ancient manuscripts as 'Cultural Patrimony of humanity'. A few Spanish, Japanese, English, Germans, Italians and French researchers visited. M. Ould Dadi, from The National Foundation of Ancient Cities roamed the desert, in 1991, to catalogue and to microfilm what there was. In 1993 a young French woman who was a journalist and was taking part in an automobile rally formed an Association of Libraries of the Desert funded by Rhone Poulenc (a major French company with medical interests). Then in 1997 a woman specialist from Le Louvre, visited Chinguetti for a week to train the 'Conservateurs of the Desert' to preserve their parchments.

Several hours later we left. Our profound admiration, out of time and out of space, made us feel all lost and whilst re-emerging into day light we decided to climb one of the towers to look at where we had been. Distant views were smeared by the clashes of light and the curtains of sand. Jacques always so calm, gave me a much needed hand on the steep stairway and later on you introduced us to Qi Gong. How extraordinary for a man who worked in precast concrete. Thank you Jacques for teaching me the pressure points which helped relieve my too often present sinusitis.

It was so hard to return to where we were, whilst not being there anymore. Our bodies and minds shredded to nothingness, not yet back in the correct time. All the afternoon, as we explored the old city opened to us by this unbelievable collection of writing, we fought and fought in ourselves the overwhelming force which could have been keeping us there, down, forever. Finally we went back to our auberge and reclaimed the books written by our hostess. It was a strange and difficult moment to understand. How could we still be so much caught up in the past and moving out to Europe the next day?

Dog Rocks

Sally Haiselden

I found every reason to stay another day, then another in Aswan. I convinced myself I needed to rest after the tough Sudan leg of my cycle ride home, Khartoum to Cambridge. I told myself that I deserved to indulge in beer and varied food. My stomach was still bad. It was so bloody cold. But basically I was scared to go it alone. And I was lonely.

So I went to see my friend Eva's German acquaintance. As a doctor and long-term resident of Aswan he knew exactly how I was feeling. He prescribed some tablets for my stomach that would 'thicken me up,' he said. In case they didn't, he listed two medicines to buy in Cairo, which would kill any combination of bacteria, amoeba or parasite I might be harbouring. He also advised switching to the west bank, the less touristy side, of the Nile to recover the flavour of Egypt and to escape the Tourist Police.

'Anyway the road will be less busy that side so you're less likely to be knocked off your bike,' he added helpfully. 'Oh but you'll need a dog rock.'

As he seemed to know what he was talking about after years of living in Aswan, I acted upon his advice. I found two stones that fitted easily in the palm of my hand and put them in the pouches on the outside of my handlebar bag. Round the very next corner I had to use them. The rubbish heap on the edge of Aswan came alive. Grunts became barks, scavenging trots, obsessed sprints towards my bike, from all directions. I was scared but knew I had to ride through the pack. I could see the bared teeth of a black shape to my right, and could picture them sunk into my calf, rabid saliva dribbling into the wound. It was time for the dog rock. The first one landed just in front of the teeth and stopped the jaws in their tracks, turning the animal back into the whimpering tail-between legs mongrel it really was. I don't know if I out-cycled the others, or their honour was satisfied, seeing off this 'thing' on a bike. Relieved but shaken I didn't know then that this scene would replay itself on an almost daily basis all the way to Turkey.

So I had plenty of opportunity to ponder the conundrum of why the dogs reacted as they did. My research confirmed that they rarely chased a foreigner on foot, or a local on a bicycle or any other combination of person and transport, remaining quiet and inert in the dust. But a foreigner on a bike seemed to send them into a frenzy. I'm still unable to conclude why.

The edge of settlements were the worst areas for ambush, where packs of strays scavenged amongst the refuse. Police and army checkpoints often had untethered guard dogs lurking menacingly. Once in Sinai I was passing a razor-wired UN observation post reading all the 'Do not...' signs when to my horror I realised the Alsatian was outside not inside the wire. The nearby soldiers made no attempt to control it and it looked the kind of canine that would become aggressively indignant if a dog rock hit it so I aimed near it. My dog rock zinged off the 'Do not throw missiles' sign hung on the wire, I'm sure the soldiers fingered their rifles, the dog careered towards me and at the same time my water bottle fell off my carrier. I needed it desperately, being in the desert, and so with the blue berets silently malevolent, I zoomed back, grabbed the bottle and executed a tight turn before the dog cottoned on. It was as graceful and smooth as any ballet move but difficult to ever repeat and I pedalled off in a manner as frenzied as any dog.

Altitude Sickness on Kilimanjaro

Françoise Hivernel

Wednesday 15th February - Day 4

This is the fourth day of our climbing adventure and I wake up after a bad night's sleep, what with the rain and with my heart having decided to play an irregular tune. I am really anxious about the coming day's walk. We extract ourselves from a rather wet tent, but luckily the rain has stopped. We put on our walking boots with some difficulty - dampness does not make for easy sliding in and out of clothes or shoes - and emerge for breakfast feeling rather under the weather. So some strong and very hot tea with cereals and scrambled eggs was heavenly. The world is dry again and frosted as it had been the day before and the sun is shining. Before leaving, I took some vitamin C hoping to re-energise myself, then a dose of Diamox (altitude sickness pills) and after a while found my pace. This was an amazing feeling. After all these years of having difficulties walking in mountains, heart pounding, breathlessness, I had at long last found a pace which suited me and I didn't have to stop every two minutes! We arrived at Mawenzi Tarn Hut at 13.00h. We did very well, it only took us four and a half hours, whereas it took the porters three and a half hours, and we went from 3,600 to 4,330 m (730 m). It was a steep ascent but very beautiful too. We crossed several valleys whose sides were dotted with the theatrical Senecio, emerging each time to stunning views of the jagged summit of Mawenzi with its needle-sharp spires. Mawenzi is the second summit on Kilimanjaro, but lower than Kibo which is the highest and best preserved. The third summit Shira became inactive and collapsed into itself about 500,000 years ago.

I have just read an old Wachagga legend which says, "Once, in ancient times, when both were still smoking their pipes, that of Mawenzi became extinguished. He went to his bigger but younger brother, Kibo, to borrow fire, and received i A short time later, while taking a nap, the fire in his pipe went out again. And again he went to borrow from Kibo. But this tim the latter became angry and thrashed him so terribly with his club that even now one can see his bruised, battered and torn surface and sense his attitude of austerity, adopted after this unjust treatment. The Wachagga believe that Mawenzi is ashamed of his appearance, therefore covers his face with cloud at every opportunity".

I took another dose of Diamox at 11.30 and the last around 15.00h just before having a nap, feeling very virtuous ar happy at how the day had gone. You, my son, the amazingly fi and never tired, went for another walk with Kagea. I woke up a hour or so later with a nasty headache. This is not fair! The day has been so perfect. I am also starting to have stomach cramps - precursors of diarrhoea. The headache went after two Nurofen but I have no appetite and just have soup. Kagea tells me that I need to drink more! And you and Kagea are very concerned about me. Our blissful solitude of the past days is ended as quit a number of other tents are pitched in the area, which is at the junction of several tracks leading to Kilimanjaro summit. Of the people camping there probably none will attempt the climb of Mawenzi. Sheer rock walls all around guard Mawenzi's summi and no walking route exists to the top. It wasn't climbed successfully until 1912. The basalt is friable and dangerous, the summit only reachable via icefall climbing. One needs a special permit to attempt it and also has to prove not only that one is a experienced climber but also has the right equipment. We had hoped to go and see if there were any animals watering at the tarn but it is now freezing. Our tent seems to have dried itself during the day and we decide to catch up on the sleep we miss last night. But summit day is getting closer and we toss and turn, unable to go to sleep, and feel very cold. I am not sure whether it is due to the altitude, as we are now well over 4,000 m, or to our inner anxiety. I then remember the survival blankets I had brought and we wrap our sleeping bags and ourselves in one of them, pretty noisy stuff as they are made of aluminium and we now look like parcels ready to be baked in the oven. We speedily warm up and blissful sleep comes shortly afterwards.

Thursday 16th February - Day 5

Today is the last day before the summit. We had a warm night but I repeatedly woke up feeling very thirsty, my mouth totally dry, tongue sticking against its sides and palate, unable to swallow, desperately wanting water. I feel that if I don't drink I won't be able to continue breathing either. I do not know if this is due to dehydration and what it is doing to my brain! Since yesterday we are not only storing our drinking water inside the tent, we also wrap it up in a jumper so that it doesn't freeze. I did not think about taking a thermometer with me on the trip and it is only now 'a posteriori' that I am wondering what sort of icy temperature we are experiencing. On waking up this morning, I was still under the grip of a very strange, powerful and disturbing dream, and I am not sure whether it was due to being so warmly wrapped up in the survival blanket, or to being thirsty, but I dreamt with all the lucidity of someone awake that a gigantic force was shaking the ground I slept on. This strange force was completely overpowering, but its message was very clear: Do not attempt to climb up to the summit. The mountain spirit forbids it and will give you no help in achieving this. The mountain spirit was pointing out that my days as an expedition leader were over and that I had to surrender all this to you Christophe. I was so sure that we had experienced some seismic activity that I asked you when you woke up if you had felt the tremor and you said no. This in a sense was even more unnerving, but in another way, strangely reassuring, as I realised that somewhere, something in me already knew what I had to do, but that my dream had needed to shake me into acknowledging it. But, of course I had had to go to Mawenzi Tarn to hear clearly that message.

During the five long hours it took us to reach the Kibo Huts we spoke about my dream and what it said about you and me and agreed that I should stay behind. All I have noted in my diary is that it was a "bloody long hard walk". I guess that since I knew that the mountain spirit had placed a limit on how far I was to go, the motivation to continue was dissolving fast. Unpleasant diarrhoea didn't help either and I was glad to be able to make use on the way of a couple of newish looking wooden toilets. These had been built thanks to Norwegian financial aid and assistance, to protect the environment. We were now using a fairly well frequented track leading to Kibo Huts, and I admired the fact that there was no litter visible despite the great number of tourists. To give an example, there were around 7,000 visitors in 1985, but in recent years this number has escalated to over 25,000 people (some even say 35,000!) attempting the Kilimanjaro climb, of which only 30% normally reach the top! We are now fully into the desert alpine zone, having reached an altitude of over 4,400m (over 14,000 ft), and I can see no vegetation apart from lichen growing on some scattered enormous boulders and a few desolate tufts of tussock hard grass. This is a desert which has been likened to a moon landscape. It is made of porous lava and ashes which cannot retain any water and therefore cannot sustain any plant life. Whatever is there relies on the mists and clouds and occasional rain and snow as well as water coming from the melting glaciers, but this is greedily absorbed by the substratum. It is regurgitated lower down the slopes, coming out in the gullies which we crossed a few days earlier.

The lunar space between Mawenzi and Kibo is called the 'Saddle' and is a vast plain, so it is just "plain" trekking, one foot after the other on a fairly soft brownish grey track for 7 long and slow kilometres. And all the way, the huge oppressing mass of the mountain is looming closer and closer, with the track leading to the crater rim ever more visible and looking impossibly steep. You and Kagea nudge me on as I am failing. Apparently there was a herd of long-haired elands in the plain in 1988, but we do not see them, however we do hear the piercing calls of rock hyrax, and this is as far as wild life goes.

We finally reach Kibo Huts around 14.30h, a god-forsaken place 4,703 m up, having gained 373 m in altitude. We are now just at the foot of Kibo summit. It is a surreal place, ending on one side into an endless precipice and a sky void. It could have been from there that an audacious hang-glider jumped in the 70's and fell to his death. I remember this as some of our friends working in southern Kenya near the northern side of Kilimanjaro had their petrol rationed to enable the rescue expeditions to search for him. His body was never found. We bypass a long stone building with a corrugated iron roof, which sleeps around one hundred and twenty people on bunk beds. Outside there are tall anchored aerials, presumably for the mountain rescue team and communication with the outside world. The only things moving with any sign of energy are ravens strutting around purposefully, scavenging in the fine volcanic ash, which is getting everywhere, especially under finger nails, and my skin is starting to crack. We go and register at the Park authorities' hut and have our names ticked off their list. We are now being accounted for, not one of the casualties, not yet at least! Just another 150 metres or so to go, above the hut,

63

just at the beginning of the track going up to the summit, our tent is pitched. I work out with the map that we are probably at about 4,850m (almost 16,000 ft). I remember thinking that at least I had made it higher than the Mont Blanc in the French Alps, which stands at 4,807 m. How weird it is that these strange bits of long-forgotten knowledge resurface in my disconnected mind. Perhaps it is developing cracks like my skin and allowing these rusted memories through. I am spent but glad also that I made it as far as here. It is important for both of us that I should be there as a witness to your climb to the summit, your rite of passage into manhood and my grateful bowing to my next stage of life. But bodies can never be ignored for too long in these surroundings and it is necessary to make a visit to the toilets before its dark and I trek down back to the level of the huts quite easily. All the toilets are built on the edge of the cliff. I enter with care. They are all, of course, squatting toilets and amazingly disgusting. Sides and floor splattered with the insides of discontented travellers – vomit, diarrhoea, you name it – who did not reach the hole in time. Well I did and peered through it to discover the void underneath my feet as well as through the back wall window. Everything goes into infinity, down the cliff side and, I guess, disintegrates pretty quickly at this altitude or is scavenged by the birds. Still, with my wonky hip, squatting down is difficult and there is no way that I am going to pull myself up again by grabbing any part of the walls, so I am glad that I brought with me my walking poles, which I have learned to use as levers. Making it back to our tent is hard work, just over a hundred and fifty metres of slow breathless toil.

It is nearly dinnertime and we have about half an hour which we decide to use to assemble the equipment which you will take with you tonight on the climb to the summit. We know that Kagea will come for you at 23.30h. and then that you will be climbing all through the night in order to reach Uhuru, Kibo's summit, at daybreak next morning. It will take you around seven hours and this is on top of the five hours we have already done today. Then there will be another three hours coming back down to Kibo Huts, a short break and another three hours down to Horombo Huts. In all nearly eighteen hours' walk - *hapana mzuri* (not good) - for me. The best description of the climb which I found so far is: "The scree, which is comprised of small pebble-like ash cinders is frozen and therefore easier to climb; ... but for many the ... reason to start so early is that it is dark and therefore one cannot see the vast distances ahead". And again: "The climb is not difficult in mountaineering terms; you could say it is equivalent to scrambling up a staircase rather more than 3 km long. Or you could say that it is equivalent to clambering up the side of nine Empire State Buildings laid end to end at about 16 degrees. But then at 4,710 m, where the final ascent of Kilimanjaro begins, there is little more than half the density of oxygen present on Manhattan or at the foot of most staircases. So in effect the aspiring climber attempts the equivalent of those feats with the equivalent of only one lung. The result is agonising, there is no other word for it".

You are getting restless and edgy and there is no socialising around tents tonight as everyone is concentrating entirely on preserving energy, both mental and physical, and willing their bodies to the top. You will be wearing my warm mountain trousers, which, being several sizes too big for me, suit you well, two pairs of socks in your walking boots, several jumpers under your anorak, gloves and taking hand warming packs as well, which go on releasing heat for up to seven hours. The temperature at the top could be anything between -18^0 C and -26^0 C. We check your head torch which you will wear on top of your balaclava and add spare batteries to the kit together with a specially insulated water bottle, high energy bars and Kendal mint cake and, of course, your camera for the summit picture! It is now 18.00h and time for dinner. I watch you wolf down all the food on offer, yours and mine: spaghetti, meat, soup, everything, whilst I have one spoonful of soup and two strands of spaghetti, my food for the day added to a small piece of chicken I had for lunch. You are not depriving me of anythin I am just not hungry and I wickedly think that at least you'll ha something to throw up, if the stories that most people get sick a true. It is less painful than retching on an empty stomach.

You attempt to get a few hours rest and sleep uneasily whilst I watch over you. Kagea calls at 23.30h. You get kitted ou and the two of you go out into the night and I am left on my ow wondering. My body reasserts itself. So far I have had three doses of altitude sickness medicine today and decide to take on more as I can't breathe and am again very parched too. I sleep i fits and starts, never cold with that wonderful aluminium blanket. I need the loo and try to get out of the tent but it feels a if the zips are frozen, or have I so little energy left that it takes f ages to open them. I cry out of exhaustion. I make it down to th loo and back without the need for a light as it is still nearly full moon. I follow you in my mind all the way up there, but am als relieved that tomorrow we will be going down for good. Some pains in my calves, so take Nurofen again and eventually fall asleep.

Excerpt from *Safartu: travels with my children*, 2015

Front Running
Sally Haiselden

Recently I have been running more often along overgrown paths through fields of cassava and sunflower. I purposely run more flatfooted and stomp to scare any snakes. Sometime a twig or stem rubs my ankle and I goosestep away. Each time I wonder if my route is a wise one.

I have been in training for the Kampala half marathon. It is difficult here to find the best time to run. There is the problem of temperature and of people. Nobody runs. Why hurry and it's too hot anyway. A muzungu attracts a huge amount of attention when walking, once running you become hilarious entertainment. You really have to be in a good mood to face this and to stop choice swear words from exiting between laboured breaths. The toddlers are the first to spot you and whoop themselves up into a frenzy of repeatedly saying, 'Muzungu, muzungu,' or the Acholi equivalent of, 'Mwono, mwono.' I often shout, 'Acholi, acholi, acholi,' back, which silences some and gets a laugh from some adults. The teenagers just stop and giggle as I approach. A few really cool ones say something to you in English like, 'Why are you going so slow?' (You try it mate. I have been pounding these roads for over an hour.) The drunks, available as your audience at any time of the day, decide to run with you much to the amusement of their friends. The older men and women I always greet out of respect and they often observe, 'Ah you are for exercise. Well done.' And the women my age, what on earth do they think? Some of the ladies in the market give a cheery wave and mime joining me from their sedentary positions. I am dressed in shorts, sweating, having time to do something totally unnecessary in their eyes. And what do I think of them? What on earth do we have in common? I look at them

67

and often think, 'Excuse me madam, but you have something on your head. In fact it is a washing up bowl containing a pumpkin, a small jerry can of water, a tablecloth and some cassava.' We are worlds apart.

The half marathon was one of the most bizarre races I have completed, once I found the other runners. I was up and out pre-dawn on a bodaboda motorbike taxi, hurtling down to the start at Kololo airstrip in Kampala. As I progressed, other bikes shot out of the gloom carrying fellow competitors all dressed in the buttercup yellow shirts of the sponsors. As more and more converged, we were a luminous wave in the pinkening dawn. I arrived in plenty of time for the usual queue for the toilet. Except the ladies' convenience was rather inconveniently locked so I had to look for a bush along the perimeter but there seemed to be a man with a gun behind each one. With 15 minutes to spare I headed towards the biggest huddle of yellow, assuming it was the start line as there were no signs or announcements to guide runners. I asked a muzungu guy if he was doing the half. He replied that he was waiting for the 10k to go off. A Ugandan nearby overheard us and said, 'The half marathon has left.'

'Pardon?'

'It's gone.'

'You mean early?' I was stunned. Nothing happens early here.

'Yes.'

'Really?'

'Yes. They went that way,' helpfully raising his arm, flicking his wrist in a very non-specific direction. I asked someone who looked as if they could be an official and he confirmed the information. 'Oh yeah. Climb up that bank and go through that yellow arch you'll catch them.' So off I set with a handful of other early-late arrivals. After 100m we hit a junction, no signs, no marshals. I followed a Chinese girl who looked efficient. At the next junction an official told us to go back the way we had come. When I pointed that out to him he said, 'Okay, okay, you take this short cut and you will catch the others soon.'

Short cut? You don't short cut in a race. After a few minutes I caught up with a bunch of runners and settled into a comfortable pace. It was 6.50 am. The race was due to start at 7am. I looked round at my fellow competitors. They were wearing everything from the goodie bag: visor, sweatband, bag with water bottle. Many wore a T-shirt under the race one. They were in leggings or nylon tracksuits. I felt hot just looking at them. The bags bulged with stuff. It then dawned on me. Daniel in the VSO office had commented, 'Yes, the MTN marathon weekend is one of the social events of the year in Kampala.' They weren't competitors but participants with snacks, sunglasses, car keys in the bags. They were taking no notice of the length of the race they had signed up for. They would run, shuffle, walk until tired then short cut back or even better, hop on a bodaboda to the finish. The few foreigners were distinguished not only by their skin colour but from their streamlined lycra, dressed as competitors, travelling light.

People's race numbers were colour coded. Red for full marathon, blue for half, black for 10k. Not that it seemed to bear any relation to the amount of running being done. I was wearing red but doing the half. My friend Helen had mistakenly entered me for the full marathon. No problem I thought, this is Uganda; everyone will do their own thing. At 12.5km the route divided. An unhelpfully forceful official took some persuading that I knew I wanted to run 21k instead of 42. I was allowed to turn right into the inclines and traffic of central Kampala. Kampala is built on seven hills as is Rome. The drivers on these seven hills make those in Rome seem like Sunday afternoon dawdlers in comparison. The traffic police had tried to hold them at bay but had succumbed to mob rule in a bid for survival. The roundabouts were a fray of taxis, incessant hooting and swerving runners accelerating past accelerating vehicles. Uphill. I tucked in behind a yellow shirt and did not look.

At one of the roundabouts about 18k into the run I spotted some Japanese tourists. As I passed I overheard them comment, 'Sugoku haiyai,' meaning, 'Very quick.' I felt flattered. My watch showed 1 hr 40 mins running time, with 3 km to go. I felt good. I strode on to gathering applause. I heard sirens then the time truck passed, chased by two elite Kenyan runners. Some of the comments and applause as I followed in their wake was directed at me. I wasn't running alone, and my style was gone to pot into the potholes and hills. It was about 8.30, hot and the men's nylon trousers were dripping sweat. Vaseline, lots of, sprang into my baked brain. Then it dawned on me. The spectators saw my red number and thought I was running the full marathon. If so, I was on course for a time close to a Paula Radcliffe world record. I shuffled on uneasily, through growing attention, studiously avoiding eye contact. I am not sure what really happened to those last three kilometres. Signs started to appear: '3 km to go,' then '6 km to go'. It was all uphill and the field of runners around me was just wiped. Even I, the now suspected female elite runner. All wiped except of course those participants on the numerous bodabodas that kept pulling up in front of runners, passengers briskly hopping off to run the last few hundred metres to the finish line. With one km to go, I passed Helen sat outside her house. A race hardened runner herself, she quipped, 'You're winning!' Great. As Kololo airstrip approached the frequency of 'Well done muzungu,' increased. I kept trying to explain and to apologise. 'No, no! I am running the half.' 'No, I am not the first woman back.' 'Well done muzungu.' I entered the stadium to some applause. I was mortified. 'I don't even look like an elite runner.' Just when I needed to, for the first time ever I could not muster the energy and coordination for a sprint finish. 'What will happen when I cross the finish line?'

Nothing. So was it all in my sun-baked imagination?

I rapidly took my race number off and hobbled into the crowd. A lovely Indian man gave me a bottle of iced water. Then it was announced, 'Will so and so and so and so and SALLY HAISELDEN please report to the finish line.' WHAT? Followed by, 'And the first female runner to cross the line is……Sa..nti from the Uganda Police.' Pause. 'Will the Red Cross please come and help, the competitors have collapsed at the finish.' Not Sally but Shanti.

I 'walked' back to Helen's for breakfast, coffee and a shower; I can't remember exactly the order of need. 'You owe me big time. At least one beer,' I said.

'There's a race in Jinja in May,' she replied.

'Right, I'll register you.'

'Ha, but it's only a half!'

One for the Malagasy Road
Jane Wilson-Howarth

Having already spent so long travelling the whole length of
Madagascar on buses, I did not believe that the journey across
the Great Red Island would take only a day. But we had time
and, confident of Malagasy unpunctuality, we turned up at the
bus station at seven-thirty for the scheduled 6am start. The *taxi-
brousse* did not look about to leave, so we had a leisurely
breakfast and returned to discover we were to have three
'chauffeurs' making us think this was going to be a tough journey.
Finally began the usual pre-departure tour of the town, touting
for more passengers, and we left Morondava, surprisingly
punctually by Malagasy standards, soon after nine.

By the time we reached Mahabo, only 30 miles east of
Morondava, the two co-drivers had demolished a whole bottle
rhum and were giggling like schoolgirls. After ten more
kilometres the reasonable, if potholed, metalled road
degenerated into a deeply rutted track, terribly deformed by
heavy lorries. This was National Highway 35. It could have been
worse: it had not rained for a few days so the mangled road was
at least negotiable. The baobab horizons gave way to grasslands
dotted with palms. The road meandered miles and miles across
the great flat western savannah: through the kind of habitat that
covers nearly three-quarters of Madagascar.

The suspension broke. The trio of chauffeurs went into a
huddle to discuss what to do. More giggles. Eventually they settled
on the usual local solution to this problem: binding the suspension
leaves together with inner tube. Further discussions, games of tag,
and the repairs took an hour and a half. Continuing along the
appalling road, the two drunk chauffeurs got drunker and we
nodded off, until we were woken by attempts to bump us out of
another huge boggy hole in the track. Often we stopped to survey

the best way through waist-deep pools that blocked the way. In places, we could drive around, but in others scrub and trees forced us to drive straight through. The extra 'chauffeurs' were clearly just cheap substitutes for four-wheel drive. They often had to push the car out of the mud and enjoyed wading and falling around in the muddy sludge. The sober driver then took great delight in driving off at top speed, spraying his drunk colleagues with soup-thick brown water, pretending to leave them behind. The giggles became even more hysterical; tears rolling down their faces as they became helpless with infectious laughter and fell back into the water.

Only about sixty miles of the road was in such bad condition but it took all day and half the night to negotiate. It was a long time after dark before we finally reached good tarmacked road and stopped at a *hotely* for some food. We were so hungry that we even enjoyed the usual lukewarm rice and thin chicken stock with fat globules congealing on the surface. We washed the fat coating from our palates with mugsful of *ranovolo* –'golden water' made by burning a little rice onto the bottom of a saucepan then boiling water in this. Onward and we then had to make a huge detour north, almost as far as Tana, in order to join the only road across central Madagascar: the direct route had deteriorated so much that it was completely impassable.

The contrast of being on a normal road was such a relief that the sober driver decided it was now safe for him to start drinking and by one in the morning he was so intoxicated he had to pull over for a sleep.

We woke just after dawn to realise we'd arrived in Antsirabé, the 'Place-of-much-salt', named for the thermal springs.

Excerpt from *Lemurs of the Lost World*, 1995.

The Beginners Guide to being a Development Worker

Sally Haiselden

The first thing you may think you need is a powerful, white four wheel drive vehicle with your own driver. It can convince the local population of your legitimacy, a show of money and a symbol of support, that people in faraway lives are thinking of them and making decisions to help better their lives. It is also a machine with the strength to push the development worker through the worst of road conditions in order to meet and greet and dispense ideas and expertise. It is usually white, which keep your driver busy whilst he waits for you, washing off the rust orange dirt.

You then need the initials of your organisation emblazoned on the side. My Toyota reads, 'Donated by UNICEF to Kitgum Core PTC - supporting the implementation of BRMS'. Not the catchiest of advertising but the majority of the population recognise the light Cambridge blue colour of the UN in all of the many guises it operates in.

Are you lost with the abbreviations? That is another skill a development worker needs; to be able to decode the multitudinous contractions of NGO (non-governmental organisation) names and their programmes and to be able to use them in reports. My full role here in development speak would be; 'VSOU vol TE with UNICEF at KCPTC working with CCTs, DPO, DPP, DEOs and DIS on implementing MoES' BRMS' (see below for a translation).

So those are three Basic Requirement Minimum Standards (BRMS) for a development worker. The next is that, regardless of political correctness, to be convincing, it helps to have a white skin. Whether comfortable with it or not, across generation and gender, at least in my corner of Africa, respect

74

and gravitas come from the historical perspective of what the whites did in the past and how they are still here to help now. My experience during these initial weeks is that I am sure the reception I would have got with a darker coloured skin, regardless of the white vehicle would be very different. The majority of the girl pupils curtsey when they extend their hands to greet me, some even remain kneeling as I pass. When I talk to my college colleagues and greet headteachers, many much older than myself and with far more experience, there are smiles almost of relief, definitely of joy; 'You are welcome', eyes dance and teeth gleam. As I explain what my role is, there is no suggestion of, 'We've heard it all before,' or 'Who are you to come and tell us what to do?' I am sure they have and some do think that, but they are wise and very polite.

So what can a development worker do that they cannot? First and foremost I symbolise money and resources. I can be the answer to everything. But once you explain that it is not your remit to build more classrooms or find more teachers, there is still the warm, expectant smile. And again, this may not be politically correct, but 'we' (the white, 'educated' inhabitants of the developed world) have a confidence, a 'can do' attitude, creativity, imagination, an ability to problem-solve. And why is this? Because of the way we are educated? Because we have had a range of experiences? Because we are here because we want to help? Or is it just because we are fresh to the situation, are not ground down by more problems than solutions, the daily grind of living here, of finding enough money to keep the family? I think it is the latter.

As a development worker you also need a large reserve of resilience, physical and mental. Ricocheting over roads that stretch the definition of the word, to reach far flung schools, your arms ache from holding the handle above the window to prevent

75

becoming unseated or whacking your head on the roof. Your neck aches too from keeping you head correctly aligned. You are often on the go all day, from 8am to 8pm, in areas so remote there is nowhere to get lunch. After the hunger pangs of your stomach saying, 'feed me', you survive the rest of the day on small sips of water and adrenalin. For your companions it is a fact of life.

You have to be strong mentally too. Life is quiet in the evenings and is when you are reminded regardless of the welcomes and camaraderie of the working day, you are a foreigner here. You become I think, a victim of your skin colour and status. You go home to your good house, with more mod cons that your colleagues have, but are socially isolated. Fellow development workers themselves are a strange breed too - just because you are one of the few whites working here does not mean they want to make an effort to engage in conversation or to socialise.

Bigger questions hit you sometimes too. Why are the majority of the population living in thatched mud huts? What would they be wearing if the markets weren't full of second hand clothes sent from the western world? What exactly does 'western world' and 'developing world' mean? Why should NGOs be providing services that are really the responsibility of the government? Why are so many initiatives of the NGOs broken or unsustainable? Why does over 30% of the Uganda Government's budget come from foreign donors? And how will I, one primary school teacher, suddenly become development worker, make any sustainable difference? Then you have to remind yourself that it is the same as in any situation, anywhere-relationships. If you inspire one colleague, encourage one pupil then you have achieved.

These are what you really need to be a development worker: an inquisitiveness, a humility, an understanding of solving problems in small steps and of going out there every day, willing to learn about where you are and to do no harm through your actions, words and what you are perceived to represent. Corruption, dependency and false hope are just around the corner otherwise.

If you are a reflective, respectful, development worker, you do ponder all of this during the quiet, solitary evenings.

*****

That translation in full;

VSOU vol TE with UNICEF at KCPTC working with CCTs, DPO, DPP, DEOs and DIS on implementing MoES' BRMS means…
Voluntary Services Overseas Uganda volunteer Teacher Educator with The United Nations Children's Fund at Kitgum Core Primary Teachers College working with Coordinating Centre Tutors, Deputy Principal Outreach, Deputy Principal Pre-service, District Education Officers and District Inspectors on implementing The Ministry of Education and Sports' Basic Requirements Minimum Standards.

The Emperor's Visit
Françoise Hivernel

The sound of the alarm clock ringing, entered my subconscious
and then drizzled uncomfortably into my consciousness, but I
was way behind being properly awake yet. What in the end
brought me back into the world of the living, was what I can only
call a "strange" noise. Strange because I couldn't link it to any
association that I knew and because of that lack in memory I
suddenly woke up. It was very cold in the tent although I was
feeling very warm on the old metallic bed on which I was
sprawled inside my sleeping bag, on top of a comfortable
mattress with two thick blankets on top.

The noise became closer and sounded as if somebody
was tripping into the guy ropes of the tent. Of course it could
have been one of the men bringing us the hot water to wash
outside, hot water which wasn't going to last for long given the
temperature, but our men had been working with us several
years and wouldn't get entangled with the tents guy ropes,
suddenly an unfamiliar shadow appeared on the wall of my tent
and angered and scared me at the same time. I crawled off my
sleeping bag and then jumped off the bed and unzipped the tent
and there he was, nearly face to face with me, a soldier with a
weapon in his hands! We looked at each other for a while and
then I remembered that of course, today, His Majesty the
Emperor was coming to visit the sites. The soldier withdrew
quite quickly, and I am not sure whether it was because I scared
him or else. In the meantime, still shivering in my pyjamas, I
looked around and noticed that our camp had been swamped by
a large number of armed men, and as it was time to get up
anyway I withdrew quickly inside the relative warmth of the
tent.

Now was the time to get dressed warmly for the beginning of this interesting day. As I threw on layers upon layers (thick socks on my feet, already into some of the long legged undergarment pants) I came to the conclusion that the day of His Royal Highness had indeed started very early and in a way not very kind to us his guests. Not a very pleasant thought but, we were in Ethiopia, in October 1966, under the reign of His Majesty Haile Selassie. We had been working on sites at an altitude of 2,000m, and the temperature there varied widely. At night it froze, but during the day the thermometer climbed up to over 40°C. A matter of dressing and undressing in the extreme, without forgetting the alcoholic drink to make us feel warm at night!

Anyway, once padded against the weather extremes, I walked to the "tukul", the centre of our working lives. This tukul was a round hut affair, not as the traditional house of the rural Ethiopians were, small and low ceilinged, ours was aiming for the opposite. It had a large and high circular ceiling and in its middle a series of long tables which could easily sit up to 20 people. We had this structure built for us last season and were inaugurating it this year. Little tables were placed around the circular walls on which we did the work required after the daily excavations, and only one window was pierced into the walls with a shutter inside which we kept closed most of the time. It was entirely built with eucalyptus wood and clay was smeared on the walls inside and outside and the round roof thatched. A very smart building indeed, into which we were never cold as we were in the tents nor too hot! There was even lighting inside, procured by a small generator, providing light too to the kitchen hut.

For those of you who may wonder how all this comfort was paid for, I must hastily announce that our excavations there were financed by the Ministry of Culture in Paris, and that although we were supposed to accommodate to widely different temperatures, food was a sacrosanct theme, and our meals carefully and artfully prepared by a Cook and served by Mengasha the ever present man doing most tasks in the camp, all of this with as much wine as we may have wished for... An unbelievable thought, especially for me who during the next few years would have gone over Kenya's border coming from the UK and settled to a diet of a tin of sardines shared between four of us for a meal!

So after having had our copious breakfast of cereals and bread and butter and jam and omelette and tea or coffee we soon warmed up and prepared for this historic day. Jean, "The Leader", was ready with plans and informed us that the choice for the day was between fun and serious work... with a twinkle in his eyes! "You women in the team can all choose a group of nice soldiers and keep them occupied whilst we men will go and make sure the sites are okay for the Emperor or you can come with us telling the men were to go..." So at 7am after breakfast we each collected our team of workers who had arrived outside the tukul and taking excavation material went off to the sites, which we were going to show to His Majesty this afternoon at around 2pm "Dana Imezgun" (Thanks if God Wills in Amharic). We wanted to make sure that the sites had not been disturbed during the night by animals digging as sometimes happened. We planned to take him to two sites Garba, Acheulean period, dated to around 0.8 million years ago and Gombore, a Pebble Culture site hovering around 1.6 million years ago.

It took us a good 15 minutes to walk to the first site and another 15 minutes from there to the other site because the paths leading to them were narrow and up and down and no driving was possible. This meant that his Highness would have to walk.

We then came back to the tukul around 11.30 had a quick wash and eat a served lunch with several courses lovingly prepared by our Cook. Time after that meant getting ready for His Majesty! It is hard to imagine what getting ready for Him meant, but the men had to put on a suit and shiny shoes which given Jean's absent mindedness meant having one shoe from one pair and the other from the other (no matching colours of course…). So the poor men would be sweating, whilst we women were donning on nice cool dresses however with high heel shoes. I dreaded to think what would happen on the narrow paths to the excavations! The first and only time I ever experienced such a thing. When the time to get ready arrived I shove the soldier in front of my tent and zipped myself up privately inside the tent and started on the transformation required by protocol. When I came out and put my high heel shoes on I physically felt the appreciation of the soldier guarding my tent which had been missing before.

Now I must try to recreate, for you, the environment we lived in for four months of the year and which we were about to compulsorily share with his Highness. We were on a high and vast plateau near the river Awash. From our tents we looked directly at the cut that the river made 500m away from us and at the scrub covering every side around us. It was a vast and quiet arid landscape. The vegetation was yellow and scruffy with a few acacia trees here and there. Perhaps the look was due to the time we were there, perhaps during the rainy season it was all green and wonderful but somehow I doubt it, given the perennial vegetation left. Looking around my tent, there was a rather flat undulation, but in the very far distance all around us we could vaguely observe mountains looming on the edges of the inside plateau. This enormous plateau created by the river Awash and dissected by its dry river tributaries, little valleys and hills gave life to that flat emptiness. Directly across from where my tent opened, I could see a hill which was called Kella and were I had explored badly eroded Late Stone Age sites. We would not be taking the emperor there, as it would mean crossing the river again and at least 1½h to reach. On the right, in the distance was the village of Awash and on the left, out of sight were all our goodies: the Acheuleans and Gomborreans sites which would definitely be seen by His Highness. Then behind my tent was the camp with everyone's similar abodes, the big tukul, the kitchen and a few run down thatched constructions.

So back to our perturbed routine. We all finally lined up near the tukul to welcome the several Land Rovers accompanying the Emperor. Jean welcomed him on our behalf and we were briefly introduced to him one by one. It was beginning to be funny, as for the women it mainly meant trying to find our equilibrium on high heels shoes which was not as easy as it may have sounded, but we all managed to curtsy without falling. Then came the shock for me of looking at him: at his size! In all the pictures I had seen depicting him, he was on his own and it is impossible to judge the height of the person without references. But now he was there standing on shoes which had a double sole giving him a few more centimetres in height and still being smaller than I was, a little midget in size but certainly not in power. Meanwhile his troops which had been pestering us since early morning were now as stiff with self-control as lifeless statues. There were endless discourses in Amharic between his ministers, Jean and Him including some explanations about the sites and then the signal was given to start walking, which with luck was taken at a slow pace and all the women of the team managed to reach the sites without too badly torn ankles. Jean with his two different shoes spoke enthusiastically about the ancestry of the sites we were

82

approaching, but as it seems that only males were allowed around his majesty I couldn't get what he was saying and we arrived at Gomborre our oldest site, situated on the edge of a small tributary of the river Awash, stone dried at the moment. Suddenly standing on the edge of the site without any desire to twist my ankles any further I gasped... what was this tiny animal trotting and sniffing at our precious Gomborean site and shame of shame pissing on bones which were 1,6 million years old?

His majesty had brought with him his tiny and I presume very expensive lap dog....and of course it did not matter whether the beast was freely watering our carefully dug artefacts, but the shock on the system was there, even for Jean who might have lost a few sentences of what he was saying. I am not sure of what happened afterwards, but an official was very quickly sent to retrieve the beast however not managing to walk as gingerly on all the exposed artefacts, bolas, choppers as we might have hoped... From there we went on to the Acheulean site Garba dated to around 0.8 million years and with a very different and much more evolved set of artefacts including bifaces and cleavers. Imagine if you can, His Majesty and his entourage and us in the extreme heat of the afternoon. I believe that some Ethiopian ministers had to walk back to our camp before all information on the sites had been given, but the Emperor stayed and showed no extra sweating! The afternoon went on and we slowly came back to the camp. An aperitif was served to his majesty and we contented ourselves with fruit juices. Despite the length and growing heat of the afternoon I admired how His Majesty seemed very curious about all the artefacts antiquity and never showed any boredom. His tiny size grew in spite of us into a rather impressive intellect. He eventually left together with his crowd as night time was coming and invited us to his Palace in Addis Ababa. After that we quickly went to our tents to change and welcome the usual feeling of freedom, his troops having withdrawn and given us back our precious sense of liberty. That evening diner was even better than usual with so many question we had for the men who were at the front and especially for Jea and with the amount of whisky and wine available, the cold outside the tukul did not exist any longer.

About three weeks later we went to the Palace for the reception which His Majesty had invited us to. Again we were dressed "up to the nines", women with high heeled shoes easie to use there than at our site, and we entered the palace, having been brought in to it by our Land Rovers driven by Jean and us The guards took the keys from us and went to park them. In the enormous room where the reception was held a great number of people were milling round His Majesty who was there, standin way above us at a pulpit where he remained during the whole time. Size is such a fascinating issue and it started me to think along a line which I had never explored before!

One Egyptian Summer
Sally Haiselden

At this time of year, dusty, congested Cairo reaches uncomfortable temperatures. The well off that can, especially non-working mums with school children on holiday, pack up the household, including cook, nanny, housekeeper and driver, and head to the cooler calm of the north coast and its fresh breeze, light blue waters and white sand. An Egyptian author describes it better than me, 'The Maryut coast….is the forgotten coast of Egypt. ….with clear water that reveals rocks and sand, enticing you to hold out your hands and scoop up water to drink, and forget that the water is salty.'

Salma and her household have an addition to their family this summer-me, the Mary Poppins-esque tutor to Nadia, 10, Tarik 8 and Majid 5.

From Alexandria, west to Libya, this Mediterranean coastline is nowadays packed with large compounds of holiday homes and apartments, each jostling for proximity to the sea and demanding a view of it. Wresting the land to develop in the first place entails negotiation with the local nomadic Bedouin. Until recent years no one has had to decide whom this desert belonged to. Now with the rich invading, requiring luxury accommodation and flaunting extravagant tastes, the Bedouin want their cut of land price, rent and their own house built on the land they now say they own but their ancestors merely wandered over. Driving along the four lane highway, heading west you pass fairy-tale castles and crenelated apartment blocks with names like 'Hacienda Bay' and 'Porto Marina', interspersed with glitzy shopping malls like, 'M Porium'. There is accommodation for thousands where 15 years ago there was just desert. The engineering required to supply power and water to this seasonal population equates to a magician conjuring out of an empty top

85

hat but it works; there has been constant power and water these past few weeks.

Salma's holiday home, near El Alamein of Rommel and Montgomery fame, and just five minutes' walk from the sea, is in one of the older compounds, built for diplomats, hence its name, 'Diplo'. Low, whitewashed bungalows, with verandas for sprawling on to catch any coolness blowing in from the sea, shaded by firework bursts of shocking pink bougainvillea, look out onto lawns of immaculate grass, watered each early morning by an army of workers – Egypt is a very hierarchical culture with a large population acting as servants to the better off.

Sitting on the beach you can watch this played out, not just by Egyptians but by Filipinos, Nigerians, Sudanese, Ethiopians, Ugandans all dancing attendance on the holiday makers, some families having a nanny for each child, a dog-walker, a maid for each adult – handing towels to their mistresses as they leave the sea. And here I am, like one of these, but not, as what I can provide, English and my accent is an expensive, therefore rare commodity. I am sure I am the only white British staying in Diplo. However watching the Egyptians walking past on the beach, you may be surprised by the range of hair and skin colour parading before you and you are reminded of the mix of genes that may have been left behind by soldiers in the war, and the flux of peoples across the Med and from the East. You hear as much English as Arabic. If I didn't speak I might fool a few into thinking I am a very fair resident but my short hair and mannerisms speak of a different place. However some on the beach will also be British passport holders, a legacy of British colonialism.

I am fascinated by the spectacle put on by moneyed Egyptians on holiday. They are living the American movies, being those glossy magazine adverts. Salma's husband heads down to the beach on his scooter, shirtless, wearing reflective sunglasses, dog tags dangling from his neck. Ibrahim the driver follows in the jeep with the bag full of towels and snacks. In the supermarket the Egyptian housewives are ponderously slow down the aisles and at the checkout. In fact they are not really housewives. They may choose the food but certainly do not cook it. They are immaculately turned out. The more secular women model the latest bikinis with transparent short dresses over the top to add some modesty whilst shopping. They do not have to push the supermarket trolley – they have a young man to do that for them. A certain section of the female population wear tight, brightly coloured turbans, hiding all hair and then plastering their faces with the most garish make up. Even the more traditional women still make a fashion statement, long tight fitting dresses with slightly looser full length jackets on top, the jacket just open enough to show their curves, and their neckline and wrists wrapped in jewellery, some with the Egyptian evil eye on them, traditionally taken from the eye of Horus, a symbol of protection, power and good health. Many of the smiles are botoxed, the wrinkles smoothed by cosmetic surgery. All of them are utterly at the centre of their world around which everyone and everything else orbits. They cannot see the queue forming behind them.

Salma comes from a wealthy, well-connected family. She is an only child whose every want must have been met growing up. She decided she wanted a tutor for the summer as her maiden aunts had had one as children who spoke with a cut glass accent, and they still mimic her to this day. Also Tarik has been identified as being behind with his reading. I have realised why. Salma's idea of parenting is to buy the children whatever they want. She buys Tarik books but then doesn't sit and read them with him. When we finish a book together he bounds over

87

to tell her – she may hear but doesn't look, focussed on her i-phone and Facebook. She doesn't know any better. Apart from what I teach the children I hope rather naively that my politeness, my 'pleases' and 'thank-yous' and my evident respect for the servants, Hiba the cook and Elsa the nanny, will be noticed by them. But they don't need to be. Nadia the eldest really does ring up her aunt in Cairo who is about to visit and say, 'I want the first Harry Potter book.' She will get it but I am unconvinced she will have the dedication to read it herself. Now if someone read it to her… Nadia is spoilt but will sometimes really surprise me with her consideration. I have just realised though these are only instances when the conversation, event or action will have consequences for her.

I do not understand where all this wealth comes from. I think it is perhaps a mind-set. Salma and her husband have to maintain the status they were born into and this is more easily communicated by outwards signs of having a lot of money to spend. Money attracts money and opportunity so that is perhaps how they can afford an international school education for their three children and a new home in a new suburb of Cairo. Salma does not work and Kamil can spend two months of the year holidaying on the north coast. It helps for Salma to have a father who is a doctor in Qatar. He gave the two older children Mac Air laptops as Eid presents.

If you go down to the beach just after sunrise the other half of Diplo's population is out, the servants. They are only allowed to swim at one end of the beach, the less pleasant, rocky part and are closely watched by Diplo's security personnel. Yet that does not seem to bother them. Watching them frolic in the sea is like watching a group of children from around the globe playing together. It is a diaspora from nations stretching east to Indonesia and south to sub-Saharan Africa and beyond. Every

morning they congregate to relax and socialise. Some bring
music, some arrive in their master's flash Mercedes. Some swim,
some cannot and wallow in the shallows. Some have their own
children with them. That's a thought – do they have to work too?
I talked to a couple of servants today when I was out for my run.
I watched the African lady mimic the running of an Egyptian
man who had just passed them. As I reached them I stopped and
asked them where they were from: Nigeria and Java, Indonesia.
'What do you do? Cooking? Cleaning?'

> 'Everything,' they answered.
> 'How is it in Egypt?'
> 'Good.'
> 'How long have you been here?'
> Maryam from Nigerian answered, 'I am almost reaching
> one year.' Her companion has been here for five years.
> 'Have you been home in five years?'
> 'One time,' she answers.
> 'I have two children at home,' Maryam added and

gestured how old they were by using her hand to show their
height. The servants get free board and lodging and work long
hours so it must be possible to save most of their salary. Their
Egyptian employers must treat then relatively well to want to
work so hard away from home for five years.

I sit on the beach with Salma and the children in the
afternoons, partly in, partly not in the group. Other friends with
other bungalows in the compound arrive with big cool boxes full
of drinks and snacks. I am greeted. Some of the movie star like-
friends of Salma's quiz me out of her earshot as to how Nadia
and Tarik are doing, what I am doing with them. After that I am
largely ignored, partly due to the language barrier I suppose and
because I sit there reading. However, it is a sometimes an
uncomfortable place to be. I am a guest, yet not as I am there to

tutor the kids. Yet I am not a servant as I eat with the family and
have my own room in the house. They are not the friendliest
section of society – perhaps it is a strain to live a fiction of
appearance and wealth. I feel most at ease with Ibrahim the
driver. He was a tour guide before recent concerns about security
in Egypt meant less tourists visited. He is easy company as he
has nothing to prove. Although I have free board and lodging,
will be paid and have been given a free return flight and have
spent time in a place where the sun shines every day, the sand is
white and the sea blue and warm, this is a strange position to be
in. I have spent three summers with Salma and her family. I am
not sure I can do it again. I do not think she would have any
understanding of why.

Lake Baringo
Françoise Hivernel

From the hotel we moved onto the fruit and vegetable market, a huge affair full of the most fantastic fruit that I can remember, especially the mangoes, and we stocked up as much as we could before continuing our journey through Kenya. The tarmacadam road used to come up to an end a few kilometres out of Nakuru, but no longer. A nearly perfect new road was unrolling itself under our wheels and we soon crossed the equator on that smooth surface and I certainly did not complain about this improvement. In the past, the rutted surface shook our bones badly all the way to Marigat on Lake Baringo. The landscape had nothing especial, scrubland with acacia trees and red laterite soil, but I loved it, like an old friend. We finally reached Marigat, much sooner than expected, thanks to the new President, Arap Moi, a Kalenjin, whose home town was Kabarnet and who had decided upon having been elected to spend money on his people and the roads leading to his home town. We discovered that something akin to a three lane motorway was under construction by Israeli contractors to link Marigat to Kabarnet, up the escarpment, where only seven years ago there was a dirt track. This time we were not going to go up the escarpment but would remain near Lake Baringo and our camp was to be in a bird reserve area known as Simon's camp - next door to a posh hotel. It was very very hot and the moment we stopped the Land Rover and let you and Chris out... wait for the now familiar story... you, Gregoire, rushed to a big acacia tree under which someone had had a barbecue or cremated his ancestors (I am only joking), stripped naked and started smearing yourself with white ashes from the fire! It was surrealistic. Ian rushed for his camera to fix for posterity this amazing phenomenon: a very blond and very white three-and-a-half-year-old communing with nature and

91

repeating without knowing it what people all over Africa are still doing: rubbing ashes or ochre all over their bodies! Besides, ash is of course sweat absorbing, but this is only a rather down to earth comment added by a rational and practical minded mother

All these years we all believed in your father's ethnographic explanation for your behaviour, without of course having ever checked it with the individual concerned, as all self-respecting scientist should always do. One day much later, as I was recounting this at a dinner party which you and Chris were attending, you burst out laughing and started mocking me. Of course it wasn't that at all Mum. "We had been playing games in the Land Rover as to which one of us was the Best Incredible Hulk, and when we stopped I just ran and rubbed myself with ash to prove to Chris that I was the Incredible Hulk, not him". I suppose you had the colour at least if not the pectorals!

Anyway, we set up our tents; ours was a large and tall family affair this time as you were no longer babies and needed more space. It was such a pleasure to pitch a tent on a grassed area and so much easier too than on stony ground, as we had to in Kibingor. We chose a patch not too close to the lake shore, for fear of crocodiles. Then we installed the rest of our base camp (kitchen, dining table, place to store archaeological samples and so on). There were shower blocks close by in the camp site, so we had luxury unknown in previous years when I camped in a much more remote area. Another perk of this camp-site (albeit not offered by the management) was that at night the adults would stealthily cross into the posh hotel grounds through a gap in the barbed wire fence and use their swimming pool. Oh the pleasure of swimming under a sky full of stars. Alice (an anthropologist and one of your Dad's ex PhD students joined me sometimes in swimming races and afterwards I lay exhausted on the side of the pool at midnight, losing myself in the infinite sky

(I did not have Alice's stamina). Eventually we were caught and had to buy a pass - but we did argue for a reduced price and got it as we were staying for a couple of months. And this is where you became a proficient swimmer; it is also thanks to that hotel's fish and chips that you always escaped from our cook's traditional food of ugali (maize meal flour) that Ian was too soft-hearted to make you and Chris eat, or could it be that he was also probably glad to escape from it himself. If it had been left to me, you would have both starved and then when really hungry would have eaten what cook had made! There, what a dragon of a mother.

Living in Simon's camp site meant living close to a lot of wildlife of all sorts and sizes. There was a huge tortoise hundreds of years old (maybe not that old) and absolutely enormous. You and Chris used to try and ride on her back, but she didn't seem that interested in moving, and how do you coax such a heavy weight into action? There were also extraordinary birds, amongst which your favourite was the "go away" bird, so called because his call said just that, Go Away, Go Away! Some terribly stern looking marabou storks (which sounded like springs from old mattresses when they took off) also strutted about in a self-important and absent-minded way. One day you and Chris rushed back nearly in tears saying that you'd seen rabbits hanging from the trees and could I come and rescue them...a closer look showed that these furry rabbit-lookalikes creatures were in fact fruit bats, hanging upside down in the position that all self-respecting bats take up when going to sleep. Who needs school in such an environment, there is so much to learn all around, and it's more fun to see your subject alive than flat and still in a book.

Excerpt from *Safartu: travels with my children, 2015.*

The Hospital
Jane Wilson-Howarth

An hour before sunset we reached Ambatoharanana. I was dying for a pee again. Abdulla invited us to see his *hôpital*. I accepted with as much enthusiasm as my bursting bladder allowed. I prayed that his hospital would be small. Abdulla led us through the village: a muddle of tiny houses, most thatched and all perched on stilts. The 'hospital' was not much larger than the other houses. It too was on stilts but had a corrugated iron roof which made it stiflingly hot and airless inside. There were four beds, each with a mosquito net full of holes. Beneath one, lying on plastic sheeting instead of bed linen, lay a man who groaned and rocked his aching abdomen. Perspiration poured off his emaciated body. Abdulla demonstrated his training and how ill his patient was by prodding him sharply in the stomach. The invalid curled up and his groaning grew louder. I felt sick. *Aides sanitaires* [like Abdulla], who are male, educated and leading village figures, are given a whole year's training to provide a basic primary health care service in rural Madagascar. They organise immunisations, treat what they can with penicillin, chloroquine, aspirin and antiseptic, and may refer patients to the doctor. He showed us his meagre dispensary while I tried tactfully to ask about the man with belly-ache. Would the doctors come and see him? Shouldn't he be evacuated to Ambilobé?

'Maybe tomorrow,' came Abdulla's answer.

Abdulla asked if we wanted to use the bathroom. Baffled, but hopeful still of finding somewhere discreet to squat, I said 'Yes', and he led us out between the little huts to the edge of the village and waved vaguely towards some kapok trees.

Excerpt from *Lemurs of the Lost World, 1995*

Yoghurt Pot Run
Sally Haiselden

I became good at evacuating into a yoghurt pot, clenching my buttocks and tearing up the road in Khartoum to the clinic for a laboratory diagnosis. A Westerner is conspicuous. A Westerner gingerly carrying a yoghurt pot is intriguing. A succession of foreigners carrying yoghurt pots in the same direction is entertainment for the locals. The doctor could give you a rapid answer if you could keep your insides from coming outside. Getting home via the pharmacy was a race against time. Was it just a coincidence that it also sold yoghurt?

First published in *How to Shit Around the World* (Travelers Tales, Calif.), 2006.

Egyptian Whisky
Françoise Hivernel

We were on our way back from Ethiopia, via Egypt and had ha
a rather difficult time in Cairo, no money to speak of except for
an array of various foreign coins, but it was a rougher time too
reality, after a war with Israel. At the last minute and after
having visited what we could in a city still recovering from the
fight, I noticed some green whisky bottles that someone was
guarding manfully on a small trestle-table in a shop. After a las
turning of my pockets I extracted the bargained amount. And
soon after we embarked on our plane with the bottle and flew
home.

Now quite some time later I opened the bottle of whisk
from Egypt. I cannot quite remember whether my friend was
there or not, but I do recall that whilst eagerly awaiting the hars
first gulp taste, only a tepid watery one came into my mouth...
another try produced the same result... After a few moments
wondering what had happened, I turned the bottle upside dow
and noticed that its bottom had been cut very neatly round and
stuck back together. Good bye to my alcoholic dreams and I
dumped the bottle with strong words.

AMERICAS

Wedding Guest in Colombia
Stephanie Green

I would like to give three pieces of advice to travellers planning to transit through Miami airport. The first is to make sure you fill in the immigration form correctly. If your next stop is Colombia it is especially important to fill in the form correctly.

Elaine and I were travelling to Bogota for the wedding of her son, Philip, to Sonia, a Colombian girl. After the tedious business of fingerprinting, eyeball recognition and answering questions on computers that didn't work properly and with only unhelpful guards to ask for advice we trailed through the airport to the transit desk. I amusedly watched Elaine approach the finger-print recognition device from the wrong angle and then do convoluted manoeuvres to get her fingers in the correct place while a surly official glared at her. Eventually she was sent through the double doors in the direction of the departure lounge.

I managed to have my finger prints and eye-balls recognised without a problem but the surly official told me not to follow Elaine through the double doors but to follow the yellow foot-steps which were painted on the floor. I did as I was told. I reached a large room and a machine-gun toting guard motioned me to sit on a chair alongside three other people. I waited there for ten minutes.

Eventually another guard beckoned me forward. 'You are travelling with more than ten thousand dollars in cash.' she barked at me.

'Chance would be a fine thing.' I replied.

Feeble attempts at humour are not appreciated by US customs officials. It seemed I had put a tick in the 'Yes' box that said I was carrying more than $10,000 in cash. It is a suspicious statement when you are travelling to one of the drug capitals of the world. To compound the problem, when asked, I had no idea of where I was staying in Bogota as I was just following Elaine, she had the address.

Eventually after much questioning and probing it was mutually agreed that the reason I had put a tick in the box that said I was carrying more than $10,000 when the reality was that I had just enough dollars for a cup of coffee and a sandwich was that I was stupid. It had nothing to do with the fact that I hadn't been able to find my glasses in the bottom of my bag and the light in the plane was dim and I'd just woken up. It seems that carrying vast quantities of cash that could have been used for buying cocaine may have had me thrown into a Florida jail while simply being stupid allowed me to sit in Miami airport for two hours before boarding the plane to Bogota. I happily settled for being stupid.

I had no qualms whatsoever about travelling to Colombia. I know it was considered to be a dangerous country for travellers. I know in the nineties it was considered the drug capital of the world, that the drug cartels of Medellin and Cali were rich and vicious and that the left-wing terrorist organisation FARQ had staged high profile kidnaps and had waged war on government officials. I was aware that twenty-three members of the judiciary were murdered during a siege in Bogota and the involvement in that atrocity of the drug barons and the government still remains uncertain. But that was twenty years ago and the Colombian government, with help from the US, has made great strides in ridding the country, or at least banishing them to the border with Ecuador, of the drug cartels and their production and processing of cocaine and the FARQ guerrillas. In Medellin the infamous cartel leader Pablo Escobar, who once ruled the town and was considered to be one of the richest men in the world, is now relegated to a legend. A tour takes tourists around the areas related to the drugs trade, the highlight of the tour being the spot where Escobar was shot.

The officials that we meet in Miami airport are surprised that we are going to Colombia, 'Are you sure you want to go to Bogota?', 'Why are you going there?' they ask with amazed and concerned expressions. I'm surprised at their reactions. Haven't they heard that Colombia has cleaned up its act and is now considered to be a safe place to travel to? Or, as they are at the cutting edge of drug smuggling, do they know something I don't know?

We are met at the airport by Elaine's sons and whisked off to a hotel in Bogota around the corner from the bride's father's house. We spend the following day meeting relatives of Sonia and driving around town chasing the delivery of a wedding dress, rings and the various essentials for weddings. Then the next day we left the thin cool air of Bogota to travel down to tropical Meglar where Ben, the bride's father, has what he sometimes refers to as a farm or sometimes as a ranch. It is a large house designed to accommodate many people. It has a swimming pool, and open air dining area and kitchen and is surrounded by fruit trees and the land falls down to a river. Ben is a gregarious, generous and hospitable host. As well as Philip and Sonia and their adorable toddler Isabella, Philip's brother and step-father have also flown over for the wedding so we travel in two cars to the farm. The plan is for the men to go out on a stag night while we are there.

If the stag night (or bucks night as the groom, a resident of Australia, insisted on calling it) was anything to go by the wedding might be interesting.

The participants arrived back from their night out in the town at 7am just as dawn was breaking and we were thinking about going for an early morning swim. The laughter and singing were raucous and there were shouts of delight when they discovered the stock of tequila that the bride-to-be had hidden from them. They turned the stereos away from the house so it wouldn't disturb us but that wasn't a successful move as the music was on at full blast and echoed off the mountainsides so we got the echo as well as the original music. It must have woken the inhabitants of the town slumbering in the valley below. The dawn chorus of parrots, macaws and tropical birds were drowned out, the cicadas silenced. The leaves of the avocado, papaya and banana trees must have trembled in the sound waves; the humming birds that came for an early morning sup amongst the hibiscus would have been startled away. Was the caiman that had startled us the previous day as we'd strolled along the riverbank now in turn startled by the pounding salsa beat flooding from the house?

After half an hour we decided it was pointless trying to sleep, we mentally cancelled our plan for an early morning swim and lay in bed singing along to the music. It sounded like a wild party but when we peeked out we could only see a dozing groom and the father of the bride salsaring with the taxi driver that had brought them home then stayed to join the celebrations.

At 8am the father of the bride arrived in our room looking for absent members of his party, found two women in bed and decided to join us. Shouting 'Mi amor' he tried to get in bed with Elaine but the groom had followed him in and hoiked him out shouting, 'that's my mother!' He then tried to get into my bed but was foiled because I was in a bottom bunk and every time he approached he banged his head on the upper bunk. Very drunk, concussed and rejected he retreated. When we heard footsteps and shouts of 'mi amor' approaching for the second time we had the sense to lock the door. It was 9am before the music ceased and it was safe go into the water for our now not so early morning swim and for the maid to emerge from her room and cook us a breakfast of eggs, sweet bread and café con leche.

The members of the stag party didn't re-join the world until late in the afternoon and the jagged conversation was about visits to nightclubs where the influential father of the bride had people moved so they could have the best seats, of bottles of tequila consumed, of 'female friends' purchased to test the fidelity of the groom and could they have more paracetamol please.

The following day the drivers of the two cars taking us back to Bogota were probably still over Columbia's nil alcohol limit. We drove down the two-mile-long dirt track, choking on the dust, through the busy town of Melgar and onto the toll road for the 50mile drive back to Bogota. The driving in Columbia is fast and erratic, lane discipline is unheard of and cars constantly make sudden swerves to avoid the impressive potholes. On the outskirts of Bogota we ground to a halt. Bogota's roads are wide and multitudinous but still unable to cope with the traffic. There is now a policy to restrict the traffic by allowing odd and even number plates to travel on alternate dates. We were travelling with the father of the bride in his large and comfortable four-wheel-drive with the even number plates. His other large and comfortable four-wheel-drive with odd number plates was sitting at home waiting for him to use tomorrow.

We crawled through the streets of South Bogota past the favelas spilling down the steep hillsides and into a tough looking area where working girls in too tight, too short dresses lean in doorways. We crawled passed the impressive, mainly political, wall paintings which have transcended the genre of graffiti and have become street art. Then it's into the more salubrious areas North Bogota, the further north we get the smarter become the streets. We stop for a meal of tough steak, rice, potatoes, plantain

102

and avocado in a small café. Elaine generously pays; it costs her all of £10 for the five of us. Philip and Sonya, the prospective bride and groom, go for a pre-wedding talk with the priest who informs Sonya that if her husband strays it is her fault and she must forgive the weakness of men.

The journey to Bogota was only 50 miles but we rose 2,800metres and the air is thin and the wind is chilly. The temperature is nearly 20 degrees lower than in tropical Melgar. It dawns on Elaine and me that the flimsy summer dresses we brought with us for the wedding, on the assumption that as we are near the equator it would be hot, are inadequate. Because goose pimples are not an attractive fashion accessory we set off the next morning to buy a warmer cover-up to match our outfits. We hit the shops at 10am but they are still closed and we wander around for an hour until they open. We are back in the same area, the Zona Rosa, late in the evening for the bride's hen night, the bars clubs and restaurants that had been shuttered when we toiled around the shops were now open, blasting out music and packed with customers. The outside tables were empty; a sharp wind is whistling through the tree-lined, fairy light lit streets even the Bogotanos are complaining about how cold it is. A guest who has flown in from tropical Medellin thinks the temperature is arctic and shivers and complains constantly. Although Bogota is near the equator it is very high in the Andes and in a dip surrounded by even higher mountains and the wind is chilled by its passage over their tops.

The hen night is a much more subdued and lady-like affair than the stag night, two rounds of cocktails, which are the same price as one would expect to pay in London, a meal, coffee and back to the hotel by 1am. We are all sober but as the wedding is at 1pm the following day that is probably for the best.

103

The wedding was held in a venue at a hill-top complex on the smart northern fringe of Bogota. The wedding was preceded by the christening of eighteen month old Isabella. Having a child out of wedlock and then to christen and marry at the same time was an event frowned upon by some of the older conservative members of the family. Columbia is a very Catholic country. But the family still turned out in droves, after all a party is a party. The guests were dressed splendidly for the occasion, and the bride wore a fabulous white dress and arrived in a vintage car accompanied by the very proud father. The morning had been cool and cloudy but in the afternoon the sun shone illuminating the peacock colours of the silk dresses of the ladies. We sat under a bower of white flowers and tried to follow the long ceremony, as neither Catholics nor Spanish speakers this proved difficult. Elaine and I were both interested in the amount of cosmetic surgery that the affluent women of Bogota had undergone. We could see gleaming teeth, pert bosoms and stretched wrinkle free faces where when we knew the age of the woman we would have expected discoloured teeth and droopy skin but what enthralled us most were the ladies' buttocks. Maybe I'd lived a sheltered life but I didn't know that a well-padded buttock was deemed to be a thing of beauty. In Columbi it is. I was fascinated by a very pretty girl wearing tight leopard-skin whose breasts and bum stuck out massively in equal measure but in different directions.

After the wedding it was a time for interminable photographs, the same as any British wedding I have attended and then into the beautiful colourfully painted hall for the meal and drinks. There was disco music but mainly there was salsa and all the guests young, old, children and even me got up and danced. It was a lovely joyous family occasion.

104

The following day we wished the Bogota family good-bye and travelled to Almeira, to the land of coffee plantations and gentle hills although the journey there was over a far from gentle mountain. The road was tortuous and very busy; over-taking lorries labouring up the mountain-side meant death-defying feats around blind bends. We arrived in Almeira with a great sense of relief.

After three days in Almeira we set off for home and this brings me to the second piece of advice I would give to travellers planning to transit through Miami airport: don't try to pass through customs with a half-eaten hamburger in your hand baggage.

This time in Miami the customs and immigration officials had been transformed from sour and surly to happy and helpful. We're not sure why, maybe this shift just enjoyed working together or maybe they've been sampling the confiscated chemicals from the Bogota flight. Whatever the reason all the officials were cheerful and as an added bonus we didn't have to negotiate the mal-functioning computers to record finger-prints and irises. We were already on record.

I went through the passport and customs control ahead of Elaine.

'Why did you go to Colombia?' asks the official pasting on a concerned smile.

'For a wedding.'

'Who's wedding?'

'The son of my friend.' I turn and point to Elaine who is next in the queue, standing behind the red line.

'Was the bride beautiful?' the official asks.

'Very beautiful,' I tell him pointedly, 'and Colombia is a very beautiful and safe country. We were made very welcome and had a wonderful time.'

He looks at me as if I might need a full frontal lobotomy then smiles, hands me my passport and transit visa back and waves me through the double doors.

Elaine, standing in the queue behind me, has attracted the attention of a glossy coated spaniel. Elaine likes dogs she bends to stroke it and chats to the uniformed lady holding it. She is pleased the dog reciprocates the affection and seems happy to be with her. It is a while before it dawns on her that this is unlikely to be a 'bring your dog to work day' and that this a sniffer dog and he is taking an inordinate amount of interest in her not because he recognises a dog lover but because he has detected something in her baggage.

Paranoia sets in. Weeks of talking about the drugs, the trafficking and the dangers of life in Bogota has taken its toll. Reading the guide-books that stressed the dangers of travelling alone and advised to steer clear of many areas of Bogota had instilled in us doubts about the country. Had the affluent middle-class family we'd been made so welcome by really made their money from educational publishing? When people jumped into action when Ben made a request was that not because they liked him but because they feared him? Even though we had had no perception of crime or drugs or organised cartels during our stay the thoughts planted in our minds stayed there.

Elaine had completely forgotten about the half-eaten hamburger festering away in the bottom of her hand baggage. In mitigation it had been a trying and hectic few hours. We'd visited relations of Sonia's in Almeria, looked round coffee plantations, eaten and, as had become routine, made very welcome in various house-holds. We had decided to fly back to Bogota for our flight home rather than risk the tortuous mountain road again. Unfortunately as we reached the airport there was a horrendous thunder-storm. In normal circumstances I love thunder storms,

106

the bigger the better but when I am flying I prefer calm weather. The lights went out in the airport and when they eventually came back on we found our plane was delayed. Sonia bought both of us a hamburger because she said it was unlikely we would have time for breakfast if we were to catch our early morning flight. I ate mine Elaine took one bite of hers and stuffed the rest in her bag hence the interest of the sniffer dog. The dog must have thought it was his birthday after weeks of sniffing nothing but deodorants, perfume and unwashed underwear with the occasional bonus of a treat when he sniffed out drugs. Here he was within inches of real meat. No wonder he wasn't going to leave Elaine's side, no wonder she was his new best friend.

While the dog handler wrestled a salivating spaniel to the ground Elaine was beckoned forward. With her mind working in over-drive she approached the customs official who had just sent me on my way through the double doors.

'Did you like her?' he asked.

'Like who?' Elaine replied, puzzled.

'Your new daughter-law.'

That confirmed all her fears: not only had she had drugs planted on her becoming an unsuspecting drugs mule but the US customs had her on the radar because she had stayed with and had just become related to a known drug dealer. The fear of arrest and the rest of her life spent in an American jail over-ruled the logical thought that I had gone through ahead of her and had been quizzed by the same official and probably told him the reason for our visit. She was so nervous her legs could barely carry her along the route of the yellow footsteps into the inspection area.

I was waiting in the lounge on the other side of the double doors. I guessed why Elaine hadn't followed me through;

she'd been made to do the same detour I'd taken two weeks previously. I just couldn't think why she'd been detoured.

Eventually she emerged, shaken but relieved. The customs officers had decided not to prosecute her for bringing undeclared meat into the country but had confiscated her cold, half chewed hamburger. I told her about my conversation with the passport control man and that eased her fears of being a marked person.

We had a seven hour wait in Miami for our flight back Heathrow and so the confusion coming through the passport control at least passed some time and the thought of her being arrested for smuggling hamburgers into America, the home of the hamburger, did amuse me. It took a while for the incident to amuse Elaine.

I think my third piece of advice for any traveller planning to transit through Miami airport on the way to South America is: don't. If there isn't a direct flight, then take a plane that allows transit in Madrid, it's a civilised airport with nice views, good coffee and no need for visas. My advice is to pay whatever extra money is required to avoid transit through Miami.

Peruvian Cures

Jane Wilson-Howarth

Railway and bus stations are always easy places to buy drinks and snacks but in Peru I was puzzled when offered the choice of cold or warm Inca Cola. It wasn't until later in my medical education that I learned of the gastro-colic reflex whereby there is a tendency to open the bowels a few minutes after taking an ice-cold drink. When suffering from travel-induced unreliability of the bowels, taking an ice-cold cola just before boarding a bus will have you tapping the driver on the shoulder so you can get down and relieve yourself on the roadside. I was impressed that Peruvians understood the gastro-colic reflex.

They also seem to have worked out that changing the body's acid-base balance can help combat acute mountain sickness. When heading up in to the Andes, locals recommend chewing coca leaves and lime; they say it speeds acclimatisation to altitude as well as making the journey fly by. It is probably nicer to take than Diamox too.

In the Canadian Wilderness
Françoise Hivernel

We left Ottawa after hiring a car. My eyes desperately stuck on
Arnold's engine, in front of me, as if he could pull me along! It's
not that I couldn't drive, but that having landed in Canada's
capital a few days previously for the first time in my life, I was
launched back very suddenly into being in charge of a car, after a
few comfortable days relaxing at my friend's house. We left the
civilised capital city with loads of other cars and my two kids,
but after a few miles of being glued to Arnold's car I relaxed and
started to tag along.

 We didn't go very fast given the loads we were carrying.
I had two large canoes tied up on the roof of the car and inside
my two children and our backpacks, all our food for a week and
a tent. Why for a week you may well ask? Well we were on our
way to a week's canoeing trip in the protected wilderness of the
Algonquin Provincial Park in Ontario. It is a huge park of 7725
square kilometres, which has one of the world's most famous
canoeing areas.

 After a good many hours of driving due west of Ottawa,
we stopped at Arnold's brother's house and spent the night there
followed by a thorough hospital examination and bandaging for
Christophe, who had managed to twist his ankle very badly
whilst playing basketball with all the kids the day before. This
came as quite of a shock... Chris was strong and almost an adult
and we were now left with just three adults (two women and a
man) and five children including Christophe! However we
decided to go for it and I took my wounded son and his
additional walking sticks with his brother into the car.

 We spent a rather long time cutting across the southern
part of the Algonquin in a beautiful lazy sunny day and carried
on for another hour totally immersed in the magnificent setting

of our surroundings. The colours were gold and green and rust red, it was mid-August and it was hot. After a turn to the right we stopped at the Magnetawan Lake access 3. I let Arnold and Louise do the things which had to be done with the authorities, as you cannot go into this dreamland freely. The rangers checked our papers for the period we were allowed to enter and then gave us all the important guide lines. We were told that we must not spend more than a day in all the places we had registered to go, as people did not like to meet others. We were warned to be careful of bears at night and off we went. Not very far of course as, in the first instance it meant unpacking our cars, making sure that our five kids were helping with the sorting out of the luggage and the loading of the boats. In fact it took us two or three hours to organise everything. As usual we didn't think ahead! It was a lot to do... And of course Chris the eldest of the children, who was walking with crutches, was not much use.

Anyway we eventually went to park our cars and we got on board. Chris and I were in one boat. I'll just let you imagine how he got into the canoe and managed to sit down with his walking sticks... We had Greg and Henry (both 15 years old) in another, Louise and Daniel (11 years old) in the third one and Arnold and Julian (13 years old) in the fourth. We tried to pack all the gear and food securely, as well as we could. The canoes were quite heavy, but this was normal as we were carrying with us all the food needed for a week's trip in the wilderness. We were also aware that a canoe could easily overturn and then all its content would sink, unless they were safely tied up to the inside of the canoe. During that first part of our journey we were finding our rhythm, as well as a way to make the canoes run well, and how to work as a team of two. It was a slow and cautious start, and I am not sure that we looked very much at our surroundings, but despite of this we eventually paddled along

111

and landed where we were supposed to, according to our map for the first night. We unloaded the content of our respective canoes, found roughly smooth places to put up the two families' tents and started unpacking some food. It had been a long and tiring day! I was the most amazed at Louise who had back at home, prepared food for the whole week's trip. Everything was under plastic bags with a label for the day of the week to be used. So having found the appropriate day we opened the packs and started to get our taste buds used to the strange flavour to savour and... we discovered Logan Bread, made by Louise! This is the most prized food for canoeists as it lasts forever and is guaranteed to fill your guts enough to survive.

Looking at the recipe once back home, I discovered that it is called Logan Bread because it was first used on Mt Logan in the Yukon. Mt Logan is well over 19,000 feet! Our first act as real survivors was therefore to taste our bit of "Wheat flour mixed with brown sugar, powdered milk, honey, molasses, oil, salt and baking powder, dried fruit, oats, nuts and seeds". It was thought of as "delicious", on the first day, but by the end of the trip, it had become the last thing we wanted to eat. The other noticeable act that evening, was for Arnold to engineer a rope across a high branch and to pull the rest of the food up out of the reach of bears. During the week this became a ritual, but no bears ever came. However, almost every evening we saw some loon families swimming back to the crooked edges of the lake or the stream we were in, coming to the shallow sides to spend the night. These loons had a hollow laugh like cry and a white belly surrounded by grey to black plumage on the head and neck. I seem to remember that after that tiring first day we all collapsed happily under our tents and slept very deeply, without noticing the harshness of the ground and not even able to watch for very

112

long the sky so full of stars; even Christophe and his crutches had already adapted to our rhythm.

The next day started with giggles between the two tents and then erupted into life as our kids were messing around. After breakfast we had to reassert our power as parents and order our kids to help with un-pitching the tents, and packing and reloading the canoes. Although we were not quite there with the process of mastering the handling of canoes, of the oars, of going straight, we started to compete with each other, at least Chris, me and Arnold. However, reality soon intervened as we arrived at a point where we had to unload the canoes, do a "portage" (meaning: carry everything by hand), load the canoes again, paddle for a while across another large bit of water and arrive at another "portage". Now I don't know if you can imagine how exhausting it is to carry an aluminium canoe, two people are needed to do that, unless you are a very, very strong person. With both your arms up for half an hour at least and your body doing a strange dance trying to avoid the mosquitoes, up and down a rather slippery path, under trees in a hot and airless atmosphere, this is the amazing reality! Chris on crutches couldn't help and neither could Daniel, the youngest one. We were therefore only six able people out of eight, and there were four canoes to carry on top of all the rest we had to do, this arithmetic left us rather uncomfortable! One trip there with a canoe and two people carrying it, then back. Another trip there with all the gear of the canoe (food and sleeping equipment) and back and another trip with our backpacks, plus the additional trip for the last canoe. Arnold had scheduled three "portages" on that day... hopeful man, and by the end of that second one, we were knackered and stopped as soon as we could, ill-tempered and exhausted. No bear came that night despite our fears, so we did manage putting up the tents and organising food and ill humour evaporated with the adults bathing in the nude to the disgust of our children.

On the third day we never caught up with what we were supposed to do but the part of the lake that we were on was beautiful. We slowly dreamt ourselves into a watchers mode and saw several moose swimming across from us as we paddled close nearby. We didn't notice any fear in them, but despite this we remained very quiet and careful. It was a dreamy day and we just slowly pushed along on a sea of white lilies. The beautiful white flowers were drifting gently as our canoes approached. The sky was blue and full of sun. There were no mosquitoes either and it was bliss! We reached land in the afternoon and decided to stop there and relax, but that evening, a couple of people came in not too pleased to see us, we gently explained to them that with our five kids, one of them wounded we just didn't manage... and they left rather grumpily to relocate on another part of the island.

On the fourth day we had decided, maybe because of the unhappy couple of the previous night that we were going to try and go back; our muscles were taught and our minds not relaxed. A series of taxing "portage" occurred again, as well as the need to spend one night in a place we hadn't planned to stay but the next day by around midday we were back to our entry point. All in all a seven days trip cut down to five, not bad you could argue, especially as we did not turn over any of our canoe or fall into the water.

We reloaded our cars and we set off, ravenously stopping for lunch in a tiny town, no more Logan Bread for us, though there was still quite a lot left, and the kids feasted on "poutine" heartily. Later on I discovered that "poutine" is a well known recipe, despite its rather revolting look. Fries sprinkled

114

with fat flaky cheese and topped with brown gravy! Yuk... but after having had only cold food for five days, who is to wonder!

Having come out of the wilderness, reality changed and we started to look at ourselves, caked in mud, with some apprehension but no one gave us a look of surprise in the restaurant. After a few more hours on the road, our next destination, Pen Lake, appeared. I still have a lovely photo of myself rediscovering the natural colour of my feet in a washing bowl, by the pile of canoes, whilst the kids were happily taking out boxes of games in the tiny wooden cottage on the edge of the lake. Chris had managed to survive the journey and happily set aside the walking crutches. Louise, Arnold and myself could now rest after another adventure in our very long friendship.

The Worst Guide in the Amazon
Stephanie Green

We arrived at mid-day and I was allocated Lodge No. 13, Tarantula Lodge. I did think that No 9 Toucan Lodge that Clare and Marc were allocated or No 5 Jaguar Lodge that Terry and Susie were allocated at least sounded inviting. My combination of No 13 and Tarantula only sounded ominous. I didn't perceive number 13 as being unlucky, I'd grown up at number 13 Holtby Close and had had a happy and uneventful childhood but I was concerned about the Tarantula part of the name. I know that in the Amazon one must expect a certain amount of unpleasant wild-life but I would prefer not to share my accommodation with large arachnids or even be reminded that they were living in the vicinity.

Tarantulas may have been lurking under the grass roof of the hut but throughout my stay they didn't make their presence felt. The small but vocal green frog that shared my toilet did. He ribbeted away cheerily all night and ribbeted away angrily when I had the audacity to use the toilet and make him dive under the toilet rim for protection.

I was travelling with my daughter Clare and her boyfriend Marc. Along the way we'd picked up Terry and Susie. At the Lodge, a three-hour boat ride down one of the many tributaries of the Amazon, we were introduced to two Swiss girls Joanna and Deborah and Alex a young American man. Clare and Marc had been following the well-worn Lonely Planet trail through South America and into Ecuador and had already bumped into, and got along well with, Alex and the rest of the group seemed to gel immediately. Later that afternoon, after lunch, we were led to one of the long, motorised canoes. Canoes motorised or paddled are the only means of transport in this part of the Amazon basin. Hector was our driver and Victor our guide. We went upriver to a dried-up lagoon (it was the dry season) and some members of the party swam in the river, I declined and wandered around on dry land. A wise move I decided as darkness fell and Victor made us point our torches across to the other side of the bank and red pin points of light glowed in the torch-light: the eyes of caiman. These small caiman may not be considered dangerous to adult humans but I preferred not to put that theory to the test.

We fell in love with our guide Victor, his knowledge of and enthusiasm for this area was infectious and although his English and our Spanish were limited (except for Alex who spoke fluent Spanish and helped translate) we were able to understand him. Sadly, because of his lack of English, Victor was only a temporary guide. The following day we were introduced to our guide for the next four days: Parajito. If we had fallen in love with Victor, we didn't have the same feelings for Parajito. Evidently Parajito meant little bird and he had acquired his nick-name because he was so good at mimicking bird and animal noises. He gave us a demonstration; he was very good at mimicking bird and animal noises but unfortunately, as we found out over the next four days, he wasn't very good at being a guide.

The first day started off fine. We were taken downriver and went walking in the jungle, looking at plants and insect life: the wild coffee and chocolate bushes, the plants that were used to extract quinine and the hallucinatory drug ayahuasca that is widely used by the shamans in native medicine. He was knowledgeable about the plants and insects but became irritated when Terry proved to be a better wildlife and insect spotter than he was. Terry was so good at spotting small traces of wildlife that we christened him Terry Nutkins, much to the puzzlement of the Swiss girls and Alex who hadn't watched British children's

117

television in the nineteen eighties (they were also puzzled by us calling the rubber boots we were issued with wellies). By the time we visited a native village to have lunch, Parajito was irritating us. Maybe it was because he wasn't Victor or maybe his habit of marching ahead through thick vegetation letting branches snap back into the faces of the followers or ploughing on regardless on overgrown paths without waiting to see if all of his party were with him. Maybe it was when we had the opportunity to learn how the maize was pounded and a weak alcoholic drink was produced Parajito sat back, ogling the pretty girls of the village and drinking all the samples of the alcoholic drink. Whatever it was we were becoming disillusioned with Parajito; we wanted Victor back.

It was at our night walk that he started to excel in the competition for the worst guide. We were told to meet at 4.30pm. At 4.15pm I was filling my water bottle and collecting my allocated wellington boots when he appeared, shouting at me for being late. Like a naughty school girl I scuttled down the steep wooden steps to the waiting boat, forgetting to go back to Tarantula Lodge for my torch. He was disgusted 'Madam, never go into the jungle without a torch,' he said and he repeated this at frequent intervals.

I walked with Alex, following the light of his torch, initially through deep mud climbing and crawling over branches and overhanging trees then upwards through steep jungle pathways where Parajito frequently stopped abruptly causing all the rest of us to canon into each other in the dark. In the distance bullfrogs called and Parajito called back to them. Around us there were other screeches and calls but Parajito seemed to prefer his dialogue with the bull frogs. 'If they're male bullfrogs shouldn't you reply as a female? Asked Clare.

'Females are silent,' said Parajito.

118

'Exactly,' said Clare.

Then at his next abrupt stop when we all cannoned into each other once again and became helpless with laughter he became annoyed because, he said, our silliness and laughter were frightening away the wildlife. He steamed back to the boat leaving us to find our own way through the forest paths in the darkness. We managed to follow the path down successfully but it left us with a difficult climb and crawl through mud and over fallen branches and collapsed trees in the pitch black night. We helped each other through (although I was more the helped than the helper) and eventually arrived back on firm land where a clearly defined pathway led back to the river. I did suggest that we stay quiet for a while and see if he actually came back to look for us but although the idea appealed we were hungry and wanted our dinner so we went straight back to the boat. Hector sat in the stern smoking, Parajito sat in the bow sulking.

From then onwards our relationship with our guide was downhill all the way. He had hissy fits when we didn't do as we were told, he stormed off and left us in the jungle when we were laughing instead of being quiet, he had no concept of time and would tell us to meet in half an hour and then ten minutes later he would appear and harangue everybody for being late. He was rude and unhelpful and we didn't get to see any animals. It wasn't his fault we didn't see any animals, it was the dry season and we had been warned that the pink river dolphin would have left for deeper waters, the jaguars would be in denser jungle and other animals were likely to be feeding away from the sluggish river. Logically we knew it wasn't his fault but at the end of our four days with Parajito we were ready to blame him for anything and everything.

The day after our night walk when going downriver, he asked Hector to stop near a large wasps' nest and explained to us about marching wasps. He thrashed the paddle in the water making a loud crack and from the direction of the nest came a thump, thump, the eerie sound of angry wasps marching. He thrashed the paddle again and the noise increased in speed and intensity, the wasps were getting angrier. He lifted the paddle once more and Hector took the decision to leave the angry wasp alone, he put the outboard into gear and we hurriedly left the area, the abrupt acceleration leaving Parajito flailing in the bow of the boat and the rest of us giggling to ourselves. Then it was onto the village to meet the shaman. A chance to swim, a chance to have learn how to use a blow-pipe and a chance for Parajito to ogle the girls in their swimsuits and to make salacious remarks about the girls' technique with the blow-pipes.

Yet it was on our last day, the day we walked around the dried up lagoon that Parajito surpassed himself. We were looking for anacondas he said, they hung in the trees and we were told to spread out and look high into the trees. He did his usual act of charging off through the jungle leaving us trailing in his wake. For a while we thought we were lost in the Amazon forest for ever but eventually we re-grouped. Joanna and Deborah joining us eventually, we were getting worried about them but they strolled unconcernedly into the clearing, they said they could hear our laughter from far away. Parajito may have been right it was our laughter not our useless guide that stopped us seeing any wildlife. Whatever the reason there were no anacondas to be found.

Parajito then led us across the centre of the dried up lagoon, where the runnels of water ran between banks of deep mud, and he marched on ahead leaving us to find our own way through the quagmire. Susie got completely stuck, the Swiss girl abandoned their wellies and waded through barefoot and Parajito disappeared. When we eventually caught up with him (except for Susie who was firmly stuck in the mud and Clare who was helping her) I voiced the opinions of all the group that he shouldn't just walk off making bird noises; he should take responsibility for the group and see that we got through difficult terrain safely. 'It is not my temperament,' he said.

'Then you're in the wrong job,' I told him.

'Stephanie, no longer wants to look for anaconda,' he said, turned on his heel and he went back the way we came towards the thick mud, we trailed in his wake and met up with Susie and Clare. They were less than thrilled to be told they were going back through the mud-bath they had just extricated themselves from. This time I got stuck, leant forward and fell, so I was up to my waist in mud, this time he did come to help, along with Marc, and I was ignominiously hauled out. I got stuck a second time as we crossed the next water-course this time I was up to my knees in the thick, black, glutinous mud and again him and Marc hauled me out.

At the third and last water-course Clare, Terry and I left the others and went towards what looked to be an easier route, they got through OK but I had no energy left in my legs and when I went to cross the mud I once more got firmly stuck. I moaned 'I just can't go any further, leave me here to die.'

Terry and Clare said 'OK, been nice knowing you,' then Clare had a change of heart and said 'She is my Mum so I better help her.' As instructed by Clare I stepped out of my wellies and ploughed through the mud in bare feet and Clare went back and retrieved the boots. I did wonder why I hadn't done as Joanna and Deborah had done and jettisoned the boots at the first batch of mud, it was much easier in bare feet.

Back at the boat, all of us covered in mud, we found Hector had gone and we had a non-motorised canoe to paddle home in and we were the paddlers. Other motorised canoes passed us full of clean, sweat free passengers while we paddled for all we were worth in the mid-day heat of the Amazon, the perspiration stopping the thick mud drying on our hands and bodies. Parajito lazed in the back occasionally adjusting the boat's direction, after nearly an hour of this hard labour he said 'only another hour to go,' after ten minutes we rounded the corner and our lodges hove into view. For once we were grateful for his lack of sense of time.

There was a plan for a short bird-watching walk in the late afternoon. I couldn't face anymore Amazon mud and Susie had feet embedded with thorns (maybe keeping the wellies on was a good idea, after all) so we stayed behind, lazing in hammocks, drinking cold beer, reading our books, watching a troop of monkeys squabble in the trees beyond the dining area. We kept a wary eye on the resident tarantula that was curled up on one of the easy chairs, ready to wake at dusk, amble across the back of the chair and startle whoever had, unaware of its presence, elected to sit next to it.

As darkness fell the other groups arrived back, showered and sat down for dinner. Our group hadn't arrived. The other groups had finished dinner but our table was still set waiting for us. Susie and I were getting concerned. We wandered down to the landings: no sign of them. We were worried; they should have been back two hours ago. We heard the sound of a boat engine in the distance, it came nearer and then passed on by. This happened three more times. By then we were starting to get seriously concerned. Then we heard another boat engine and this time as it came nearer we could also hear the sound of laughter. 'That's them,' we said. It was. Our illustrious guide had managed to get them totally lost in the jungle. He didn't have a clue where they were and he didn't have a torch with him. They had wandered about for a while, only Alex had a torch but the battery soon went flat, somehow, in the dark, they had managed to find their way back to the river and stood on the bank shouting. If it hadn't been for the lovely boat driver, Hector, knowing they should have been back long ago and setting out to scour the riverbank for them they would still be there now.

Yet despite, or maybe to some degree because of, our hapless guide we had a wonderful time. As a group we bonded, we ate drank and laughed together and helped each other along. We may not have seen the more dramatic animals of the Amazon basin, the tapir, the pumas, jaguars, the capybaras or the anaconda and boa-constrictor and I'm not sure that I'd want to bump into the last two when we were floundering around after Parajito in the dark. We did see many caiman, including a very large one that was always in the same spot opposite the landing to the lodges. This caiman was so immobile that we suspected it was a model put there by the lodge owners to persuade us there is wild-life here. Yet although it would have been good to see these animals the best part of the trip was just being there. To see the beautiful butterflies and birds, to watch turtles tumbling into the river as we approached, to hear troops of monkeys chattering in the trees. We watched what seemed an entire village of all generations play a noisy game of what as a child I called 'British Bulldog' on the sandy banks of the river. I even became fond of the lodge's resident tarantula. It was just good to be in the Amazon.

On the last day we had a three-hour journey by canoe back to the nearest road. Hector drove, Parajito came with us. It was a suddenly animated, informative charming Parajito. When we came to shallow water and it was obvious we would have to get out and push he belatedly took account of my age and general decrepitude and insisted that 'madam' stayed in the boat while the younger members of the party got out and pushed.

123

On our last night at the lodge we had been muttering into our beers about what tip to leave. We decided that Hector deserved every penny (or dollar) but Parajito deserved nothing. When we came to leave the smiling, suddenly helpful Parajito we back-tracked on our decision and left both driver and guide the tip recommended by the travel organisers although our effusive thanks and farewells were only given to Hector.

ASIA & AUSTRALIA

Visiting Australia
Stephanie Green

A visit to Australia wasn't on my bucket list. In fact it was way down the list of places I wanted to visit but a very good friend, Julie, lived there and I did want to see her so when an aunt died and left me some money I decided to spend it on the airfare to Australia. I subscribe to what a friend describes as 'the theory of low expectations' the theory being if you don't expect much you won't be disappointed. I find it particularly useful for family Christmases. I expected Australia would be much like England, we speak the same language (sort of), drive on the same side of the road and if Neighbours is anything to go by the weather isn't that much better. Although I was looking forward to seeing Julie I had low expectations of Australia.

I landed in Darwin late at night, Julie collected me and we stayed at a hotel. In the morning we breakfasted on fresh pineapples and papaya while sitting in a Jacuzzi in a small garden behind the room. Bright white and pink parakeets squabbled in the hibiscus bush behind us. So far October in Australia didn't bear much relationship to October in our mutual home town of Hull.

After a trip around Darwin we ate a fishy barbeque at the Darwin yacht club and watched the sun set over the beach. beach we couldn't stroll upon because sea-water crocodiles had been spotted during the day and evidently to stand on one of the stonefish that thrived on the beach could prove fatal. After our first night in the hotel we went to spend the next two days with friends of Julie who were two years into a four-year term as Governors of the Northern Territories. We sat under the portrait of The Queen and were treated to a wonderful meal of giant prawns and seafood served by a waiter from Huddersfield. The second night we ate corned beef hash, still watched over by The

126

Queen and served by the same waiter from Huddersfield and then retired to the sitting room to watch an old episode of The Bill: the TV programs and language might be the same but life in Australia in October still didn't bear much relationship to an October in Hull.

Julie lived in Alice Springs, making a living painting and making pots. We drove the very long, very straight road from Darwin to Alice Springs and after the first tedious miles of the journey through scrubby bush with only the odd termite nest to give interest, the bush faded away and we were in the desert and I got the next pleasant surprise about Australia. The Australian desert is not the uniform beige that I expected of deserts, it is red with rock formations and silver and purple shrubs and the sky is a clear bright blue and there is colour everywhere. And this part of Australia is not in the least bit like England or another other country in the world, it is totally just Australian, with kangaroos and emu and wallabies and exotic birds and strange plants and endless sun and endless trucks, the road trains, which thunder along this mostly empty road. We intended to stop overnight in Ellis but the bar of the first hotel was full of drunken men, mainly aborigine, and the atmosphere was threatening so we drove out of town laid sleeping bags in the truck and slept overnight. I slept peacefully but Julie – more aware of the dangers of the outback, especially as today was the day social security payments were made and drunkenness was rife amongst the Aborigines – was on higher alert and slept fitfully.

We reached Alice Springs the next day at noon. I thoroughly enjoyed my time in Alice Springs. While Julie worked, I went on day trips, in a four wheeled drive through rough rocky terrain and dried up river beds. I went to Uluru and the Olgas on the only day in the year that it rained and I was unable to look out of the window at the scenery because of the mizzling rain on the window (the nearest it got to being like October in Hull). I did wonder why I was on a coach travelling for 300 miles just to see a large rock but when I got there the sun came out and then set changing the colours of the rock. There was something inexplicably magical about this large rock in the middle of the desert. We visited a fig farm that was set on the route of the old railway that went from Adelaide through to Darwin, the farmhouse was the old railway station and I slept on the roof of a truck and marvelled at the brilliance of the night sky. I went to Aborigine settlements and found it impossible to get my mind around the solution of how white Australia could right the wrongs done to the Aborigine people. Each morning, before the temperature rocketed into the high thirties I followed the trail of a large snake, out of the garden and went for a walk, often to the telegraph station which was the reason for the settlement of Alice Springs.

When it was time to leave I felt tearful, there was so much more to absorb. But work and family had to be confronted and on that Thursday morning at Darwin airport the temperature was at 42 degrees, a sure sign that a hot, uncomfortable summer was arriving in the desert.

I flew from Darwin to Singapore and looked out of the window of the plane at a perfect volcanic island with white beaches set in an azure sea. I wanted to go there. I wanted to travel more and see more of the world. I wanted my preconceived ideas of countries and people to be as shattered as my preconceived ideas of Australia had just been.

Since that day I have travelled more to Asia, Africa and South America and I'm still searching for that perfect island sitting in an azure sea and I'm still finding that my pre-conceived ideas about people and places are likely to be totally wrong.

128

Australians Abroad
Jane Wilson-Howarth

I spent one winter in Ladakh working for Save the Children and was one of the few foreigners to brave the climate. Even when the sun shone, maximum daytime temperatures only got as high as -11∘C. For most of the winter months there were five other expatriates in town and these included an Australian couple. They were doctors and were quite rude about their compatriots. They said, 'The only way Australians judge a place is on grounds of expense and the only places they like are cheap. "Really cheap" to them means really good.'

The roads to Leh were usually closed by ice but a few tourists flew in and within minutes of touchdown, everyone in the central market knew exactly how many more foreigners had arrived. People would volunteer that information as I wandered past the vegetable salesmen.

I found myself queuing in the bank behind a man who looked as if he had been travelling for a while. I sparked off a conversation, 'What do you think of Ladakh then?'

'Oh yeah, it's really cheap.'

'You like it then?'

'Yeah it's great.'

'Have you climbed up to the palace then?'

'Nah. Just chillin'.'

Down Under
Jane Wilson-Howarth

The shivering had stopped now and, pressed closely against Jill for warmth, I could feel her nodding off. The blackness was absolute. There was no sound except for Jill's breathing and the occasional drip, drip from the cave roof. I strained to hear something more. Surely that was a sound? Or was I starting to hear things? People found after days or weeks lost in the dark are often mad.

I still didn't understand how we'd got so terribly lost. I'd come looking for blind, white, cave-adapted animals and my mind wasn't on route-finding. We'd crawled down a much-used passage, found some small white invertebrates browsing by some effigies visited by Hindu devotees of Shiva: broken pieces of glass bangles said that even sari-clad women came down here to smear red powder on the stalagmites. We – in our big boots, caving helmets and lights with 4-inch reflectors – were not so intrepid. Yet there wasn't much hope of rescue. Not for days. It would be six days before weekenders would come again. Six days.

We'd ventured beyond the temple chamber to search for blind cave shrimps in an underground stream. As we turned back, I realised to my horror that the cave that had seemed so simple on the way in, presented choices of side-passages every few feet. The tunnels were arranged in a herring-bone pattern and now we were scrambling along unfamiliar corridors.

'I think we're lost, Jill.'

'Let's try following the draught. That might show us a way out.'

'No, let's go back to where the cave looked trampled. I saw some arrows there.'

'But do they point to the way out or the way in?'

130

We'd crawled and scrambled as the lights grew rapidly dimmer. I felt more frantic. I knew that once we were lightless we would never find our way out. There were no rescue services, not here in Nepal.

Then negotiating a small climb, I dropped the one light that was still working. Fumbling around in the mud I found it, but it wouldn't relight. I cursed under my breath.

We were now in a chamber so small that we couldn't stand up straight. 'Let's go back to where there is more room.' We blundered into each other and into the cave walls and failed to find a bigger space. 'Let's sit and wait.' We played consequences, but the subject kept coming back to bodies and death. We sang a few cheerless songs. Silly things occurred to me. One of my aims on this trip was to search out small wildlife, especially animals adapted to life underground. I'd collected some insects already but if we didn't get out, I would have killed those springtails and sandflies for nothing. I hate killing things. If we died in here, how long would friends at home remember us for? It is odd to contemplate your own absence from the world – especially when you are in your twenties.

We'd left our rucksacks in a little teashop close by. The teashop owner knew the caves, but if we didn't return he could make a lot of money by selling our cameras and other belongings. It wasn't in his interests to come and rescue us. And would anyone find us even if they did look? We'd probably wandered a long way off the main route to the effigies. We were in big trouble. We didn't even have any water to drink. And we hadn't bothered with breakfast. The springtails I'd collected were probably new to science, but at best all their discovery would have earned me would be a publication in an obscure entomological journal. Not many people would be impressed by a description of a 2mm long, dung-eating insect. This was not a discovery to die for.

A fluttering sound. Was I hearing things again? Bats were leaving the cave for the night. We must be near the surface 6pm. We'd been underground ten hours now. I strained to hear more. Perhaps we could leave via the same crack as the bats, but I despaired to finding the bats in the blackness. They'd be gone soon. I woke Jill. 'I think I heard something – let's shout... HEY

Was that a reply? We shouted again. There *was* a reply. Muffled and distant but a human voice.

A glow became visible. I hugged Jill. A smiling face appeared at a small hole in the roof. His fist was completely encased in candle wax. 'I coming different way madam. You was there.' As if we could do anything else. A few minutes later the light re-appeared way below us. We scrambled down towards it and the smell of candle wax. We cursed our aching, cold, seized up limbs. The bare-foot teashop owner who led the rescue party asked, 'You no happy madam?'

'Sorry! Don't I look happy?' He responded with one of those difficult-to-interpret head-waggles Nepalis do so well. 'You we are happy-very, very happy...'

Later I asked him, 'How do you know the cave so well?'

'I coming inside caves for nine years' time; here my wives can't find me. I having big wife-problem. They fighting at times.'

He knew the cave well but we took many more wrong turns on the way out. Back in the deliciously smoky teashop, the two wives didn't look pleased to see us – or him, especially when I bought a bottle of Kukhri rum to celebrate our salvation.

Decades later I went back to the caves to a picnic spot now called the Manjushree Park. It was hard to recognise the scene as lots had changed over the years and because of earthquakes. There was no sign of the tea-shop, but now the caves were hyped as 'one of the longest, adventurous and real caves in South Asia'. They were all locked. Maybe others had been lost in there. Maybe others had not found their way out. Locals talked of places inside where there was no oxygen. Maybe someone had died in there.

A Phallus and Two Snakes
Jane Wilson-Howarth

A few years back – before the earthquake – we organised a trek
along the route that tourists and expeditioners used to walk on
their way to Everest Base Camp. Now everyone flies so these
Middle Hills in this part of Nepal feel quiet and off the beaten
track, yet there are plenty of tea-houses and places to stay, or
simply loiter over a hot lemon or a glass of thick sweet tea. For
me the Middle Hills are far more appealing than the high
mountains, although I'm always inspired by mountain views. I
imagine the himals as avuncular, if distant, as they look down on
mere mortals. They are not things to be conquered, though I
admire those who choose to try.

I have made a lot of journeys to limestone regions and
love to visit caves. Caves may be an odd interest but the
creatures that live or shelter in them intrigue me and in many
parts of the world locals are drawn to them too. This is especially
true in Nepal where stalagmites are seen as embodiments of the
greatest of the Hindu trinity, Lord Shiva. In the eastern middle
hills at about 1500m above sea level, there is a limestone ridge
overlooking the confluence of the great rivers of the Dudh Koshi
and the Sun Koshi. The forested ridge is punctuated by many
caves which are well known throughout Nepal. Local friends in
Kathmandu said that the caves are impressive and very
beautiful, as well as centres that attract hundreds of people to
worship there four times a year – including for the Halesi mela, a
huge festival in the cave in the Nepali month of Chaitr (mid-
March to mid-April).

We approached the temple to the Mahadev through the
most wonderful forest that was alive with so many butterflies
and birds. I saw gorgeous scarlet minivets, and iridescent blue
hummingbird impersonators: the lovely sun-birds. Then we

134

arrived at the top cave to find the ground concreted and ugly concrete steps leading down into a deep dark pit about 10 x 10 by 15m high. It was dank and odiferous. One thing I've concluded from living for years in Nepal is that my aesthetic sense and the Nepali ideas of beauty don't always coincide. Barbed wire seems to be used a great deal in temples and there can be some terrible juxta-positioning of power lines and golden stupas.

Doves and pigeons cooed and fluttered on the rocks above the cave entrance. Inside there was a big colony of leaf-nosed bats. The assembled avian and insectivorous residents let their excreta freely rain down onto pilgrims and ourselves, and I found myself picking beetle body parts out of my hair. Even from my unwashed perspective, having taken 11 days to walk to the cave, it veritably stank.

We joined locals descending the hundred or so concrete steps and arrived at the phallic symbol of Shiva, the great god of destruction and recreation. It was a disappointingly small and stumpy lingam even if well decorated with scarlet powder. Since size matters, legend has it that it continues in the cave below and even deeper underground too. A woman in a bright red sari approached, genuflected at the stump and threw a coconut hard at its base. As the coconut smashed and the 'milk' ran out, several sleek, well-fed rats ran in to fight over the biggest pieces. More bits of insects rained down from the bat colony above.

As often happens in such places, a man approached me and in fluent English explained the significance of the place. This cave is one of the three largest locally and represent the three eyes of Lord Shiva. My informant pointed to the 'cow's udder'-shaped stalactite that constantly drips 'milk' onto the lingam and he told me how this represented the cow in heaven who can fulfil peoples' desires. He also took me to two large stalagmite columns that stand together and explained that pilgrims can test

135

their worthiness by trying to squeeze between them. Only the virtuous succeed. 'Try madam!'

I did and got through albeit with some difficulty, feeling thankful as I scraped the skin off my hip bones that caving back in England had given me some unusual skills.

The lower cave was much more attractive, although its floor had also been concreted. Slightly to my surprise the words of the Buddhist mantra *Om Mani Padme Hum* were painted in letters two metres high in the main chamber. I never have got over a desire to classify holy places into one religion or another, but Nepalis never have a problem with mixing things up. 'Hindu, Buddhist, never mind!' they say.

These caves were the final destination on a 100km trek from the end of the road at Jiri. We'd managed about 5000m of ascents and 5500m of descents with a maximum height above sea level of about 3500m. Over a week-and-a-half we'd traversed ridges and trekked through rhododendron forest and had wonderful views of Everest. Our final day was a five hour walk along the limestone ridge where the bird nerd in me was pleased to be able to stop and watch a hen harrier mobbing a kite. And the children were delighted when I discovered a metre-long slime-green snake. It was muscular but took no notice of us until six-year-old Alexander poked it with a stick and it slipped away into the undergrowth. As we walked down to the grass airstrip of Lamidanda, there were long discussions about whether it could have killed us or not. Our local guides were sure it was highly venomous. I wasn't convinced.

Soon we'd fastened out seatbelts and were bumping along over ground that looked and felt like fired brick. I was sure that flying in Nepal – the country where pilots joke that the clouds have mountains in them – was far more dangerous than any snake. The little propeller-driven plane seemed to struggle to get up speed and I grew increasingly uneasy that the pilot didn't seem to feel the need to leave the ground. Then – shockingly – the airstrip disappeared as we shot off the edge of the world and without gaining altitude were suddenly at least a thousand feet above the ground. Phew – we were safely airborne.

Only a few days later I was back to work, looking at improving health care in two districts in the lowlands of central Nepal. I visited the hospital in Hetauda. It was 2pm so the work of the day was done but a skeletal little boy squatted in the empty foyer area with his arm in a bucket. I asked the Nepali professionals I was with what was wrong with the boy. 'Snake bite victim.' I was told.

He'd been bitten at 10am, the bite incised, a tourniquet applied and now his arm was soaking in a strong solution of purple potassium permanganate while 'under observation'.

'Who is observing him?'

There were discussions and some shouts and a Health Assistant, wiping food from his mouth, joined us. He reported that the tourniquet was being released every 30 minutes.

'When was it last released?'

He didn't know. No-one knew. I pressed for more information and it transpired that the tourniquet wasn't being released but only moved a little. The boy was at risk of losing his arm. No-one really knew whether anti-venom was available locally. There was definitely none in the hospital but the local public health chief said, 'It is my idea that it is available in the bazaar.'

'Will someone buy it for this patient?'

'He is poor only. No-one will buy it.'

I asked the Health Assistant to check the boy's pulse. The HA was clearly too frightened to do this and as I approached the boy, who was quivering in terror, he told me not to touch the patient for fear of being envenomed myself. I squatted down by the boy and put a hand on his shivering shoulder. I asked him about the snake. His description suggested either a harmless species, or a viper. As viper venom kills tissues locally and the bite site wasn't inflamed I told the assembled company I was sure that the boy was going to be all right. I took off the tourniquet. I was aware of a lot of mumbled disapproving comments from the medics present.

The following day the public health chief announced to me, 'We saved that boy!'

I tried not to show that I was slightly miffed that I'd be given little credit not only for saving the boy's life but also his arm.

Coming or Going
Stephanie Green

I decide I have to have more courage using the Waray language. I need to speak the language at every opportunity and I have to accept that I will be laughed at, for the laughter isn't meant unkindly. Tomorrow I am going to Borongan and I will buy the ticket at Duptours using only Waray.

I prefer to use Duptours vans; they are more expensive but they have some tread on their tyres, and sometimes leave at almost the specified time. You can tell that Duptours is a more up-market carrier. They have a notice in the window saying, 'Sorry but we do not allow chickens or pigs to travel in our vans.'

I try my Waray on the girl in the ticket booth:

'Usa tiket Borongan, buhas returning (the word returning is replaced by a circle in the air because I can't find the word, in my very thin list of English/Waray words, for return) kakulop, alayon.'

'Bu-hasss,' hisses the man behind me.

The girl looks at me blankly.

'Usa tiket Borongan, buhas, *'twirl in the air'* kakulop, alayon.'

'Bu-hasss,' hiss the rest of the queue.

The girl still looks at me blankly but at least she's not laughing.

I turn to the queue, 'bu-hasss,' I say. They all nod and smile, so at least I've got word for tomorrow right. I try again.

'Usa tiket Borongan, bu-hasss, *'twirl in the air'* kakulop, alayon.'

The girl still looks at me blankly. I decide she is the product of a small gene pool. I give in and write down which van I want to catch, give it to her and she sells me a ticket.

It seems that there is no such thing as a return ticket. I have to buy my ticket back to Tacloban when I arrive in Borongan. I had also got my kulops (afternoon) and my kakulop (yesterday afternoon) mixed up, so had actually asked to go tomorrow and return yesterday. Even so you would have thought the girl would have realized that.

The attempt at Waray may not have been a great success but at least I managed to get to Borongan and back and I can now pronounce bu-ha*sss* correctly.

Rising to the Trot
Jane Wilson-Howarth

We'd risen before dawn. The slightly sulphurous air hung thick, warm and misty. We negotiated cracked paving stones over stinky storm drains, splats of red betel spit and razor wire protruding from buildings. Someone had nailed a tiny spirit house to a banyan tree. A crazy *Ko-el* call came from a cuckoo and crows shouted surprised *Aggh, Agghs.*

This is a troubled country where everyone stares but everyone smiles and people put themselves out for outsiders. The sounds, spicy smells and paan-sellers in Yangon reminded me of scenes I'd experienced in 1976, the first time I visited India. This didn't surprise me as Burma had, after all, been part of 'British India' albeit for only 62 years, and – I learned – large numbers of Indians moved in to take administrative jobs for the Raj. Yet local manners, gracefulness and roadside shrines recalled destinations further east, in Thailand and Indonesia. This truly felt like a cultural crossroads: the bridge between south and south-east Asia. It also felt very last millennium. Already it was clear that the infrastructure needed money (as do the health services). What did I know though?

The station was seething with families and impossible amounts of luggage. Neon lights shone harshly. Three-metre-high railings stopped anyone getting close to the trains. We waited, watching small children in their best going-out clothes playing tag amidst the packages and cases. We hoped we were in the right place, wrong-footed by having been rendered illiterate, unable even to read numbers. There was simply nothing recognisable in the Myanmar language.

That had made even buying our tickets challenging. A couple of days earlier we'd gone to the station, intent on taking the night train to Mandalay. The ticket office didn't look as if it had been functional for years. Someone official-looking directed us over the railway line. On that side there was nothing that looked remotely like the kind of place you'd buy a ticket. Another official pointed us out of the station to a different building. Knowing that the grand colonial railway offices where being converted into a hotel, we had very little idea where to go next, but then down an alley I spotted a shed with corrugated iron for a roof. It looked like the kind of place cattle might be auctioned. It didn't have many walls. Inside there were rows of ticket counters. The wallessness of the building allowed the air to move a bit so it was a little cooler inside. Tree sparrows were enjoying the echoes that they could make. There was a big sign in English saying Complaint Centre; it alluded to a small red post box, definitely a relic of the Raj. A couple of counters seemed to be manned. We approached one and the official asked whether we would travel Ordinary or Upper Class. We wanted Upper Class. He pointed behind us to another set of counters and told us we needed Number Two.

The counters were labelled in Myanmar only but we plumped for the second counter from the left. It was unmanned. S made the bold move of putting his head into the office to ask for help for a ticket on the night train. We needed counter six. The man there established that the night train was fully booked for the next couple of nights. I wondered whether this was the time to offer a bribe. I didn't. We asked for a ticket to travel during the day, but for that we were assured we needed to return to the railway station.

We doubted that was true. A koel joined the negotiations shouting increasingly manically so it sounded as if the heat had completely fried its brain. It was early. We were not yet frazzled. We had time and explained we wanted to travel the day after tomorrow. We were directed to counter five. The man at counter five directed us to counter seven and someone else to counter eight.

The official at counter eight needed to see our passports. We didn't have our passports with us. Fortunately, our hotel was close by and when we returned to counter ten with them, buying tickets became straightforward.

Back at the station before dawn, ready to travel, nothing seemed to be happening. We wondered if there would even be a train, but then suddenly everyone at the station roused themselves and became animated. People surged through a tiny gate and onto the platform. We joined them. We examined our flimsy tickets and didn't have too much trouble identifying the only Upper Class compartment. We'd been allotted seats numbered with a back-to-front C and a J. Our carriage could have been a relic of the Raj. It was bile green, smeared with the grime of decades. The four tiny ceiling fans for the whole compartment looked inadequate but weren't moving anyway. There was evidence that the seats had been reclinable and they'd once had built in cushioning. This was disintegrating but at least it had been recovered in stout military green cloth. Some of the tray tables still almost functioned too. This was really, really not Upper Class travel but it was going to be a small adventure.

Six o'clock on the dot, the train gave a lurch then, as if reluctant to start, almost imperceptibly began to move. A large bat, beautifully silhouetted against the rose of dawn, overtook the train. Through the open windows I saw once-white concrete tenements festooned with feisty little wall-weeds, drying laundry and yet more razor-wire. Progress was slow enough to catch snippets of unintelligible conversations. The speed built from walking pace to perhaps 30mph, which caused the poor old train to creek and rattle and crash.

143

We were soon clear of Yangon city and looked out acro the vast fertile delta of the Irrawaddy. I stuck my head out of th window for a better view, narrowly missing a mouthful of red spit emanating from a betel-chewing chap further up the train. The lush countryside was flat, dotted with tiny thatched houses on stilts and the occasional breast-shaped pagoda. Women in bi brimmed hats squatted in paddy-fields, planting. People move about on ox-carts, bicycles, motorbikes, scooter-trucks, two-wheeled ploughs and other improvised modes of transport. We passed a line of commuter-ducks marching off for a day's work in a drainage ditch. Giant pods dangled from big-buttressed kapok trees. Flame of the forest and red silk cotton trees were in glorious bloom. Some bore white blossoms which took to the ai screaming, as they transformed into egrets.

A handsome man in a white shirt, bleached quiff and a big smile was moving through our carriage speaking earnestly each passenger in turn. He had the kind of obsequiousness I associate with evangelists. When he came to us, he handed us a small tract. I thought of refusing until I realised this was the breakfast menu. We could choose from:

> Deep fried sparrow
> Deep fried eel
> Fried Rice
> French toast
> On Toast
> Hard boil egg
> Red Bull
> Shark

Normally I'd have ordered something as unusual as sparrow but I love these cheeky little birds so chose On Toast. Further into our travels I worked out that nouns are sometimes lost in translation, so a café will advertise TEA – SNACK – COL or COFFEE & COLD. The Deep Fried Sparrow was actually Sparrow Bananas – the tasty little yellow ones. Our menu had also failed to mention what was On Toast; it proved to be two fried eggs on white sliced bread. And Shark was simply an energy drink. We enjoyed our On Toast and managed to gulp down glasses of over-sweet Nescafe without spilling much despite the train lurching at random. The whole train rattled and raunched. Over some sections, it rocked from side to side, but mostly it dodged and bucked like a creature trying to break free.

A three-year-old boy in front had been studying us with great seriousness over the back of his seat. I wondered if he was frightened of us but his face broke out onto a sunshine smile when I shared some segments of orange with him. His Mum turned to grin at us too when she saw where the fruit had come from. I wished we had a language in common. Actually everyone seemed genuinely friendly and always returned our attempts at offering a greeting, which was something like "Mingle about". Folks were even more interested when they learned we were English. I took this as a colonial connection but of course that was not it. They smiled, "Manchester United", "Wayne Rooney!" "Chelsea".

The train stopped often but never for long. Families and food-sellers climbed aboard. They strode through the train with huge trays of food balanced on their heads, never dropping anything. The vendors shouted unintelligibly in Myanmar. The only one I understood was an old man who used three languages, "Ye – paani – water – ye." That 'paani' was the only time I heard Hindi spoken. After one especially big jolt, water – fortunately it was clean water – poured through the roof behind us. The supply to the loo was incontinent. This, of course made me think I had to "go'. I'd been putting this off as I wasn't confident my knees would allow me to pee without mishap.

145

My knees are worn out from too many Himalayan treks. I'd had surgery and stem cell treatment to my right knee six months earlier and my surgeon had forbidden what he called "deep squats". No problem, I thought: life in the UK seldom requires deep squats. I'd worked hard on my rehabilitation exercises (at least in the first two months) and strengthened my quadriceps and practiced the balances my physio had suggested. I'd returned to cycling and no longer needed to wear my knee brace but could see that using the lavatory was going to demand some special skills. It was quite clean but there was, of course, no pedestal (and certainly no loo paper). There was also nothing to hang on to. I am a veteran of squat loos though so normally this wouldn't be a problem. My challenge was that I'd rather neglected my exercises in the month before this trip. And a half squat was difficult to maintain while guarding against head-injuries due to random train-lurches. Looking at the speeding track down the modest hole between my legs induced a touch of vertigo too. I told myself to man up and cursed my idleness. Other silver travellers know the wisdom of pre-trip conditioning and so should I. Eventually I emerged with a bruised elbow but dry-knickered and unsullied. I even managed a well-directed and very refreshing bottom splosh with the scoop provided.

The smiley man with the bleached quiff came by often and when a passenger made a lip-smacking kissing noise, I took a moment to realise this was not a proposition but the accepted way to attract his attention. Smiley was kept busy bringing boxes of delicious-smelling, thoroughly-fried unrecognisable food. Sadly when we tried to order "some of that" they cooked especially for us, and it didn't seem as good. I think they slipped in lots of monosodium glutamate.

The countryside changed. Low hills appeared on both horizons and, now that we had left the delta, the land was parched. This was a tough region for scratching out a living. We had a map but it wasn't easy to follow our progress northwards as most of the signage at each tiny station was in Myanmar, a script that although based on Sanskrit has so evolved that we could identify very few letters. Most looked like circles with various pieces missing or twiddly bits added.

The unpredictable motion made us feel a little unhinged as the train lurched and bucked like an unbroken horse. I even wondered if trying to rise to the trot might make me spill less of my drinking water because we had to drink somehow, but this just dislodged the blocks that served as seat cushions. The temperature had risen to around 40∘C and sweat dribbled from my nose and down my back. Someone started the ceiling fans but they were completely ineffectual. The smiley man changed his shirt so continued to look immaculate.

The bucking continued. There were often huge crashes as one compartment was wrenched out of synch with others. Some jolts left one carriage more than half a metre higher than its neighbour. It genuinely seemed only a matter of time before there would be a derailment. It amused us that 384Kyats of the 9500Ks ticket price was for life insurance. Discomfort and speed probably explained why so few people – locals or tourists – travel the entire distance between the two great cities, from the former capital of Rangoon (Yangon) and another old capital, Mandalay, despite the cost being less than for one stop in the London Underground.

By the time we reached Pyin Mana Junction we knew that the ten-and-a-half hours timetabled for this 650km journey was unrealistically optimistic. Indeed all the journeys we made on this visit to Myanmar were optimistically timetabled. Probably it is better that way. A bevy of smartly dressed police and soldiers joined us.

Alarmingly one carried a machine gun and two others rifles looking as if they might have seen service during the Korean War. Their uniforms were crisp – as soon as these military men had decided on seats, they removed their shirts and dangled them with their weapons. The military are very much in control here, and unbeknown to us at the time (March 2015), colleagues were doing battle with demonstrating students ahead of elections later in the year.

We came to the ten-year-old capital of Naypyidaw, Royal City of the Sun, and crossed several empty five-lane highways, wondering why, if the planners really anticipated serious levels of traffic, these were interrupted by level crossings. Twelve hours into our ten-and-a-half-hour journey vendors offered chilled Myanmar and Tiger beers and half bottles of Grand Royal or High Class whiskies. We gazed out at a spectacular sunset, feeling ready for a sundowner. A can of Tiger beer hit the spot so that as we rattled into Mandalay after 15 hours, battered, sweaty and bruised of bum, we felt suitably mellow and ready to do battle for a taxi.

First published in the anthology *To Oldly Go;* Bradt Travel Guides, 2015

Pilgrimage
Seeta Siriwardena

It has been instilled into the minds of most Buddhists that they must visit four important places of worship in their lifetime. They are:

The place where Lord Buddha was born at Lumbini, Nepal.

The place where he attained Buddhahood at Buddha-Gaya or Bodhgaya, Bihar, India.

The place where he preached his first sermon at Saranath, Uttar Pradesh, India.

The place where he passed away in Kushinagar, Uttar Pradesh, India.

Wealth and social class determine how pilgrims travel. The wealthy travel by plane, stay in good hotels and add sightseeing trips such as visits to the Taj Mahal and the Red Fort in Delhi. The less wealthy organise group travel, charter a bus, employ cooks, take ample provisions and stay at designated sites for pilgrims. This latter method has a tour leader and invariably has numerous toilet stops which is a real bonus as there are no toilets on the way to these extremely remote areas. When a toilet stop is requested the male passengers use the right hand side and the females the left hand side of the road just beyond the grass verge and if lucky find a suitable shrub as a screen. Friends of mine call these "parippu stops": parippu means lentils in Sinhalese, and the fields around Bihar were planted with lentil bushes, acres and acres with no houses to be seen. No sane person does the pilgrimage on their own.

In the early 1960's against all advice Jeeva, my husband and I decided to do this trip on our own. We were young, in our late twenties, and at an age when we thought anything and everything is possible. We left our two-year-old son with my mother, obtained the necessary visas and travel documents and flew from Colombo to Bombay. From Bombay we took a bus to Aurangabad, and another to the Ajanta and Ellora caves. These caves date from AD 200 to AD 650 and are covered with Masterpieces of Buddhist religious art with figures and depictions from the Jataka tales. The architecture of these is at least as interesting as the myriads of rock paintings on the walls These cave halls are as large as cathedrals, we had a torch but n binoculars and disappointed with our lack of preparation, we le after a couple of hours.

Outside waiting for a bus we met a young Indian coup and Jeeva soon discovered that the man was a doctor and a Buddhist, a rarity in India. He was doing the Buddhist Pilgrim route with his wife and invited us to join them. They gave us a lift in their car as far as Allahabad from where we took a train t Gorakhpur and another to Balrampur where we had booked a night stay in a hotel.

From the railway station in Balrampur, we took a tonga to the hotel that we had booked. The tonga is a horse drawn tra it is built like a dog cart, the passenger sitting on a plank of woo facing the back, sliding off continually, and seeing the view ahead only by twisting the neck. It is not 'done' to sit beside the driver so Jeeva and I sat facing backwards. Our tonga was pulle by a beautiful white horse. Its head was decorated with white feathers and bells. He was pawing the ground restlessly. We to the driver to take us to the Balrampur hotel and he gently whipped the horse into action

It was late evening and we did not see any other vehicl on the way to the hotel. The horse dashed through the flat country side with his decorated bells ringing in the air. There was an occasional lit house visible far away. We finally stopped at the hotel, which turned out to be the former palace of the King of Balrampur.

We got down and two men in full turbaned uniform, stood at the bottom of the three steps and another one directed us to our bedroom. The bedroom had an enormous bed with two huge stuffed tigers on either side of the headboard. And at the door there were two further turbaned men in some form of full ceremonial dress with swords tucked into their waistbands and a spear held in one hand.

I took one look at the face of the men who had swarthy complexions, were muscularly built, six footers with unwelcoming faces. We were the only guests in the place. We looked at one another and I said 'I want to go back!' My husband, although a six-footer, was puny compared to these tall well-built men. I did not want to stay there, as we had visions of not surviving the night. However, the tonga had already left for the gates of the Palace.

Jeeva who was an eight hundred metres hurdles champion, a cricketer who played for the university, who had also done the ten-mile open air swim from Mount Lavinia to Colombo, ran as fast as he could all the while calling out to the tonga-driver to stop.

He finally managed to stop the tonga and I ran, the 'fall' of my sari streaming out behind me like a peacock's tail. Once I'd caught up, we rode back to the railway station.

We explained our position to the station master and he said, 'Alright, as you are pilgrims you can use the station waiting room and for your own protection lock yourself in till morning.' He handed us the key. We ate the biscuits from my suitcase – supplies so we could avoid eating unhygienic Indian food - and slept. The following morning, we were woken up by very loud knocking on the locked waiting room door. Jeeva opened up and a man came in shouting that we had no right to lock the door. He was so furious he hit Jeeva and soon the two men were rolling on the floor thrashing one another. Jeeva took most blows while I shouted, 'Stop, stop, we are not Indians! We are Sri Lankan Buddhist pilgrims!' At the word Buddhist he suddenly stopped, fell on his knees and said how sorry he was to upset a Buddhist pilgrim and the two men shook hands with one another.

The two men, now friends, went out to look for a place to eat. Jeeva came back with something looking like flat bread on a piece of yellow leaf of a tree that had just fallen on the ground and was peppered with sand. I went back to eating my now rapidly dwindling stock of biscuits yet again.

We got onto the next train which was to take us to Lumbini just across the Indian border in Nepal. We had booked a couchette for two but it turned out to be a sleeping car for four with two berths on top and two at the bottom. We had been allocated the two lower berths and I settled down to watch the passing countryside. There were numerous stops with vendors selling food and the ever popular 'chai' or hot milky tea at each stop. Towards evening two burly North Indian men got into the compartment and climbed on to the top berths. Jeeva and I talking in Sinhalese wondered whether we were safe on the lower berths and whether we would end up like roti or flat bread, when with a loud crack the berth over my bed tilted and was stuck at an angle held wedged between the door and the lower berth. There was nothing we could do as the train was travelling through the countryside so we informed the car attendant. We got down at the next stop and boarded a bus to Lumbini. Here, in a grove of Sal trees (*Shorea robusta)* which are no more, was the place Lord Buddha was born.

The principal sight at Lumbini is a stone pillar set up by King Asoka 2600 years ago, and is made of attractive sandstone.

There is no doubt as to the authenticity of its location as Cunningham's Archaeological Report confirms the site. Pilgrims have been coming here for over 2000 years but the nearest railway station is about seven miles away. We next took a bus to Buddha-Gaya, the place where he attained enlightenment and we wandered around the lovely leafy site with the sacred Bo tree surrounded by gold railings. At the end of his Enlightenment the Buddha wandered to the nearby river and was offered a meal of milk rice by the daughter of the village headman called Sujatha. At the time that we visited, this particular area of the river was dry and the area was desolate. We wondered whether this was the same river mentioned in the Jataka tales. Jataka tales are a collection of Lord Buddha's five hundred and fifty previous lives. When Lord Buddha was born as a squirrel he lived in a tree beside the river. One day during a very heavy rain the dray fell into the river and the babies were swept down the stream. He ran along the river bank, and as he could not swim he dipped his tale into the water, pulled it out then sat on it and squeezed the water. And so he went on till the God Sakra saw this, came down from heaven and walked towards the squirrel, and said, 'You're very foolish, even a man or an elephant cannot empty the sea'. The squirrel said, 'Perhaps you're right but I do not know what to do, and I'm doing what I can'. God Sakra saw the determination on the face of the squirrel and made himself big, walked into the river and took the babies out.

We both noticed a man dressed in the garb of a local inhabitant had been following us on and off since we came to Buddha-Gaya. He never came too close but hung about a few yards away. In this lonely spot he summoned up enough courage to come up to us and ask for money. When we refused he became abusive and persistent and we were quite concerned. And as the man did not understand what we were saying, we started to walk away from him fast. He followed us.

On the far horizon, we spotted a cloud of dust rolling towards us. And we made out that the rolling ball to be a bus, in the middle of a cloud of dust. We decided to run to catch it. My husband ran like the wind and stopped it just in time. I trailed wearily behind him, and the man who was following us was left behind.

From Buddha-Gaya, we took a train to Benares. This town is famous for the hundreds of shops that sell Benares silk saris. It looks as if each and every road is crowded with these sari shops with the sari displays looking like mini rainbows hanging down from the shop windows. Traditionally saris are all six yards in length, and Benares saris are so light that it is reputed that the entire sari can pass through a ring.

After succumbing to the inevitable, and with two saris safely tucked under my arm we walked to the Deer Park in Saranath. This is the place where the Buddha preached his first sermon to the five disciples. It is a tranquil place, and has the most expansive Buddhist ruins amongst the two and a half acres of stupas and monasteries scattered around. A stupa is a mound like structure containing Buddhist relics. They are built of earth covered with stone or brick. Stupas vary in shape in the various Buddhist countries but the majority are circular in shape. Some however are bell shaped, some are cone shaped, some are like pagodas and in some countries simple mounds with a spire on top.

The landmark here in Saranath, is an octagonal brick tower on a ruined stupa mound built by the Emperor Asoka, who spread Buddhism throughout his empire.

We took a bus to Kushinagar, where Buddha passed away. Here in the temple there is a twenty-foot high statue of the

Buddha in the recumbent state. Wherever one stands in this temple and looks at the face of the statue, the eyes appear to be following you. The Buddha, it is said to have told his chief disciple, 'I have now come to the end of my life. Please make me a couch as I am tired and want to lie down.' The disciple made a couch with robes and Lord Buddha lay down on it and passed away peacefully in a grove of Sal trees, saplings of which stand to this day.

There is one place in all India where one can recapture something of what early Buddhism meant in art and sculpture and that is Sanchi. Asoka founded the great Stupa there and of course one of his pillars is erected there.

We met the head priest, who was a Sri Lankan and held in great veneration by the local people. At the end of our visit, he walked down with us to the railway line and held up his hand to the next train that came by. The great juggernaut of carriages stopped, we climbed in and were taken to Delhi where we had a booking in a hotel. In this part of the country if one is travelling in first class or in an air-conditioned compartment one could hold up your hand and the train will stop for you.

My husband's friend from their time at the University of Colombo, Peter, was the Trade Commissioner for the Sri Lankan Government in Delhi, and he had invited us for dinner at the very luxurious Ashok Hotel. Looking around for a place to sit in the crowded lobby while waiting for him, a lady beckoned us and invited us to sit with her. We did so and discovered that she was an American from Texas on a world cruise, and the next port of call was Colombo. Peter joined us and while talking he asked me if I had bought any silk saris, and I confessed to buying two. He said that a new law had being passed banning the import of all silk saris, I was heartbroken and started to weep silently. Barbara, the American lady patted me and said she will carry it

155

in her baggage and that I could pick it from her when she comes to Colombo. True to her word when the ship docked in Colombo she visited us and handed the two Benares silk saris to me. I still have them with me.

Dithering in Delhi
Jane Wilson-Howarth

I'd just flown down from Leh. I'd been working with Save the
Children and shy, self-effacing Ladakhi people. I'd been helping
with roving clinics to remote mountain villages in "Little Tibet".
Delhi was an assault on all my senses – the heat, the eye-stinging
atmosphere, the stink of vehicle fumes, the filth, the in-your-face
poverty, the pushy lepromatous beggars, the blaring car-horns,
the clashing colours and the press of people. Everywhere I went I
was propositioned.

Men sidled up and whispered, 'What you need,
madam?'

'You want hashish, madam? Opium?'

Beggars put hands to their mouths and fixed me with
pitiful stares. If I gave them money they pursued me relentlessly.
Other hopefuls followed too so I developed a comet's-tail of the
destitute.

'I be your guide memsahib. Very good guide. Very
cheap.'

'Baksheesh!'

'Hello – taxi.' Or, barring the way, 'Hello – rickshaw.'

'Special price for you, memsahib.'

'I be your boyfriend, yah?'

'Nice carpet. Very cheap for you only.'

'You have husband at home, madam?'

My chaos of blonde hair made me stand out like a boil on
a bottom. Later – while living in Pakistan – I took to wearing the
local shawar kameez and covering my head with a dupatta, so I
was less obviously foreign. On this trip, though, I didn't know
much and although I wasn't provocatively dressed, I wasn't
especially modestly covered either. I didn't know then that
young Western women are seen as promiscuous. I hadn't heard

then that there is an appetite in the subcontinent for porn involving well-rounded blonde women. I was ignorant and just hoped to carry on as if I was in London. I plunged into Palika Bazaar, the underground market. I knew there would be plenty of foreigners down there and hoped to attract fewer stares. The heat was suffocating. I poured sweat but it was a treasure-trove of gorgeous fabrics. I tried something on and got groped by a bald fat sweaty man in a fitting room. I fled. I wanted to hide away. I didn't want to explore any more. Travel is all about taking risks. Playing safe and keeping yourself in a bubble reduces the joy, the spice. But suddenly after conquering those mountain passes and coping with queues of sick people, I wasn't as intrepid as I'd thought.

I was staying in a middle range, government run tourist hotel. Even there I felt hassled. I was obviously on my own. Men endlessly knocked asking how many people were staying in my room. They said they had to check I was paying the right room rate – the single occupant rate. I wasn't convinced but maybe they were just doing their jobs.

At least the hotel restaurant was under-used and hasslers, hawkers and gropers were firmly kept out. Next morning I sat on my own taking a leisurely breakfast, slurping bad coffee while I wrote home. Someone came and sat at my table. There were 20 others he could have chosen – all empty. He didn't greet me. I didn't look up. I frowned determinedly at my letter, acting as if I was deep in a creative process. He didn't take the hint. I neared the bottom of the page. I had no more paper. I had to look up and engage with this man. I expect my face wore a frown.

'I am disturbing you, madam.'
I didn't respond.

'I felt compelled to talk to you, when I came to know you had been in Tibet.' I must have frowned an even deeper frown. 'I saw your bag, madam.' He explained, pointing to a colourful shoulder bag that hung on the back of my chair that I'd bought in Leh. It had TIBET in big letters across it.

I looked at him. Keeping my face blank. He was a small slight man, smartly dressed. Respectful. Serious.

'I have always wanted to travel to Tibet only. There are so many wonderful animals there.'

Suddenly he had my interest.

'The snow leopard. Red panda. The impeyan pheasant. I long to see these species.'

He was a fellow-biologist.

'I am one conservationist. Indeed,' he said with a proud sparkle in his eyes, 'I am the man who has saved the Great Indian Bustard!' His expression said I should leap to my feet, shake him by the hand and exclaim, '<u>You</u> are the man!' But I was a little unclear what a bustard looked like. I'd a vague idea it was a clumsy great flightless creature. The word bustard made me titter inside. I already felt comfortable in this little chap's company. I was beginning to regret being a grump.

It took very little prompting for him to tell me about his conservation efforts in Rajasthan. As he uttered Rajasthan, I conjured up opulent palaces and lakes full of wildfowl. His passion was endearing. Then came the proposition. 'I am also alone here in Delhi. I am thinking we must spend some time together.' My heart sank. He was older than me: charming but not my type at all. He continued, 'You will be needing to take presents for your family. I will show you best places, and get you best prices. We can have nice times.'

He looked so solemn, so sincere. He did, after all share my enthusiasms for wildlife conservation. More importantly, I judged that he weighed less significantly than me and probably wasn't as fit as I was after my months in the mountains. I could surely either out-run him if need be, or sit on him if he misbehaved.

I said, 'What do you suggest?'

'We will do one thing.' This lovely expression made me smile. 'Let us first go to one emporium….'

No harm in visiting the emporium that I knew was close by. Then we had lunch. He wanted to pay. And so we had a delightful couple of days exploring the city. He was a perfect gentleman. He had no sexual agenda and he didn't seem to expect money from me. He spoke of needing to be a good host in his own country, and because he was with me, the hassle was less, and I suspect the prices were lower. We toured the Red Fort. We looked at silks and ivory. We had earnest discussions about how ivory shouldn't be on sale but that – fortunately – much of it wasn't ivory but actually buffalo bone. We debated whether ebony artefacts should be sold. We plunged into sumptuous shops smelling of sandalwood and incense and admired inlay work and mirror-work, bedspreads and shalwar kameez outfits, intricate woodwork, brasswork, statuettes of gods, carved elephants, chess sets. I wanted to buy everything.

I don't even remember his name but he restored my faith in people and showed me that it is good to take risks and come out of your bubble.

On another lone trip from London to Delhi, I queued at check-in with a young mother travelling without her husband but with a small baby and a toddler. She had an enormous heap of luggage. I made faces at the toddler. Made her laugh. Distracted her, and me, from the boring wait. I helped the family through security and into the departure lounge. I lost track of them after we boarded.

160

Waiting for my luggage in Arrivals in Delhi at 4am though, she was at my side again. She knew I had a short stop-over before flying up to Kathmandu. I wanted to find a quiet place in the airport to relax and maybe sleep. She told me I'd be more comfortable at her house. I hesitated, thinking that leaving the airport would be more hassle. She insisted.

Relatives scooped us up and we powered through the crowds and soon we were in a quiet neighbourhood and a small flat full of excited but respectful children. I was offered refreshments then shown to a huge bed already occupied by a veritable tribe of kids. I was slightly nervous I'd miss my onward flight but excited by this small adventure. Suddenly I was being prodded awake. A smiling face and, 'Bad tea!'

'Ah, wonderful bed tea. Thank you.'

They'd sent out for white sliced bread thinking I wouldn't want the delicious kedgeree they'd have for breakfast. The rubbery bread was plastered in axel-grease-flavoured margarine and luminously crimson plastic-flavoured jam. A teenager came into the flat saying something in Hindi and minutes later he showed me to a waiting taxi and I was driven away to catch my flight feeling choked up at their kindness.

Such kindness!

Leaving Serendipity
Seeta Siriwardena

The Arabic name for the island of Sri Lanka from about AD 301 was SERENDIB. Serendipity means fortunate happenstance or pleasant surprise. It is also used for unaccountable or unintended but fortunate experiences. This word was first coined by Hugh Walpole in 1754.

Mala was woken up by a volley of shots, it was pitch dark. She sat up in bed, her eyes not able to see any light. The clock on her bedside alarm registered 12.30am. 'What are they shooting at, and who are they?' she thought. Eventually the disturbed crickets started their chirping and Mala partly reassured by that noise, went back to sleep. She slept fitfully till morning.

The children were already up and the ayahs had given them breakfast, washed and dressed them ready for the taxi that would take them to the schools in the city twelve miles away.

Mala went to the surgery in the morning as she did most days of the week and, while talking to the patients who lived in the village, discussed the gunshots that she had heard last night. Strange to say, nobody else had heard them.

The following night around the same time she heard the volley of shots again, just after midnight. Yet again, when she asked the patients the following morning, nobody else had heard them.

Mala was a General Practitioner in the village. Her husband was a surgeon in a town seventy miles away. He could come home only for the week-ends. For three nights running she had heard the gun shots but nobody else had heard them and she knew she could not be imagining them.

162

Her last patient for that morning was an elderly lady who had lived in the village all her life. Mala asked her about the gunshots; she bent down, put two fingers on her lips and whispered, 'We don't talk about it.'

'Why not?' asked Mala.

Her patient did not reply and walked away.

Not far from where Mala and the family lived there was a large army camp, and covered army trucks rushed past their home every evening. Mala and the family had just returned from living in England for five years. Sena, her husband had gone abroad to specialize in surgery. Most of their relatives had left the country to live abroad and their friends lived in the city of Colombo.

Mala realised that she was alone in this house in the village with only the maids, the cook and the gardener. Talking with them, they too had not heard any shots at night. She wondered why. But most of them had fear in their eyes, and changed the subject very quickly. Why were they were behaving so oddly.

In the late afternoon an unsigned letter was put through her letter box asking the inmates of each house and shop not to light any lamps and to switch off all the lights that night and the following night. If you do not comply you will be shot, the letter concluded.

Were these the people responsible for the gunshots that she had heard, wondered Mala, and if so who were they? When Sena, her husband, came home on Friday evening, Mala discussed the events of the previous few days and they were both quite disturbed and upset. They decided to visit their friends in Colombo, the capital city, but they had not heard any gun shots nor did they have any unsigned letters put through their letter boxes. Clearly it was a rural problem.

Sena went back to Colombo on Monday and Mala tried to settle down to work. That evening she found another anonymous letter requesting her not to buy any foreign food. The following day two police constables visited her in the surgery, and she was delighted to see them, as she could tell them about the gunshots and the anonymous letters, but before she could say anything, they asked her whether she had treated any persons with burns on their arms and hands. If she had done so the Police must be informed straight away.

She asked what the relevance was. Apparently the burns on the hands and arms were an indication that the person was attempting to make homemade bombs and were chemical burns. If she did not comply with the law, she could be taken in for questioning.

In her mind the delight in seeing the police constables now turned to horror, as at that very moment the practice nurse was dressing the hands of a young man with burns, in another room.

She wanted to get rid of the Police as quickly as possible. They had no search warrant, but Mala did not want the patient whose name was Simon to come out with his hands bandaged, and there was no way to warn Simon. Mala therefore decided not to ask about anonymous letters and the gunshots and said of course she would inform the police. She smiled sweetly and let them out.

In the normal course Mala would have offered the PCs tea and chatted about the local events but she could not do so as she was too worried about being taken in for questioning. Thoughts were racing in her mind. What would happen to the children? Who would look after them? What would happen to her? Clearly something had to be done.

When Simon came out of the nurse's room Mala asked him how he had received the burns to his hands and he repeated his original version of events, that he had burnt his hands while retrieving some combs of unripe bananas from a pit that had hot embers.

In the village there was going to be a big wedding – Simon's sister was getting married to a prosperous shopkeeper in the next village, and the wedding meal had to have numerous sweetmeats and fruits. The commonest fruit was bananas and he had to provide enough ripe bananas for 100 people. He therefore had decided to cut the partially ripe bananas from the trees which were then placed in a pit on the ground with a good thick layer of embers at the bottom, covered with banana leaves and the unripe bananas placed on top, covered with more leaves and left them in place until ripe, but they had to be checked daily so that they do not get over-ripe. In the process of doing this he had sustained burns to his hands.

It sounded a very plausible story to Mala. But what could she do when he comes back for a redressing? She called the nurse and found that she had asked him to come back in seven days.

The next patient was a middle aged man from the same road as the one in which Simon lived. After the consultation Mala asked whether there were a lot of decorations around Simon's house. He looked at Mala and said 'Doctor what are the decorations for?' Mala said they are for Simon's sister's wedding. He said Simon had no sister, and I do not know what you are getting at and said good day 'Ayubowan' which is Sri Lankan for good bye and walked out. Leaving Mala surprised, baffled and confused. 'What is going on?'

That evening when Mala went home there was another anonymous letter stating that she must stop sending her children to schools in Colombo to learn a foreign language such as English. This was a direct attack on her. She had seven days to decide as Simon would be back in seven days.

Mala's mother had given most of the landless villagers a small portion of land all around her large ancestral estate and helped each of them to build a house. This prevented outsiders encroaching on her land and acted as a good deterrent. Simon's parents were one such family.

Mala could not phone her husband to discuss these events as the phone lines to his town were not working, and she had seven days to decide on their future.

Mala decided to close the surgery for a few days cancelled the taxi taking the children to school and left to meet her husband. On the way she met up with an old school friend, Manel, in Colombo and heard that Manel's aunt, who was the director of Medical Services in charge of the pharmaceutical services, had been shot dead when she stopped at a set of traffic lights. A note was left behind to state that she and her staff should stop ordering drugs from abroad and should use only local available drugs, and let this be a warning!

Mala realised that there was a connection between this and her anonymous letter. Her friend filled her in on the current informed news and the 'underground news'.

Apparently there was a movement of educated but unemployed young people to overthrow the democratically elected government and form a Marxist government. They called themselves the JVP or People's Liberation Party, with ideas and ideals similar to the Khymer Rouge. The youths were fed up with having no legitimate way of earning a living and took the path of a faceless underground movement to upset and unnerve the population. People were warned not to talk about any incidents that they had seen or heard and eat only produce that was grown or produced locally, not to use any imported foods and not to patronize the western medical practitioners.

This started as a rural underground movement which through fear, threats and murder gradually invaded the whole fabric of society. As a result, there was a lack of knowledge amongst their friends in Colombo. This was the time that Mala and Sena had returned to Sri Lanka from England with their Axminster carpets and Slumberland mattresses to settle down. These were the hallmarks of a recently returned family from England.

Mala got to her feet and bade her friend goodbye, then got into her car with the children, and tears were rolling down her eyes as she realised what the future held for them. The children were curious and said, 'Mummy why are you crying? Did Nimal pinch you? Because he pinched me.' And the other said, 'He pushed me against the wall and took my toy car from my pocket. Don't cry Mummy, shall we go back and hit him?' Nimal is Manel's six-year-old son. Mala stopped crying and was touched and heartened by the children's sympathy and drove on.

She came to Sena's house by evening and welcome and surprise were equally evident on his face. After children had gone to sleep Mala and Sena discussed their future and came to the conclusion that in the present political climate Mala and the children would not be safe alone.

Mala's general practice brought a fairly adequate income but her husband's did not, as after coming back from England as a fully qualified surgeon with the FRCS (Fellowship of the Royal College of Surgeons), the Doctors' Trade Union called the Government Medical Officers Association (the GMOA) did not recognise the FRCS England and therefore his salary was the basic pay, that of a government medical officer of 1000 Rupees a month. This was medical politics at its cruellest as, although the government recognised the FRCS England and was willing to pay appropriately, the GMOA refused to recognise it and pressurised the Medical Directorate not to recognise it.

One of the reasons for Mala's success was that she was a local woman that had gone to England and returned to the local community. Another was that Mala's maternal grandfather was a wealthy land owner who built six schools in an area roughly twenty miles square and employed teachers who were paid by him. This was before the free education act came into force when he handed over all his schools to the government. The patients were invariable educated in these schools and Mala remembers the people saying that were it not for her grandfather they would have had no education. These schools are now large secondary schools.

In recognition of his philanthropic work the British government gave him the title Muhandiram, which equates to the rank of a minor official in the British colonial service for the low country (the Maritime provinces), and he was also appointed the registrar for the births, deaths and marriages for the area. Mala's mother, Alice, was a teacher who went to the Teacher Training school and was then appointed as the head of one of the girl's schools. Around this time Alice learned to drive, and obtained her driving licence. This was just as well as Mala's father did not know to drive. Alice also employed a chauffeur, who always sat in the front passenger seat. He was a Catholic and his name was Victor. He made the sign of the cross and mumbled a prayer just prior to Alice starting to drive. Mala had to sit in the back seat or stand in seat well at the back of the Baby Austin car.

It was a terrible dilemma. How does Mala survive? If she went back to general practice and Simon came back for the redressing to his hand, Mala would have to inform the police and thus be the next target of the JVP. If she did inform the police the JVP would definitely kill her. If she did not, and the police got wind of it she would be taken in for questioning. After a lengthy discussion Sena and Mala decided to leave the country again.

Sena took leave and drove back with Mala and the children. The very next day they went to Colombo to book tickets to London. However, a new law has been put in place saying that all professionals leaving the country had to have an exit permit issued by the Prime Minister's office, to enable travel agents to issue tickets.

Sena went to the Prime Minister's office and found that a queue of about half a mile in length was snaking its way slowly round the building in Colombo Fort. He spoke to a staff member who said that tickets are issued only in the mornings and only 200 a day. Dejected they drove home.

They had five days left before Simon had to come back for the dressing to his hands. What a significant event this was going to play in their lives!

The following day, very early in the morning, Sena and Mala both went to the Prime Minister's office together, as the exit permits were to be issued to each individual personally. They got a number and joined the already long queue, but as they had a number allocated to them, they felt a confidence not felt before.

The sun was hot as they took their place in the queue. They waited and waited. Sweat pouring down arms, legs and faces. This being a government building, there were no trees planted for shade as security regulations did not permit them – only hot slabs of concrete lay all around them. There was no shade and no breeze, although tantalisingly the brilliant blue sea could be seen in between the buildings nearby. Also governments are not noted for providing places for the general public to sit or loiter around these important buildings so consequently there was no place to sit down either.

Mala was very thirsty and she said that she was not feeling very well. She handed her passport to Sena for safe keeping and said, 'Sena, can you please get me a drink of water?' Sena stepped out of his place in the queue to look for a shop to buy a bottle of water. They were not prepared for the long wait and had not brought any drink with them. He went down a side street and wandered back round to the front of the building. There was no shop in sight, upset and dejected he was about to go back to his place in the queue when someone hailed him.

170

'Hi Sena – what are you doing here? I thought you were in England,' said the person. Walking towards him, Sena was delighted to meet an old medical acquaintance of his called Mike, who had been a colleague of his a few years back. They fell to talking and Sena explained to Mike why he was there.

Miraculously, Mike said, 'No problem, I can do it for you straight away. And I will take you to my sister.'

'Your sister!' gasped the astonished Sena in complete surprise.

'Yes,' replied Mike. 'Didn't you know? She is the Prime Minister now. Her husband, the democratically elected prime minister, was shot dead by a JVP man dressed as a Buddhist monk, and my sister has taken his place, and thus become the world's first woman Prime Minister.'

Sena explained the problem and in an instant his and Mala's passports were stamped with the exit visas. Talking to Mike further, Sena realised that the country had changed dramatically and was no longer a safe place for them to live as Mala would not be safe living alone in the village.

Whooping with delight, Sena came back to join Mala who was still standing in the queue and they walked out to celebrate the event by going to a hotel nearby for a drink of water. This hotel was the very hotel, the Grand Oriental Hotel Fort in Colombo where they had got married about ten years ago. They next visited a travel agent who said that he had only three berths available on the next sailing out of Colombo to London. They paid and got the berths allocated to them.

The large sprawling house that Mala, Sena and the children lived in belonged to Mala's mother Alice who was widowed four years ago. Since the death of her husband she had taken over the running of the land. The house consisted of a central area with two wings on either side.

The house was set amongst a plantation of rubber and coconut trees. Where these trees ended the rice fields began. Acres and acres of lush pale green rice fields surrounded the house on three sides; the other side bordered one of the main roads to Colombo. The fields were divided into roughly rectangular plots, separated by narrow grassy and muddy footpaths, which were crisscrossed by narrow canals which carried water for the rice plants.

In Sri Lanka the rice fields are called paddy fields. The word comes from the Malaysian word for a rice plant which is 'padi'. It is paddy, and has nothing to do with Irish men.

Alice supervised the entire process of planting and harvesting the rice every year. She had a retinue of people to help because all the adults living in the houses surrounding her house helped out.

In return for the work done they could either be paid a daily wage or bags of rice that they had helped to produce or even a mixture of the two. So labour was readily available and very often the young children of these families who where not attending school or working joined in. Thus Mala's children had children of their own age to play with and run around and great fun was had by all.

At midday everybody was given a meal of rice with two or three varieties of vegetables which were grown in the gardens of the house. The meal was cooked in the main house in huge earthenware pots and pans and the hot food was brought down to the edge of the field and all participated in it.

No fish or meat was cooked so as to not to upset the gods, or Devas, who were supposed to cast a benign eye on the procedure and thus was responsible for a good harvest. Similarly, no alcohol was served but after work when the workers went home the gods took their eyes off them, and they were able to celebrate.

The food was served on fresh glossy green banana leaves and was washed down with plenty of hot tea and water. The drinking water was stored in earthenware jars with narrow long necks which were washed daily. They were left over night over the embers of a fire which had rice husks burning in it. This added a lovely smoky flavour to the water and was also supposed to be germicidal. By late afternoon everybody had called it a day.

When the harvesting season was about to begin a large barn was constructed on the land adjoining the field, and the cut sheaves of rice placed in it in bee hive shaped mounds, covered in banana leaves to protect it from the rain.

The sheaves of rice were cut by sickles with short handles and curved blades, by both men and women working together. They stood in a straight line bending and cutting, all the while singing together melodiously, working from one corner of the rectangle to the other.

Alice was heard to boast that she was the only farmer in the village who grew two or three different varieties of rice each year. The idea was to find which variety gave the biggest yield of rice and which was the tastiest.

Once all the rice was cut the head farmer hired water buffaloes. These are very heavy large animals, dark brown in colour and with huge horns. They were paired together and driven round and round on the rice fronds inside the barn which were placed on the ground in a circle.

When all the grains of rice were teased off the sheaves of paddy, they were put aside and the rice collected in bags made out of jute which allowed free movement of air and was eco-friendly. This process was carried on until the paddy mounds were completely done.

The rice was winnowed by two people who constructed two tall wooden structures in the shape of an X. The structures were about eight feet apart and on the opened end of the X was placed a wide plank of wood which was wide enough for a man to stand on. One end of each X was embedded on the ground. One person would climb on to it and held the rice in a "kulla" which is a large triangular-shaped container made of cane, against the wind and gently let it stream downwards, helping to separate the solid grains of rice from the empty husks.

The rice was now ready for drying in the sun, of which there was plenty and then stored in a huge specially built wooden box which occupied half the store room by the kitchen of the house.

The following Spring, the fields were ploughed and the process of sowing the rice would start again. During the intervening short period after the rice was harvested, the water canals in each rectangular plot were dammed to collect the water and soften the soil.

This area was a haven for egrets and various types of storks as there were a lot of tiny silver fish darting around. Around the perimeter of the rice fields were short

174

Griselia trees which hid numerous kingfishers. You knew they were there because there were streaks of blue darting into the water and out onto the branches of a tree in a flash. After a couple of months, the fields were ploughed using the water buffalos tied to a wooden plough going round and round each plot.

Then the rice seeds were sown by hand. If Alice wanted a particular rare variety of rice in a particular area each seed was planted by hand.

In addition to all this she also supervised the tapping of the rubber trees daily. The rubber tappers would start tapping the rubber early morning by making a deep circular indentation in the bark of each tree and leave a coconut shell hooked to one end of the mark made on the bark.

By midday the tappers would collect the milk into buckets and then pour them into trays much like rectangular cake trays, and add the correct amount of acetic acid for it to set. The tappers would come back in the evening and take the rubber that has now become a white latex sheet to the nearby factory for processing, drying and storage.

There was a small colony of monkeys who lived in the rubber trees and were a great source of delight for the children.

Besides the rice and the rubber, the coconut plantation too needed some attention – much less than the rubber and rice but if the coconuts were not plucked at the correct time they would become a source of danger to all who worked there.

The house was painted white and set back from the road, with an oval shaped lawn in front. From the gate a wide red gravel road skirted the lawn. Three green cement steps lead to the wide veranda which ran half way around the house. The veranda had green coloured cement leading to the central large airy sitting room with high ceilings supported by white columns of pillars. This in turn led into the equally large dining room. Doors led into the bedrooms from the central area. On the right hand side were five large airy bedrooms with attached bathrooms and on the other side were three bedrooms of a similar type. Beyond these were the staff quarters and kitchens. A long passage ran from the front to the back of the house and Mala remembered coming out of a bedroom to see a monkey running down the passage to the back of the house where the rubber plantations were and where there was a colony of monkeys.

The part of the garden nearest the house was planted with banana trees and numerous other fruit trees including damson, mango, mangosteen, green and purple varieties of avocado, sapodilla, guava, lemon, lime, pineapple, and a special variety of short king coconut tree, where one could pluck the bright orange coloured fruit by hand. Alice had also planted ten different varieties of banana trees over the years.

The twilight hours were fascinating to watch. If one sat in silence the bats would come out and hang on the branches of the fruit trees, particularly sapodilla. These were incredibly sweet and luscious fruits, which had soft brown flesh and tasted of a mixture of brown sugar and beer. What fruits that could not be consumed were sent to the Sunday market for selling.

Intermingled with the noisy bats were the smells of the flowers which bloomed only in the evenings such as white and yellow temple flowers or Araliya. They were so called as they were the favourite offering to the statues in the temple. There was a small structure about two feet in height standing on top of the wooden pillar with a statue of a Lord Buddha inside. The cook had instructed all the maids and the gardeners to pray here every morning and evening.

Adjoining the house was a large double garage. Rarely were two cars ever parked there and the empty portion became a store room. This was also occupied by a large monitor lizard (V*aranus salvator*) that crept under the closed door of the garage in the morning and came back in the evening. It was about six feet in length and moved noiselessly.

Alice was reluctant to leave all these things behind but she had no option when she realised that Mala's life would be in danger if they stayed behind.

Mala, Sena and the children occupied the central portion and one wing while Alice occupied the other wing.

Mala's maternal grandfather was a wealthy land owner. When the new high level road was constructed from Colombo to the interior of the country, it divided his land into two. Mala remembers her grandfather sitting on the veranda and telling her mother, 'Alice, you take the left hand side of this land and your brother can have the right hand side. And I do not want any arguments between you two.' So it remained until it was sold.

Alice had to balance whether to stay behind by herself or to leave all these lands and her way of life for sixty years and accompany her daughter to England. She also had to balance the probability that if her daughter

177

stayed behind she could be killed by the unscrupulous politicians. It was a heart-breaking decision that she had to balance out in her mind. Finally, she decided to join her daughter in leaving the country.

Of late, Alice was saying that the house was too big for her, now that most of her relatives were either dead or had emigrated to other countries. When Mala told Alice that they wished to leave because of the political scene, they also realised that Alice could not be left alone. As Alice was a sprightly sixty-year-old and they had paid for three adult berths, Alice decided to accompany them. The shipping agent had said to Mala and Sena that the two children would be provided with fold up beds in two of the three cabins.

As they did not want news to spread that they were leaving, Sena took all the goods they had brought with them - carpets, mattresses and electrical items - to a sales room in Colombo for selling. They packed the absolute bare essentials, said goodbye only to the closest friends and relatives and joined the P&O liner in Colombo Harbour. All the way from their home to Colombo, the children kept looking out of the car window to see if there were any people following them. It was like 'cops and robbers' and the children were thrilled - more thrilled that we were the robbers being chased by the cops! The ship was an old troop ship making its last journey home to England from Australia. With each rough wave the ship encountered, it would creak menacingly as if it was just about to give up the ghost that very minute.

Mala was violently seasick, as she was having morning sickness. After many long days at sea they berthed in Durban. They were invited to disembark and, along with

178

the other passengers, they went down to the quayside. There were rows of taxis waiting to take them to the town. Sena, after holding his hand to a dozen or so taxis which had a lit up sign with Net Blanks on it, went back to the purser on the ship. The purser explained to him that as he was a Sri Lankan, he was classified as a coloured and ordered a special taxi to take the three adults and two children to the town. This was the first time that they had experienced Apartheid and were shocked by the inhumanity of it. Worse was to come!

Rounding the Cape was something most people on board the ship dreaded. This was the treacherous part of the journey round the Cape of Good Hope and after a very rough journey the ship berthed in Cape Town. Having being cooped up in the confines of a ship for nearly two weeks, the children were clamouring to go to a park so that they could run and climb. We agreed and walked towards a park.

The park was well tended, with lovely borders of flowers of varying colours and huge acacia trees giving shade. The children ran towards the swings and as they did so a large Afrikaner walked towards them and motioned them to a corner of the park, separated by a steel chain from the rest. If the size of the park could be equated to a room 15ft by 15ft, the corner reserved for the Blacks and Coloured was one tenth the size of that room with no swings or frames and only a bench. This area was separated from the rest by a steel chain fence.

The adults sat on the bench, while the park keeper stood with his back to them, with a large whip in his hand. He would frequently lash the whip perhaps at imaginary miscreants who invaded his mind.

179

Mala's five-year-old little girl started crying every time he did this. He clearly didn't want them there, so they got up and wandered towards the town looking for a place to have a cup of tea. Almost all the restaurants were reserved for Whites only. They were about to give up, but finally saw a place where two Asian men were serving and they went up to the front door of this restaurant. The men started talking to them in a language they did not understand and gesticulated to the side of the café, where they were directed to the back door.

The door was framed by a row of long nails, and from each nail there hung a tin mug of dubious cleanliness. The man gestured to them to take a mug and to stand in the queue in front of him for tea.

They could not stomach it, and particularly Alice kept on repeating that we fed our dogs at home on similar plates and mugs. And what an insult this was to her.

They walked out with the Asian man shouting insults a them and, thoroughly disappointed, went back to the ship. The next port where the ship berthed was called Port Elizabeth, where they disembarked and walked to the town nearby. They visited the shops and bought warm clothes and shoes in anticipation of the dreaded winter in England which they had already experienced few years back. They had not expected to return ever again, and so had dispensed of all warm clothes.

On a bleak, wintry morning in January the ship docked in Tilbury.

Mala visited Sri Lanka in August 2015 and was pleasantly surprised to see about thirty-five large well-constructed houses with very large gardens on her ancestral land.

Troubled Children

Jane Wilson-Howarth

Soon after we moved to the new town of Embilipitiya, I heard of the other ex-pat in town. She was a Peace Corps volunteer and with her long flowing golden hair and habit of riding around on the back of her local boyfriend's motorbike, she was the talk of the town and was endlessly pestered and propositioned by the testosterone-fired single young men of the area. Her morals were universally misjudged in this rather orthodox up-country community.

We met, of course, and Carly talked passionately of her idea to set up some kind of day-care centre for families with disabled children. In rural Sri Lanka, there were few facilities, and families cared for any challenged individual, young or old. Many young mothers were exhausted and needed respite. Carly asked me to meet some of the families, make medical assessments and see what help was needed. Up until that point, I hadn't noticed any disabled children. Carly explained that such children are regarded as a divine judgement and are kept hidden. They bring shame on the family.

One of the first 'disabled children' I met was a young woman of 20 who had been born with a disfiguring deformity of her face, median facial dysplasia, which meant her eyes were widely separated, her nose broad and she had a hare lip and cleft palate. She was shocking to look at, even for me the medic. The family lived in a small house in the middle of nowhere and kept her out of sight.

She learned through correspondence courses, was widely read and spoke good – if lispy – English, as well as her mother tongue of Sinhala. Eating was a problem – food came down her nose unless she carefully manoeuvred it in an inelegant manner.

181

The dramatic surgery to correct her deformity wasn't available in Sri Lanka and the family certainly couldn't afford to go abroad for the operations and aftercare. I was impotent to help and left their little house shocked that even their closest neighbours assumed that this girl was intellectually as well as physically challenged.

Later in Nepal, I worked with parents of children with cerebral palsy. I met one young mum who talked about her life, saying that she had sinned during her pregnancy by eating meat. This was the reason she'd been given a troubled child. It was her karma. She said she often went to the temple. The child was calmer there, closer to god. He had fewer fits. She often took expensive offerings.

Maya Visits Sri Lanka

Seeta Siriwardena

Two little girls go on a holiday to an island in the Indian Ocean.

Their house nestled on the slope of a high hill, with a valley below, and after sunset the lights of the houses on the hills opposite twinkled like fireflies stuck on a mat of greenish blue.

One light stood out from the others. It appeared brighter than the rest and did not go out like the other lights.

Maya, who was too excited to sleep that night, peeped at the light from behind the curtain in her bedroom window and wondered what it was.

'Mum, there is a bright light across the valley that does not go off at night like the others. Why is that?' She asked the next morning.

'Oh, there is a cluster of caves, about three or so, on the top of the hill across the valley. People around here believe that a fairy spirit lives there, so they make offerings of food and water to her. Maybe they also light a fire at night,' said Mum.

Maya was happy as this meant she could go exploring.

Excerpt from *Maya and the Dragon, 2016.*

Ticks and Tongba
Jane Wilson-Howarth

My heart was in my mouth as I watched our seven-year-old tumble off the path and roly-poly-head-over-heels down a steep sandy slope. I scrambled down to him. Astonishingly Alexander had escaped with little more than a slightly grazed elbow – and his mouth and ears were full of sand. The fall didn't curb his enthusiasm for charging along the mountain paths. He was bounding with energy, keen to show off his walking prowess to every local child. Perhaps we were getting too cocky though. Could we be putting the boys at too great a risk?

We'd been living in Nepal for five years and had done 11 family treks mostly following well-beaten tea-house and tourist trekking routes. Now, during the Easter school holidays, the four of us were trying to be a bit intrepid. We had a month to head to the base camp of Kanchenjunga, the world's third highest mountain in the extreme east of Nepal. Our best mountaineering flipflops and a big first aid kit packed, we flew from Kathmandu down to the bustling town of Biratnagar which proudly announces it is a mere 235 ft above sea level. There we hired a Land Rover and driver to take us to the attractive small Newar bazaar of Dhankuta where we stopped for the night. Next morning, we drove on through Hile to Basantapur (at about 2300m / 7500 ft) where so many people had gathered we could hardly get along the street. It was market day and people carried baby pigs away from the bazaar in individual little oinking bamboo handbags. We gobbled down a huge delicious lunch of rice and lentils, snatched up our daysacks and started to walk up towards the top of the first ridge. Whether it was the altitude or lassitude from sitting in a Land Rover for too long, three-year-old Sebastian was suddenly unimpressed with the idea of trekking. This wasn't a problem though as the boys weren't expected to

184

walk all the way and the shy Sherpa Somé carried Seb in an especially adapted conical basket slung from a headband.

We reached the top of the first lovely forested ridge (at about 2960m) as the weather became overcast and windy. Sebastian announced, 'Bout to rain!' We hurried on and the rain started in earnest as we descended to Chauki (at 2700m) where we were to spend our second night. We'd arranged this trip with a local trekking organisation and started out with a team of 12 minders/porters/cooks to carry our luggage and everything we needed. This included tents, food for the entire trip, a dining table and camping chairs. They even brought jars of marmalade, bottles of tomato ketchup and paper napkins. It felt like an excessively over-resourced outing. It seemed decadent but allowed us the freedom to go anywhere in the country and avoided spending time tracking down supplies of rice or other basics. We were also able to indulge in items we feel are essential, including good coffee, which although grown in Nepal and sold in Kathmandu is mostly exported to South India so is even hard to find in coffee-growing regions. The only thing we needed to buy on the trip was fresh milk, and sometimes eggs.

The next day, was our first full day of walking and took us along a ridge through rhododendron forest up to 2890m (about 10,000ft) to the village of Gupha which, as usual, was cold and shrouded in cloud. It seemed a tough place to live. It was centred around a tarn and when the sun peaked through strings of multi-coloured prayer flags flung between stunted junipers they reflected in the still lakelet waters. A craggy-faced woman encouraged Alex and Seb to approach her suckling *naks (naks* being female yaks) and pet her shaggy calves. Then we bought glasses of rich steaming *nak* milk from her. The boys were also amused to discover pens containing lots of very hairy black oinky pigs.

The middle hills of Eastern Nepal are known for *tongba* which is like hot rough Devon cider that still has the lumps in. The best is made of millet but smashed up maize, wheat or pretty much anything that will ferment can be used. The fermented mush is shovelled into a tankard and boiling water poured into it. It is then supped through a bamboo straw that sieves out the millet or grain pieces. It is wonderfully warming and the more you stir, the more intoxicating it is. The pigs at Gupha, and further on too, were fattened up on *tongba* spoils and always seem slightly drunk. They would become more vociferous when they saw people, presumably on the expectation of being fed even more mush.

We chose a scenic campsite by the tarn. Sleep came quickly but we were woken during the night by a terrific hailstorm; it frightened the boys a little. The tents were in an exposed place on the top of a ridge, so the thunder sounded mighty close. In the morning though, the boys were delighted to find heaps and drifts of hailstones. We had breakfast on a breathtakingly bright new day gazing at both the world's fifth highest mountain Makalu, and the third highest, Kanchenjunga.

'Are we really going to walk that far?' I asked Simon. 'It looks a hellava long way away.'

Simon just chuckled.

The start of the fourth day took us from Gupha along and down a ridge amongst rhododendrons covered with rich red blossoms. Huge purple orchids grew on the trees. There were white magnolias and straggly *Daphne bholua* bushes with scruffy little lilac flowers but the most intoxicating perfume. With the team cooking, pitching camp and carrying for us I felt terribly pampered but the porters seemed to find their work easy and they'd often put down their loads to arrange competitions to measure their strength. Wrestling and boulder-hurling were

186

especially popular. The boys were lost in admiration and clearly aspired to being as strong and tough. Often most of the team were either way on ahead or far behind so mostly we walked only with the chief Sherpa, Lakpa, and the two child-porters, Pemba and Som Bahadhur. Somé was so painfully shy I felt bad trying to chat to him, but Lakpa Sherpa told stories of some of his big treks and casually mentioned friends who had died in the mountains or who been disabled by frostbite. When I asked if the only employment options open to Sherpas were mountaineering which was why they risk so much, Lakpa laughed and said, 'We love the high mountains. It is our life.' It was his passion. It was also clear that the porters enjoyed their work. Days were short, loads were light, they were well fed, properly clothed and they were relatively well paid. Porters employed to shift goods around the mountains are not only paid less per day but sometimes carry as much as 100kg, for walking from sunrise to sunset. With us it was a late start after our leisurely breakfast and only two or three hours walking before stopping for a two-hour lunch break. They sang a lot and whittled a lot of bamboo flutes. Somé taught Seb some Sherpa dances. Pemba carved Alex a wooden rifle. The porters had one complaint. Bir Bahadur had brought a double-ended *madal* (drum) but he was of the Magar tribe from further west in Nepal than the rest of the team and the rhythms his fingers produced and the songs he knew were unfamiliar to the others. They complained a lot about that but they did a lot of teasing too. Three of the porters were called Kaji so to avoid confusion there was Ang Kaji (Young Kaji), Real Kaji and Spare Kaji. Spare Kaji was incredibly strong but a bit dim and kept getting lost. He was the butt of endless practical jokes. Most of the team had come down from Kathmandu but a few had been employed locally. They'd walk with us for a while, then would say they'd gone far enough and would be paid off and walk back home. Then Lakpa would find other willing help, although as the days went by and we ate through the food loads became lighter and we needed fewer porters.

Everyone except us – and Lakpa – carried ridiculous amounts of stuff. Nima-the-chief-cook often walked with huge cooking pots ad spoons. Each morning we'd receive enamel mugs of steaming sweet 'bed-tea' that Nima thrust into our tents. Then after breakfast we'd set off, leaving Nima and the team to clear up and boil up some drinking water for us. Day five began with a long rocky descent. Downhill is surprisingly tough on the thighs and knees but Sebastian didn't care. He enjoyed doing long flying leaps off boulders holding my hand or Somé's. We arrived right down at the river at a mere 650m at one of many places called Dobhan (meaning confluence). The region used to grow some of the best tea in the country, but it had been settled by Tibetans who don't understand that some people prefer tea to alcohol. All they could offer was hot *tongba* and distilled *raksi*. The pigs here, which were fed the residue, were particularly large, black, hairy, less oinky and more somnolent. The local children were intrigued by Alexander and Sebastian and wanted to poke and prod them to see if they were real. We fled and camped down by the river.

I saw Simon pull a towel and shampoo out of the luggage and head for the riverbank. I followed, astonished he could bathe in glacial meltwater. I wasn't temped and Sebastian only washed the tips of his toes. I found a tick on me, fortunately before it had found its way to any bare skin. I fired it into the river with a finger-flick. Two passing men wandered past discussing our tall thin toilet tent. 'Oh look – they have a sentry to guard them!'

The Himalayas were formed by India slamming into the rest of Asia, and Nepal is like a giant crumpled rug. The ridges tend to run roughly east-west which makes walking north-south tough. You cross one 3000m ridge only to descend to cross another. Following the mighty rivers that flow off the Tibetan plateau and have cut through the mountains is the alternative and for the next several days we walked close to the River Tamur. At this low altitude the air was hot and the challenge was negotiating all the landslides. That first river-side day we only managed nine kilometres and hadn't even gained much altitude. We'd scramble up to 500 ft or so above the river only to descend beneath river cliffs and then climb up over yet another landslide. The forested riverbanks were noisy with birds celebrating spring. The loudest were the brain-fever cuckoo, magpies and tree-pies. We strolled through villages peopled by Limboos who have a reputation for enjoying good boozy parties and where there was plenty of *tongba* on offer. In one place Alexander fell in love with a goat kid and pleaded to bring it along. We told him they wouldn't let it on the plane back to Kathmandu, which was probably a lie.

We stopped for a long leisurely lunch and watched, on the opposite river bank, a healing ritual run by three *jañkris*: men wearing white dresses and Red Indian chief style feathery headdresses. They banged drums, danced and organised the village to mime throwing something into the river. Lakpa Sherpa couldn't tell us what was going on. He seemed to think the ritual weird. I guessed they were exorcising some illness from a very chubby infant at the centre of it all. At the end of the party they slaughtered a goat. As they began their feast, gentle rain sprinkled its blessings on the ceremony. We didn't welcome the celestial blessings as we had to cross a couple of frighteningly steep landslides, which were more slippery in the rain.

Next morning, the sun re-emerged, made the land steam and rejuvenated the birds. A (very) Large Cormorant flapped

189

purposefully south. There were Plumbeous Redstarts and White Capped River-chats, swallow-tailed butterflies, tiny violets, and the occasional lizard. The route took us slowly up again, although still along the river. The rain set in again on day 9; it soaked most things, brought out the leeches and made the steep ascent ahead even more treacherous so we took a rest day (at Sekathum; 1600m). The *tongba* was good here and the boys fished for toad tadpoles and built sand-castles while we watched the white-water in the Gunsa River thundering down to join the Tamur and the snowline crept ever closer.

When the skies cleared it became surprisingly hot and Alexander was even persuaded to bathe. We explored the village, he was bitten by a village mutt, which had just lost a fight with another dog over titbits offered by a mountaineering party and got his own back by sinking its teeth into the back of Alexander's leg. He was immunised against rabies but still had to suffer the indignity of taking his trousers down so that I could clean the wound by feel in the gathering dusk and then dowse the bite in Khukri rum. 'That brown stuff doesn't smell nice!' Alexander complained, 'And that dog has made a hole in my *best* camouflage trousers!'

Day 10, the last day of March, saw us climbing up and up along narrow crumbly paths above precipitous drops. Winds funnelled down the narrow gorge made dry oak leaves dance on the updrafts. Crag Martins did aerobatics too. Superb waterfalls plunged off the tops and were caught by the winds. Ahead the vista was snow. Alexander couldn't wait to get into it. The path took us back into rhododendron forest inhabited by noisy flocks of Rufous-fronted Tits and I wondered how such tiny birds stay warm in the mountains. The way wound up and across a steep slope (45^0 in the gentle bits and mostly a lot steeper) with the river nearly a thousand metres directly below. I tried not to look down. I pretended to become absorbed in ornithology and taking artistic photos of red rhododendron flowers while I got my breath back. Lakpa said we shouldn't let Sebastian walk this section and loaded him into Somé's basket. Alexander was disgusted by the idea of being carried and steamed up the mountain-side, sure-footedly. He wanted to race me to the top. I didn't have the energy to race but was also scared that competition would make him reckless. On a previous month-long trek, I'd counted up 42 scratches cuts and bruises. He was fearless but it was a very very long way down to the river. I tried not to think about what would happen if any of us slipped. My head spun and my palms went sweaty if my foot skidded even a couple of centimetres. After four hours of not daring to put a foot wrong, we reached Amjilesa, a tiny village perched on the only bit of approximately flat ground we had seen all day. At about 2500m above sea level it was not as high as Gupha (where we'd stayed on our third night) but it felt like we were deep in the Himalayas. The cattle were mostly yak-cow crosses called *dzos*. I felt gelatinous but Alexander wanted to run more races. He found a plough and, with Somé's help, he and Sebastian took it in turns to be the *dzo* and the ploughman, and Somé taught them a bit of *dzo*-language (*hut* means to go and *hurri* to turn round).

On we went almost-contouring high above the ever more dramatic river gorge, where the cliffs were vertical and the views spectacular. There were scarlet minivets, fierce-looking shrikes, very unshy buntings and more Crag Martins. Great grand Himalayan Griffon Vulture soared effortlessly on wings that span up to three metres. They drop bones onto rocks from great heights to smash them and so get at the marrow. Ang Kaji charged on ahead and went thundering down the next descent at break-neck speed.

Eventually we dropped down to the river. Onward the forest merged into rhododendron with pine, huge moss-laden hemlocks, red birches and lots of bamboo. Finally we were awa from frightening precipitous drops but I often I had no idea where Alexander was as he was involved in hide-and-seek games. We stopped early (for which I was thankful) on day 11 a Gyabla at about 2800m, and were rewarded with good views of Nango Ma peak. We'd hardly seen the real *himals* since breakfa at Gupha on day 4. I noticed that Ang Kaji was limping and offered to check him over. His knee was infected and hugely swollen so I gave him a course of antibiotics and some of his loa was shared amongst the other porters. Even Lakpa carried a bit more.

The next day we continued through the forest past the attractive Tibetan village of Phole. Simon and Alexander celebrated the afternoon with a snowball fight amongst the juniper trees. There were prayer flags everywhere, little watercourses created to turn prayer wheels, *dzos* and even a fev yaks. The *tongba* was good, but Sebastian became sleepy and subdued. Nima made him special garlic soap which he said would protect him from the altitude. Even so he had an unsettle night. We thought we'd press on for another hour to Gunsa the biggest village in the area and little higher at 3400m. We'd paus there until Sebastian's mild mountain sickness evaporated: thus far I'd successfully treated it with Kitkat. Gunsa was a wild desolate place, with hardly even any grass growing. It was overcast, windy and very cold. We asked if fresh milk was available and the reply came 'The naks are too tired to make milk! Have some *tongba!*' It seemed that everyone must spend most of their days drunk, huddled inside their wooden houses close to the fire. Even toddlers slurped distilled spirits from dir glasses, and I was alarmed when one friendly mother offered some to our boys.

Sebastian, revived by rest, slept well and seemed much livelier next morning, so day (14) saw us setting off up. We all felt intrepid as we tacked further on up the course of the glacial Gunsa River; the forest was hopping with innumerable tiny noisy birds. There were large patches of ice and snow which made the path very slippery, but sure-footed Somé carried Sebastian easily. Frozen waterfalls on the river-cliffs looked like freeze-frame photos of gallons of milk that had been poured off the top of the mountain. We were all excited by the prospect of reaching the great Kumbhakarna glacier that flows west off the magisterial Kanchenjunga *himal*, but weren't sure how far to risk going with Sebastian. It is so difficult to distinguish mountain sickness from the cold or a cold and I was forever arguing with myself over when or if we should turn back. The scenery was spectacular but soon, the clouds rolled in again.

'Bout to rain!' Sebastian announced.

'I think it's about to snow!'

Sebastian became increasingly unhappy as it grew colder, while Alexander became increasingly excited at the prospect of glaciers and crevasses. From a spur which protruded into the river valley we could see ahead a vast ice wall and the mighty terminal moraine of the glacier which is several hundred metres high. We pressed on, Sebastian ever more miserable and on through flurries of snow until we stopped for lunch in a partially-built tea shop; snow came in through gaps in the boulders which made the walls and through the woven bamboo roof. The altitude was 3850m. Alexander went off to make a solo attempt on a nearby snowdrift and was in ecstasies, climbing up using the ice-axe (actually carried for nothing more heroic than excavating the latrine pit) and skiing down the steep snow on his bottom. Our destination, Kanchenjunga base camp, was simply a bit of fairly flat rocky ground covered in scrubby grass. We didn't need to get there but the glacier was enticing and Alexander desperately wanted to go on. Sebastian desperately wanted to go back. Meanwhile the weather was worsening and forced us to consider how much more unpredictable and treacherous conditions are at this eastern end of the Himalayas. I also started to worry that Alexander risked getting seriously cold as he was now sodden.

And so we fled back through the stinging snow and arrived in Gunsa cold and hungry with soaking wet clothes, bodies, socks, and squelchy boots. The *tongbas* were particularly warm and welcoming that evening. The weather looked even fouler further up and I wondered how many mountaineers were up there pinned down by the storm. We'd made the right decision to come down but Alexander was miffed.

Once Sebastian realised we were heading home he brightened considerably and next morning he took a very long time walking through Gunsa, saying good bye to assorted beloved puppies, chicks, kid goats and yak calves. On any descent now he would grab my hand and do long flying leaps off boulders or would launch himself to dangle from my outstretched arm as I scrambled downwards. He reported yet again 'Bout to rain,' as we walked back through drippy moss-forests. We thought we'd take a different route back walking over a 4000m ridge to Walungchung and thus avoid some of the vertiginous paths that had frightened me on the way up. So the morning of the 16th day saw us heading homewards but up from Gyabla. We started early in sunshine with lovely views of Jannu *himal*, the spectacularly shaped northern outlier of Kanchenjunga. The clouds rolled in again during the late morning. We scrambled steeply up through very fine forest with increasingly deep patches of snow. Lunchtime saw us perched amongst boulders at 3600m above sea level.

'Bout to rain!' Sebastian announced and then the drizzle arrived. Having climbed nearly 1000m, Nima-the-cook had to melt snow to make water to cook with. Ahead lay deep snow and we were at least 400m from the top of the ridge. And so down we went again, Sebastian looking forward to being reunited with various much loved puppies in Gyabla.

'When *are* we going home? I *need* to play on my tractor!'

We now had to retrace our steps along the 'exhilarating' and precipitous path through Amjilesa – even Alexander was frightened at the prospect. It was only whilst sitting round the fire drinking *tongba* that we discovered that there is in fact another and much easier path which the locals use – the high path is just for yaks. Much relieved, I was expecting the descent to be a cinch (being, by now, fit and all) but the next day was strenuous, my knees creaked as we climbed up and down and down and up and up and down through forested paths where the rain-freshened rhododendron blossoms looked particularly lovely. We plunged down a very steep gravelly path through Amjilesa, pausing briefly for a cup of delicious cardamom-flavoured tea (cardamom is locally grown on boulder-strewn scraps of jungle) – and down to the river at Solima. I fell and grazed my hand, Somé slipped and fell and even sure-footed Lakpa Sherpa slithered onto his bottom. It wasn't an easy path, but Sebastian walked and Alexander ran all the way and it was less alarming than the high route. We tacked back and forth across temporary and very insubstantial bridges (they are washed away each monsoon) over awesome white water; even a strong swimmer would have no chance at all if they fell in. Sebastian got very excited at the prospect of crossing any bridge. The wobblier they were, the better he liked them, and the more nervous we were. And it was on to a very pleasant campsite by the river. There was no *tongba* but we enjoyed a refreshing icy dip to wash away rather too many days grime. We found a warmer, non-glacial, spring-fed pond for Sebastian to bath in but he refused to wash amongst tadpoles; he just enjoyed 'fishing' with bits of bamboo. It was a fine site but the low altitude allowed beasts to thrive that we'd almost forgotten about – especially big aggressive stripy-legged *Aedes* mosquitoes and biting blackflies. A little seed tick was cheeky enough to try feeding on me; I pulled it off and dowsed myself (inside and out) in Khukri rum.

Next morning we followed the river further downstream, crossing and recrossing the river over a succession of perilous bridges – much to Sebastian's delight – and back to Sekathum and then we struck upwards again at Hellok.

Alexander complained, 'I don't want to walk with Mummy; she walks so slowly!' As I panted very steeply up a never-ending staircase, we heard gunfire. Alexander was frightened, but it turned out to be part of a funeral 'celebration'. As so often, it clouded over in the afternoon and Sebastian announced 'Bout to rain!' It was drizzling heavily by the time we camped at 2400m. Over supper I noticed a leech had attached itself inconveniently under my wedding ring. The rain had brought them out again. I took malicious delight in sprinkling salt on it so it dissolved like the Wicked Witch in the Wizard of Oz.

The forest we were into now was a wonderful mix of crimson rhododendrons, two kinds of magnolias, *Mahonia* (a surprisingly manky shrub in its natural state), violets galore and lots of giant bamboo. We loitered in a high (2800m) shallow basin of dense moss-forest with magnificent hemlocks towering over us. This was such a lovely place we decided to stop walking at

11.30 and the boys enjoyed exploring an almost dry river valley littered with huge climbable boulders and did many Everest conquests in miniature. The place was dotted with little springs where we washed our socks and I photographed purple primroses. The magnolias here were particularly lovely. The forest merged into purer rhododendron forest as we slowly ascended the next morning. The patches of snow grew larger as we walked up and for the last few hundred metres of climbing we were walking on or in calf-deep snow. I was trying to be clever kicking steps in the snow with my boots but then sank in up to my bottom. Simon was just ahead carrying Sebastian on his hip. I was floundering and couldn't climb out of the hole I was in. 'What do you do in this situation?' I shouted.

'Wish you weren't there!'

I struggled until I eventually found a patch of snow firm enough to let me to scramble out. We climbed up to the prayer flags at the 3550m pass. From there we could see snow ahead and behind and fine hemlock forest each side of the ridge. The way down was steep, slippery and difficult along a rough path lined with lilac-coloured primroses. Campsites were often not easy to find because of a lack of a combination of flat ground and water so several nights we camped in *goth*s – temporary shelters where people stay while their cattle graze.

We descended through forest where it was Simon's turn to announce that he'd picked up a tick and out came the rum bottle again. We continued to grazing grasslands dotted with violets, *Mahonia* and another member of the Daphne family, the yellow scented *Edgeworthia gardneri*; a man sat beside the path making rope out of it. We wandered through a village unappetisingly called Yam Pudding and right down to the river again so that less than 24h after being up to my bottom in snow, I was savouring an invigorating bath from a grassy bank dotted with wild geraniums. The heat made the walking tiring, but the wildlife was engrossing again, and there were plenty of bridges for Sebastian to enjoy. We watched an extrovert cuckoo (the same species as in England) for a while, then Sebastian asked, 'Why has that cuckoo bird stopped cooking?' At my request Nima cooked stinging nettles fried in garlic and bracken tips that proved tastier than asparagus.

At the fly-ridden Brahmin village of Khebang I thought not for the first time, how odd it was for a whole village to be inhabited by only one caste. When we stopped for lunch, Alexander drew a huge crowd while he wrote his daily diary. By now he was used to being a celebrity. Then it was on through fine forest and low hills, where Sebastian walked, or trotted along, well now we were at lower altitude. He wanted to visit every chicken, goat and pig. One afternoon where the path was going steeply up, Sebastian announced, 'Me tired!' and sat down. When I sat down beside him, he looked disapproving and said 'Mummy you're not strong! Why are you resting?' By now both sons had written off my mountaineering skills but I felt the judgement a touch harsh as it had taken some athleticism to support Seb's hair-raising leaps off boulders on most of the down-hills thus far.

By the end of day 22 and after another precipitous descent, we'd reached another place called Dobhan (still meaning confluence), and a nice spot for another plunge. The boys thought that bathing was an extremely bad idea but Simon and I managed hair washes, standing thigh deep in the glacial meltwater and dipping heads in by bending at the waist. It felt good to get the edges cleaner, but it was painfully cold on the head. On day 23 we walked from a place called Dobhan to a place confusingly also called... Dobhan. There are a lot of confluences in Nepal.

Towards the final day's walking, after another 1000m climb, we got back to the road. It was New Year's Day in the Nepali year of 2055 and we saw Kanchenjunga again. This felt like a good end to the trek and we celebrated with one last *tongba*. Sebastian was delighted to find waiting for us the rattly old Land Rover that had dropped us in Basantapur. The same friendly driver took us the 12 bumpy uncomfortable hours back to Biratnagar. The views of Kanchenjunga grew ever finer as we drove up and over the last 3,000m ridge to Ilam; and on through tea plantations which looked wonderfully green and attractive despite being such a neatly manicured, ecologically sterile environment. Then down we went into the lowlands. The evening light picked out recently transplanted spring rice. We passed houses on stilts and were soon back in the land of cycle rickshaws, loin cloths and big muscular mosquitoes.

Finally on the 26th day we flew the hour back from Biratnagar to friendly familiar old Kathmandu where Sebastian was joyously reunited with his red plastic sit-on tractor. It seemed an amazing decadence to dine on mulberry (fresh from our garden) and apple (fresh from Kashmir) crumble and to be able to bathe in hot water. The filth that flowed down the drain that day was a wonder to behold. In washing Alexander's hair, I discovered a tick was feasting behind his ear, and judged that it had been dining there for days. 'Hmm. This shows how you failed to wash behind your ears!'

'That,' he responded, 'is the WHOLE POINT of going trekking!'

When Alexander had to go for his two rabies boosters at the American clinic in Kathmandu following the dog bite, he was amazingly stoical, the pain mitigated by a Batman Band-Aid (especially imported all the way from America). He didn't mind the injections, he just wanted to know when we would next be going into the mountains. It had been a great adventure for the four of us and even little Sebastian said he might quite like to go trekking again if there were lots of songs and dances and pigs and not too much rain.

Death and Life in the Philippines
Stephanie Green

'Come and see Mama.' said Rosemarie. She walked ahead of me into the house.

I hesitated and she stopped and looked back at me. 'You don't want to, do you?'

'Yes,' I lied, 'I'd like to see Mama.'

I shouldn't have been concerned about viewing the body of Mama, in life she was a kind and caring lady who made me welcome and fed me at every opportunity. In death it was unlikely that she would do me any harm.

I followed Rosemarie into the house where the white coffin, lined in white silk and decorated with white silk flounces, was lying in state on the dining table. Around it a mass of white gardenias gave off a sweet and heady smell.

Mama lay in her white silk bed looking peaceful and serene yet absent. Her nails had been painted, her lips were pink and she wore blue eye shadow, her hair had been crimped. In life practical Mama had been make-up free and plainly dressed, in death she looked like the chief bridesmaid at the wedding.

The dress she wore had been bought for the occasion. It was probably the most expensive dress she had ever possessed. The white frills framed her neck and wrists and there was a lace inset in the tight bodice. I wanted to utter appropriate words of comfort to Rosemarie and to her sister Ruby, who was sitting by the coffin, but when I looked down at Mama in all her finery the only phrase that came to mind was, 'I wouldn't be seen dead in that.'

I didn't stay long with the family after seeing their Mama. It was late and I'd had a long day travelling back from a conference on the island of Camguin. As the crow flies Camguin

201

is not that far from Leyte but crows don't fly in a straight line in The Philippines. They take long convoluted journeys by ferries and boats that criss-cross between the thousands of islands that make up the archipelago. For one journey travellers may have to catch the boats and the ferries, the buses and coaches, the jeepneys and the pedi-cabs. They ride on the backs of motor-cycles extended to carry five passengers or in side cars that can take up to nine passengers if the ones on the outside are roped in efficiently.

I'd set off at dawn from the quayside on Camguin in a banca, a small boat that just about held myself, Nicole and Jean and the two crew. We were so well laden with our back-packs and copious amounts of water that we had to get out to push the boat over the shallow water of the coral reef that surrounded the island. Three hours later when we landed at the island of Bohol (after an amazing glide through pods of Dolphins) we had to wade ashore, carrying our back-packs on our heads, because for some untold reason the two crew members were reluctant to beach the boat in Jagna Bay. Wet and muddy we caught a jeepney to the ferry terminal where I caught the Fastcat to BayBay on the island of Leyte. Then it was a two bus journeys: first to Ormoc on a smart new coach with very aggressive air-conditioning. When one of the passengers asked the driver to turn off the air-conditioning because we were all in danger of hypothermia his response was, 'you've paid for air-con, you'll get air-con.' So, we shivered for two hours. After that it was a local bus to Tacloban where the air-con was provided by the absence of glass in the windows. Finally, it was a pedi-cab ride to Rosemarie's house.

It was after 9pm when, after a short pedi-cab ride from Rosemarie's, I eventually reached my house feeling tired and dispirited. I was startled by a short, fat young man in a bright yellow Hawaiian shirt emerging from the shadows by my gate.

'Good Evening Ma'am Steph.'

I racked my travel weary brain to try and place this stranger who apparently knew me.

'I have an invitation for you.' He thrust a buff card into my hand.

I looked at him blankly.

'It's an invitation to my mother's forty-day death anniversary.' This caused me more confusion, not only did I have to try and recognise him but I also had to place his mother. It seemed I knew her well enough to be invited to her forty-day death anniversary but obviously not well enough to be informed that she had died and been buried.

I told him how sorry I was that his mother had died in the hope that further conversation would elicit a name or a fact that would make me recall either him or her. But although I was told that he has to travel from Cebu, where he works in a call centre (hence the very good English), and that the death was sudden and caused by a heart attack there are still no clues given as to her identity. In the end I asked the question. 'Who is your mother and how do I know her?'

He looked surprised that I didn't know the person we had spent the last five minutes talking about. 'Of course, she is Eleanora Rodriguez-Gonzales, she owns this house and she was your landlady. I am Jojo her son.'

Realisation and surprise dawned. The last time I saw her was three weeks ago, a fit looking fifty-year-old who came to collect the rent. 'We would be honoured if you would come to her death anniversary next month. It is only across the road at my cousin's house.' He pressed the invitation into my hand again and turned to leave, then hesitated and turned back.

'I have great expenses with the death celebrations,' he tells me 'would it be alright for you to pay me the next two month's rent in advance. I will return tomorrow to collect it, if that is convenient Ma'am.'

The celebrations for the forty-day death anniversary is Catholic tradition held to celebrate the time the soul of the departed ceases its wanderings and ascends to the after-life. The Philippines is a strongly Catholic country (apart from the island of Mindanao and islands in the south were the majority of the population is Islamic). It is a religion inherited from three hundred years of Spanish rule. Many of the rituals associated with Catholicism (the nine days after burial and forty days after the death celebrations,) are incorporated into the funeral arrangements but many more Filipino traditions, beliefs left over from the old Animist religions, and local superstitions are also included. I came to think that the Filipino love of partying and celebrating were also incorporated into the rituals. Catholic tradition decrees that there should be a celebration on the first anniversary of the death but the tradition in the Visayas is for that celebration to be continued for not just one year but for the next nine years. In a country that has a high death rate it is possible to go from one celebration to the next on an almost daily basis. It is believed that the body should be interred no more than nine days after death and until the internment the family should never be left alone, day or night, and that a person should always sit with the body of the deceased. The reality of this is an exhausting time for the family who have to feed all the mourners be there to receive condolences and to answer time and again all the questions asked about the death of their loved one. A dish for contributions is placed next to the coffin which goes towards the expense of feeding the multitude but it can also be an expensive time for the family. There is often discussion about the styles of mourning in different cultures and with the implication that our rather sanitised version of dealing with death is not a healthy way to come to terms with the mourning process. But our way is consistent with our society's mores. I, for one, would not like to have a room full of friends and relatives, playing cards, drinking, telling stories and reading poems day and night for nine days. Yet it fits well with the more gregarious Filipinos who if left in peace until the funeral, would feel that nobody cared. Does all the ritual help the grieving process? I'm not sure. Rosemarie and Ruby's mother was much loved and is still missed and grieved for. Grief is grief the world over and although beliefs and rituals might go towards mitigating the loss grief is still raw and painful. Grief is especially painful if it is a child that has been lost.

Rosemarie had been correct when she said that I didn't want to view the body of her mother. Until I came to The Philippines I hadn't seen a dead person. I'd declined to see the bodies of my grandparents and my parents when they'd lain in rest at the funeral parlour, covering my fear of the dead with the statement that I wanted to remember them as they were when alive. My first viewing of a person was accidental: Rosemarie and I had been visiting a new born in the very run down and over-crowded public hospital. We were standing on the balcony outside the ward waiting for the baby's father to get supplies and for us to try and clear our nostrils of the strong smell of disinfectant and the more putrid underlying smells the disinfectant attempted to cover. A porter joined us for a smoke and chatted to Rosemarie in Waray. I glanced down at the trolley he was leaning against, protruding from the blanket was a big toe with a label tied around it; the nail was a thick, chipped yellow ingrained with dirt. I looked back along the trolley; the blanket was slipping off the rest of the man. He lay on the trolley

205

motionless, eyes closed. He looked as if he was sleeping but I knew he was dead. I felt nothing, no repugnance, distaste or fear. I was simply looking at a middle-aged man who had once been alive and now wasn't. Yet I didn't want to be a voyeur, I walked away leaving him some privacy and went back to the maternity ward where the start of this cycle of this life was in progress. Violetta and her new baby (her ninth) lay on an iron bed with a sheet of cardboard for a mattress. Medical care is free at the public hospital but the family have to provide bedding, food and pay for the drugs. While waiting for her husband to return with sheets and food the staff had slotted Violetta and her baby into old well washed rice sacks: Violetta in a large one the baby in a small one but with the same design and lettering so their outfits matched.

My second viewing of a body was in much more tragic circumstances. Rosemarie and I had been monitoring the chicken rearing project that our NGO was over-seeing. It had meant a day of walking between far-flung houses, trekking along forest paths, balancing on narrow banks between paddy fields. Talking counting chickens, filling in forms. More walking. We were staying over-night at Carla's house and having eaten we were sitting around in the compound. I had recently recovered from a bout of Dengue fever. It had been a mild bout but the residue of it left me very tired. I was dozing on the hard bamboo chair, the solid back rail sticking into my neck; in the background the talk and laughter ebbed and flowed around me as I drifted in and out of sleep. Then I became vaguely aware that the background buzz of the conversation had changed, that more voices had joined in, that the laughter had ceased and that the talk had become more intense. I was shaken awake and told we had to go to Salvacion' house. 'Why?' There had been an accident and her four-year-old daughter, Michaela had died. I thought that as an outsider, a

206

foreigner, my presence wouldn't be appropriate but I was told that because I was an outsider and a foreigner my presence would be more important and most appreciated.

With leaden legs I set off after the others: Rosemarie, Carla and her brother, Mr Torevega the municipality's veterinarian and Jennifer a young widow who always appeared if there was food, a spare man and the possibility of a party. It was past midnight, a cloudy, humid and dark night. The forest tracks where too narrow for Mr Torevega to ride his motor-bike but he switched it on and pushed it so the headlight lit our way. No night sounds echoed amongst the trees and we were a quiet party, groping our way in the dark, tripping over roots of trees. Only Jennifer made any noise, squealing and clinging onto Mr Torevga when she tripped over the roots and branches, she managed to find more things to trip over than the rest of us put together. At a branch in the tracks we came across three people heading towards the house and they told the story of the accident and Rosemarie translated for me.

Evidently Michaela had jumped on the wooden covering of a well, the covering had snapped and she had fallen in. Her teenage uncle had seen what happened and he'd gone into the well to try and rescue her, her father, Michael, had gone in after them to try help both of them to safety. When extra help arrived they managed to pull her father out but it was too late to save Michaela and her young uncle. The other party thought that they had been unable to recover the bodies and they remained in the well.

We emerged from the dense foliage of the forest into the clearing, stepping over the hedge of pineapple bushes onto the brushed bare earth of the compound. Around the house of Salvacion and Michael there were lights and movement. A short distance away a circle of candles flickered around the rim of a well. In the small breeze-block house Salvacion quietly welcomed us, insisting that Rosemarie and I take the only two chairs, black plastic ones with wobbly legs. Rosemarie held Salvacion's hands and spoke gently, I let her speak for both of us, Rosemarie knew what to say. I didn't. We sat down as Salvacion went to greet more visitors. Her sister was explaining to each new person what had happened. I didn't need to speak Waray to understand the details; her oft repeated elaborate mime explained it all. On the floor and on the bed in the small adjoining room children slept and two women propped against wall leant on each other in sleep, one occasionally snoring. Next to me on a table a child slept, she was rather unnecessarily clad in socks and mittens for it was a hot night and in the crowded airless room the heat was oppressive. Michael sat in the corner, a pink nylon jacket wrapped around him staring bleakly into the distance not responding when people spoke to him and gently patted his shoulder.

It wasn't until Salvacion leant over and carefully, lovingly straightened the dress of the child lying next to me and very, very gently stroked her cheek that I realised the little girl wasn't sleeping and that I was sitting next to Michaela. I hadn't recognised that the small, perfect face framed by black curls was that of the bright, lively child who earlier that day had run away and hidden from the strange, foreign lady who had visited her home.

Across the compound lights flickered around the house where her young uncle lived. Outside there was the sound of sawing and hammering as the men got to work making two coffins: one for a young man, one for a small child.

The funeral was the following week. We arrived at the white stone church of Barugo, built by the Spanish in the seventeenth century. We got off the bus and crossed the green

208

space in front of the church at the same time as a lorry load of residents from Bukid arrived. The municipality had contributed towards the costs of the funeral and provided a lorry to bring the mourners from the isolated barangay. The men were in the process of helping the elderly over the high tail-gate of the lorry, the preferred method of assistance seemed to be that the man standing in the lorry slung an elderly lady onto the shoulders of the man on the ground in the manner of a sack of rice and then the man on the ground staggered backwards and, not very smoothly, lowered her to the floor.

We left the hot morning sun behind as we went into the cool church and settled into the pews towards the rear. Geckos scuttled amongst the peeling paint on the walls. In the gallery above, out of sight, a choir sang beautifully.

There was a hush as the funeral cortege arrived: the smell of incense wafted through the church and a priest in his fine gold edged vestments slowly followed the boy who was swinging the incense boat on long chains. Behind him two plain wooden coffins painted white, one of them poignantly small, were carried into the church, followed by the bereaved parents; dignified and silent.

As they reached the altar a sudden beam of sunlight burst through the high windows causing a dancing pathway of dust motes to illuminate the way for the procession.

It was raining the day of the funeral for Rosemarie's mama. It was the heavy tropical rain that sweeps in from the Pacific causes overflowing drains and flooding and then stops as suddenly as it has started. It was arranged that I'd meet Joji and Amy at the office and we'd travel together to the church in Sagakahan for the service and then follow on to the cemetery for the internment. As is the habit of all Filipinos Joji was late and Amy was even later, so we missed the service. Even if they had been on time we would have still missed the service because we'd got the time wrong. We caught up with the mourners as they reached the cemetery. The coffin had been unloaded from the hearse and was been carried by six men, not through the main gates but down a rat infested, urine smelling back alley. We slithered our way through the mud caused by the recent rai trying to avoid the nastier looking debris and not for the first time in The Philippines I thought I would have found it better t be wearing wellies than sandals.

Out in the main cemetery the coffin had already moved well ahead of us. Held aloft and tilted precariously it was carrie pushed and hauled over the tombs of the both recently and lon ago deceased. There is very little town planning in The Philippines so if the living aren't the focus of careful planning detail it shouldn't be surprising that the dead aren't. But they could have least have planned to leave a pathway between the tombs and burial plots. A family purchase a plot and bury thei loved one, surround him or her with a concrete block and then subsequent family members die they place them on top of the original tomb and then concrete that in as well. The result is a series of building blocks sometimes as much of six or eight bloc high spilling out onto what was once a pathway. These are interspersed with vacant lots filled with weed, litter and water. Hibiscus and bougainvillea had seeded themselves and provid bright splashes of colour amidst the greyness of sky and concre Rising amongst the chaos of blocks are the more elaborate and larger tombs of the wealthier. These tombs are often better buil and more opulent than the houses in the shanty towns along th bay and it is not unknown for them to have inhabitants who ha moved from the squalor of a nippa hut along the water's edge t the comparative luxury of a home with their, or somebody else' deceased Papa.

The tomb of the Dorado family was across the cemetery against a far wall. We could see where they were heading because there was tarpaulin over the family tomb so the cementing in of the coffin could be done under cover, sheltered from the rain. The route to the tomb was by necessity tortuous; it was a case of the mourners finding the route of least resistance over the higgledy-piggledy tombs. The pall-bearers were having difficulty carrying the coffin and were becoming fractious, and as one dropped a corner of the coffin a good deal of shouting took place. I did hope the lid was screwed down securely. Children who had skipped over all the blocks were at the site waiting for the coffin to arrive but the progress of the deceased was slow. The rest of the congregation was scattered across the cemetery finding their own way to the tomb. We had already over-taken a group of elderly women who were finding the climb over the blocks difficult and finding the help of a strong young man not of much help at all.

Another sharp blast of rain sent Amy, Joji and I under the cover of the impressive tomb of one Juan Marie Martin. The plaque said he was seventy-six when he died but the framed photograph alongside the plaque was that of a much younger man who, with his thick dark hair and drooping moustache, looked more like a Mexican bandit than an elderly Filipino businessman. When the heavy rain eased we made our way forward. The coffin had now arrived at its destination and prayers were being said. Under a leaden sky Rosemarie and her sister stood still, sharing an umbrella with their arms around each other's waists. Their brother and father, recovering from their exertions carrying the coffin sat sharing a cigarette, the rain and the sweat had soaked their white shirts so that they had become transparent and stuck to their backs. The rest of the large family stood in groups some under umbrellas, some bare-

211

headed, some of the elderly women wearing white lace mantillas watching as the coffin was cemented on top of a cluster of tombs of late family members.

Amy, Joji and I stood a short distance away, after a while Amy leant over and looked at the tomb we were standing on and then looked around. 'We're standing on top of my grandma and auntie.' She said.

'How did they get here?' asked Joji.

'They were travelling in a pedi-cab near Wilmars and they were hit by a jeepney.

'They were killed but the pedi-cab driver just lost a leg,' said Amy in a matter of fact tone of voice.

There wasn't a lot we could say about that so we said nothing.

It seemed to take an age for the completion of the internment, when the work had been finished and more prayers had been said we slowly followed the family out of the cemetery once more climbing over the heaped blocks of concrete. The rain had stopped and the sun was coming out; steam rose from the blocks. Despite sheltering in tombs and clustering under umbrellas I had got wet and my feet were sodden. I felt as if I was steaming as much as the tombs.

As we were leaving I noticed a man, who had been standing at a distance beneath a lone tree, move towards the tomb and place a bright red hibiscus flower on top of it, its petals formed a limp, wet flash of scarlet against the slowly drying cement.

Thai Tastes

Jane Wilson-Howarth

Thais appreciate good food and they also have the reputation of eating most things that move, and many that don't. I'm generally happy to try any dish but never did fancy toe-biters – the pond living insects known for nipping swimmers. I was up-country in Suphanpuri and we'd sent out for a take-away. Within the stir-fry were delicious cubes of something I couldn't identify. They were of a smooth texture almost jelly-like and black. I asked a local what I was eating and he said, 'You take one duck. Cut off its head and pour out its blood into a bowl. This is heated slowly until it becomes solid, then it can be cut into cubes and fried.' I didn't enjoy it quite as much after that, and now whenever I eat black pudding my mind replays the scene involving a decapitated duck.

A little later, I was out walking amongst the rice fields with a local engineering colleague of my husband's. We walked along the mud banks that surround each field and a medium-sized snake slid across in front of us. I asked whether the snake was venomous and he said, 'Not venomous and not good eating. Some snakes are tasty, but not this one.' My informant's expression said that he considered this was a complete write-off as a species.

Conversations with my Landlord
Stephanie Green

After the death of his mother my new landlord arranged to come and collect the rent himself until he had bank accounts sorted out, and for the next couple of months he did so, but he worked and lived in Cebu, not far in miles but a long way on the erratic transport services of The Philippines. In third month I got the following messages. Only the account numbers have been changed.

Landlord: Steph gud morning can u just deposit the rent I can't go to tacloban

Steph: Yes if u tell me where to deposit it

Landlord: Steph can u just deposit the rent today

Steph: Yes where would u like me to put it

Landlord: Steph I use friends account as I didn't open yet. can u just deposit the rent today

Landlord: Have you deposited rent yet

Steph: No because you haven't given me bank details

Landlord: OK Maximo Garcia chinabank, lahug branch account n0111. Can you deposit today.

Steph: No banks closed now, in barugo tomorrow will deposit Wednesday

Landlord: Have you deposited amount yet

Steph: No will deposit tomorrow

Landlord: Can you deposit today

Steph: Yes in bank now

Landlord: Don't use that account he has gone to manila

Landlord: Steph can u deposit at Ronald Dimaunhan account. Equitable Bank ac no 2222222.

Landlord: Steph have u deposited yet

Steph: In Equitable PCI Bank the number you gave me is for Equitable Savings bank. No branch in Tacloban

Landlord: OK will give new account can u deposit tomorrow

Landlord: Steph my cousin will collect rent on sat morning

Steph: OK

Landlord: Steph where are you my cousin is outside now

Steph: Downtown. U said this morning it is now 4pm

Landlord: Don't give money to anybody I will text with new account.

Landlord: Steph can you send money to me at huillers, keep pin number and text when u have sent money

Landlord: Steph have u deposited yet

Steph: Brownout in Tacloban, can't send money until elec restored.

Landlord: Steph can deposit money at Lydia Laqinon, Landbank, ac 33333

Landlord: Steph have you deposited money yet

Landlord: Steph have you deposited money yet

Steph: Pls remember I have to work and can't spend every day sitting in banks

Landlord: Don't use account she has gone to Bohol

Landlord: Pls deposit money at my house mates accou

Marjorie Joy Alorro, Equiable PCI ac no 3333. can u

deposit today, text me when money deposited

Landlord: Don't use account I will send you another

Landlord: Pls deposit money Alberto Lahung Metroba

Account no 22222

Landlord: Steph have you deposited money yet

Landlord: Steph have you deposited money yet

Landlord: Steph I need the money pls deposit today

Steph: *Money deposited*

Landlord: Thank you so much! Steph can I ask you a

favour. Can u lend me 6000 pesos, I will pay you when

my loan check will be released. Will dat be OK, I need

to pay year end taxes. Can you send 6000pesos.

Steph: *No*

Landlord: *That's OK.*

King of Kipling's Jungle
Jane Wilson-Howarth

The boys were excited about the idea of going back to the jungle, especially as they knew it was home to Shere Khan, Kaa and even the Bi-Coloured-Python-Rock-Snake. The night before we were to ride deep into the Royal Bardiya National Park, Ramdin, the naturalist, told some tales over dinner. He described the time that a tiger had charged one of the working elephants. The elephant tried to bat the tiger away with her trunk. Then she ran off in panic. In her flight, she passed beneath a low branch which swept the howdah and the tourists in it onto the ground. We must have looked shocked so Ramdin continued, 'No-one was *badly* hurt but the tourists were shaken and they weren't happy that our elephant driver…'

'The *mahout?*' I asked.

'No the *mahout* is the boy who cleans out the elephant. The *phanit* is the driver with real skill and a special relationship with his elephant. That day, the *phanit* took quite some time to calm his elephant and return to rescue the tourists. They were a bit nervous while they were on the ground knowing that the tiger was still close and that the tiger was a little bit angry.'

I asked, 'Do tigers ever kill people?'

'Not usually,' Ramdin was chuckling now. 'If they do, someone comes from the Forest Department, darts him and he spends the rest of his life in the zoo in Kathmandu.'

Ramdin seemed more than casual about the risks, and my confidence wasn't exactly boosted when he added, 'Oh could I just ask you both to sign this disclaimer?'

We signed that we wouldn't sue if any of us was killed or maimed.

Next morning, when our two-year-old, Seb, approached the elephant we were to ride on, he objected, '*Haati* too big!' As

217

Seb had started to talk, he'd select the easier word from Nepali or English and *haati* was so much easier to say than *elephant*.

Seb's reluctance was short-lived. Once he had been persuaded to scramble into the big wooden *howdah* strapped onto the elephant's back, he was delighted at being up so high. We were installed on thick cushions on one elephant and Simon managed to persuade Alex to stop admiring a motorbike and climb aboard another so we were installed well above the zone where mosquitoes hunt. As the elephants jerkily, uncomfortably walked us into the forest, Seb pointed at elegant Spotted Deer that darted away between smooth-trunked sal trees. He liked being up with mischievous chattering rhesus monkeys. Six-year-old Alex chatted loudly, wanting to swing between the trees on dangling lianas like the Bandar-Log.

The jungle was tranquillity itself: even if I strained my ears, there was no traffic noise, no planes, no sounds of any kind of human activity. There was, though, an odd truncated *cock-a-do*. At first I thought we must be approaching a village, but a gorgeous deep green and red Jungle Fowl ran out from the undergrowth and I realised it had been his call. Another called from further away. Seb pointed to a rhino. 'I like one-hoseras bestest,' he said.

We meandered through forest that I expected to be pristine but trees had been pushed over, broken or gored. Ramdin saw where I was looking and explained, 'Our wild elephants are not happy. They need to roam more freely but villagers all around the Park light fires and send them back into the reserve. A few elephants over several nights can eat the village's entire rice harvest which should last a year – then everyone starves. It is not easy for them.'

Closer to the river, a spot in the elephant grass smelt of death and we peered down on bones that were still red with

218

fresh blood. Our naturalist said, 'A tiger has killed another adult tiger... this has never happened before.'

I could hear Alex's upset voice from the back of the other elephant. 'Is that Shere Khan who is dead?' Alex was passionate about playing killing and fighting games but he didn't like this real violence with real blood.

Ramdin had told us about the increasing stresses on the big wildlife in the reserve. A male tiger needs 25 square miles and when a young male comes of age, he either has to oust an established adult or move away and find his own territory. But these animals are hemmed in by the burgeoning human population in the great Gangetic Plains, so are turning on each other or they stray outside the reserve kill livestock. It was a matter of survival, a life or death struggle.

Our elephant shuffled languidly on, down and across a small river. A bright green barbet let out its strange echoey *krrow-krrow-krrow;* all the birds were noisy with pre-mating euphoria. Now we were into patchy forest with broken canopy where luxuriant tree-sized shrubs grew. The jungle was so thick it was difficult even to spot something as large as an elephant. We all heard the deep rumble of an elephant close by and our elephant rumbled back. Ganga Lal, our *phanit* seemed nervous. Another elephant pushed through the leaves but I saw Ganga Lal relax as he realised this wasn't a wild elephant but the one carrying Simon and Alex. Ganga Lal knew the jungle and soon he was kicking our elephant into a grove of sal trees. Monkeys were busy in the trees above us. Our elephant stopped and Ramdin pointed to several cow-elephants and youngsters. I could see Simon trying to keep Alex quiet as he prattled on about Colonel Hathi. We pushed deeper into the forest patch and watched delightedly as more and more elephants emerged from the

219

underbrush. We counted about 40. Our elephant ambled amongst them while we peered down on just-born calves.

Ramdin who was standing on our elephant's bottom behind the howdah then spoke to Ganga Lal who responded by laying into our elephant and kicking her vigorously behind her ears. For a moment I couldn't understand what was happening … until I noticed the large bull elephant that was heading towards us. His ears were splayed out threateningly. His huge tusks gleamed in the afternoon sun. I didn't know where Simon and Alex were. Our elephant didn't seem the least bit perturbed and didn't noticeably respond to the ferocious whacking of her skull. Maybe she liked the look of the tusker. We'd heard that wild bull-elephants sometimes visit the tame cow-elephants who may or may not accept their suitors. Ramdin said something about this being Deepgaj who "didn't usually charge" which I didn't find especially reassuring. Probably our elephant knew that the wild elephant wasn't really interested in chasing us.

I'd started to feel safe again and my focus returned to looking for beautiful birds and butterflies when another big bull elephant appeared – as if by magic – straight ahead of us. Too close. He'd come up out of the riverbed but had approached so silently that he'd taken us completely by surprise. 'Kancha!' Ramdin breathed.

This was the notoriously aggressive elephant who knew he was king of the jungle. He had the reputation of charging at anything.

Ganga Lal frantically kicked our elephant around and really laid into her with his spiked ankus. It made an odd clanging sound as metal hit skull. Behind us, Ramdin stage-whispered, 'He's coming!'

He looked really scared as he crouched down to disguise his profile. He rained blows on the elephant's bottom in an impotent attempt to speed our flight. I guess Ramdin was most worried because he'd be the first to be flattened if Kancha had amorous intentions towards the cow-elephant on which we sat.

The whacking and urgent exchanges between the naturalist and the *phanit* continued for what seemed like minutes. I tried to catch what they were saying to each other in Nepali but all I got was the flavour of their fear. And Ganga Lal's frustration at failing to get our elephant to flee. She just shuffled languidly on.

The next time I looked back though I realised I could no longer see Kancha. His honour had been satisfied. He had lost interest in us. He'd melted back into the jungle again. By this time little Seb had picked up on all the adrenaline. I wrapped an arm around my son although as I was dry-mouthed and tremulous, wondered how reassuring he'd find this gesture. He said loudly, 'Me no like this big *haati*. *Haati* no come!'

'It's okay Sebastian – he's not coming. He's gone to find some dinner.'

Seb smiled at the thought of food.

The jungle was always full of surprises. I'd lost track of the number of times we'd gone from blissful tranquillity to terror and back again in the space of seconds. And Alex was still pondering the violence he'd seen, 'Is Shere Khan really dead?'

Dog's Bollocks

Jane Wilson-Howarth

Local languages mingle and mix across the Indo-Nepali border.
The Nepali language predominates in the hills because it is easy
to understand when shouted across valleys but Hindi is more
useful in the Plains as more people understand it because of the
popularity of movies made in Mumbai. The Nepali spoken in the
lowlands is full of Hindi words, or words from 'tribal' dialects
it can be a struggle knowing even what language people are
speaking. Nepali can appear imprecise too. Now never means
immediately and the word for flower, phul, is also the word for
egg. When one wants hens' eggs you have to specify this, or you
risk buying a bunch of flowers by mistake.

I asked someone in the market - I thought - to sell me some
chicken's eggs (*kukhura ko phul*).

She started to snigger. 'Buy what, *memsahib*?' She'd heard
'dogs' eggs' (*kukur ko phul*) and exploded with merriment as
dogs' eggs could only be testicles. A little later, Guliya gave me
an anatomy lesson. She pointed out a male dog and underneath
his eggs and banana. Patiently she explained that this was the
equipment he used to impregnate bitches. She thought me a
complete idiot. After that any mention of bananas caused hilarity
too – this is slang for penis. Then oranges are a euphemism for
breasts and anyone called a radish is stupid. I began to feel
insecure when talking about food in case I inadvertently insulted
someone or made some unintended sexual proposition.
Pronunciation was also challenging, and I couldn't make clear
the difference between *char*, four, and *chha*, six. Often I'd
approach a vendor and try to say, 'Please give me six hens eggs.'
They'd pick out four. 'No, I'd like six.'

'But I *have* given you four, *memsahib*.'

'I need two more.'

222

'Why did you ask for four, then?'

I decided it was best ask for five instead. *Panch* is easier to pronounce.

That still didn't get me out of trouble. The Nepali languages contains consonants that can be retroflex, aspirated, non-aspirated and to the untrained ear the five d sounds, for example, are hard to distinguish. English consonants tend to be partially aspirated, in that some breath comes out of the mouth on pronouncing letters like b and p. I had special trouble with the pronunciation of *baanta* which means aubergine. This sounds dangerously close to *bhaanta* (vomit). Traders in the market did give me strange looks when I ask then to sell me a kilo of vomit. To them the b and bh sounds are so dissimilar they cannot understand the confusion.

And to be extra discombobulating, *kul,* means both yesterday and tomorrow in Hindi.

Points of View
Jane Wilson-Howarth

Sonia – an English woman in her early forties

I watched Moti step up onto the verandah of a dilapidated thatched hut and dive inside. She soon reappeared with the smiling tea-house owner. They brought rice-straw mats. I stirred my aching body in response to their beckoning. Creakily, I hobbled across to the verandah and collapsed onto the surprisingly thick, comfortable mat.

Moti passed me some tea. I curled my hands around the glass and felt the warmth flow into me. I let the steam flood my face. It tickled the inside of my nose. I paused before allowing myself the first sip, savouring the warm fudgy smell that made my mouth water. The tea was so hot and sweet and so delicious. What a treat it was to luxuriate in such simple sensations. There is just nothing like the pleasure of a drink when you are really thirsty or sitting down to rest when you are really, really tired, or getting warm and cosy and comfortable after you've been chilled to the marrow.

I didn't even much mind the faint whiff of cow dung you can always smell in these houses. It is normal for these people use a mud and cow dung mixture to plaster the walls and floors – actually I can't believe I just thought that – not minding the smell! And anyway what is cow-dung but processed grass! I felt rather proud of myself for thinking of it like that! I checked my arm and saw that the nasty allergic wheal had faded already; there was nothing but a slight scratch there now.

I found myself studying the two women as they babbled animatedly. The teashop owner had been so kind and welcoming that I didn't mind that their language excluded me. I studied the older woman's face. It looked as if it was moulded in terra cotta. Her eyes were dark and almond-shaped, and her high

224

cheekbones were sun-blushed and rosy. She looked so different from the Plains-people – like Moti. It was as if – by walking through the gorge – we'd entered a new country. The houses we had passed had been very different too.

I tuned out of the women's unintelligible chit-chat and thought about the day. I felt good about myself, what I'd done, for myself.

Before, I would have felt the need to tell my husband or my mother of any small achievement and seek their approval, which I seldom got. I considered that I had been trying to prove myself to someone forever. My mother simply wouldn't believe where I was now. She would never credit that I'd be this intrepid. I thought about all the things I'd done over the years to try to impress my family and realised how foolish I'd been.

Today I felt proud of myself, and I didn't need to tell anyone a thing. I knew I'd done well and that was enough. I'd achieved something, just for the sake of it – just for me. Actually at that moment, I didn't care if I ever went home. If I had an accident – or met a desirable man – I wouldn't care. Falling in love or falling off a cliff, either way, I'd have no regrets. Dying now – or disappearing – would hurt no-one, and this was a liberating thought. Really, I might never go home! Never.

I suppose that no-one would want to go through a traumatic experience but when you've survived something life-shattering and risen above it, it gives you a kind of serenity. I lay back on the mat on the verandah and closed my eyes, feeling smug and content.

A while later, I became aware of something tickling my hand. I looked down and saw – in the process of climbing up onto it – a huge black spider. A tarantula. It was the size of a saucer. It was heavy. Its hairy legs were as thick as pipe-cleaners. I froze. It seemed to be looking up into my face with its row of

225

glinting black eyes. Its jaws looked like wire-cutters. An enormous green dragonfly was struggling to get free from them.

I looked over toward Moti and mouthed, 'Help!'

She hadn't noticed anything.

I dared not move. Sweat dribbled off me. The spider started to walk further up my arm. That was it. I just panicked. I thrashed. I flailed my arms to get it off me. I ran.

Moti – a Nepali woman in her later teens

I am just thinking that Auntie is happy – when she screams. She screams like she has seen Kali and all the thugs who worship her. Auntie jumps up, flapping her arms like a vulture that has eaten too much trying to get airborne. Then she takes off: she runs up the mountain, along a small, small goat path. She's still screaming. This is very strange behaviour.

The *didi* who owns the teashop asks, 'Your foreign friend – is she mad?'

I say, 'Maybe mad; my mother thinks this bideshi is possessed. It is hard to be sure. Mostly she is harmless – and quiet. But you can never tell what she will do next. She washed my baby brother in water!'

'Unbelievable!'

'*And* she chased a cow out of our vegetable garden. The mother cow came to bring blessings on our family and the foreigner chased her away!'

'This is very strange. She *must* be possessed.'

Excerpt on how people of different backgrounds regard one another, from the novel *Snowfed Waters, 2017.*

Foreboding
Jane Wilson-Howarth

She is old now – about 40 probably; she doesn't count age in numbers – but she is content. Life was so hard when she was young. Things are better now. She still remembers – like it was yesterday – that awful time when she gave birth for the first time, alone in the neighbour's cowshed. The neighbour was angry. She had defiled that place, but what could she do? She couldn't stay inside her own house. If the baby had come out dead, its spirit would kill all her other babies. The babies to come.

It had been a long labour. She hadn't known pain like it. There was no-one to help but the baby was healthy. A girl.

Seven of her children survive. She has been fortunate. Her eldest daughter has already given her three beautiful grandchildren. She is suckling her youngest grandchild now. Her three sons are away in the big city. She worries about them. There is too much sin and temptation there, and not enough respect for the gods. And there are so many bad spirits in the Valley. They get inside as you breathe and make you cough. Each year when they return to their village for Dashain, they are coughing. Each year they come to visit their old mother, and they cough.

She asks them about the temples they have visited in Kathmandu and what offerings they have taken but they do not speak freely and she suspects that they are not paying enough attention to the gods. Perhaps this is why the mountains have been shaking themselves. Perhaps even the Great God Shiva Himself is angry. She will take a small offering to the little cave close by in the morning.

She knows that she should feel happier. The weather has grown warm after the winter and she can gather nettles to cook with her potato curry. There is still grain stored in the roof of her

227

house. It is enough to last until the next harvest. Her chickens a[...]
laying nicely. She has spread the outer leaves of cabbages to dr[...]
in the sun. She should be satisfied but today something is
troubling her. She has a feeling of foreboding.

Her husband is out in the terraces, hoeing. She sits on h[...]
verandah massaging good thick yellow mustard oil into the
baby's perfect skin. The sun warms her and makes the oil on hi[...]
glisten. Gazing at the baby makes her happy again.

Suddenly, strangely, the world falls silent. Birds,
chickens, dogs utter not one sound. She looks towards the
Eternal Snows. She feels it first in her intestines. Then it is as if
Lord Shiva's mighty hand has grabbed the earth beneath her fe[...]
and is pulling it back and forth. She throws herself away from
the house as the verandah crashes down. She crawls further
away, cradling the baby. The shaking goes on. She cannot get u[...]
The baby is quiet. She checks. He is breathing.

She is out in the open. She thinks she is safe enough bu[...]
there is crashing and thundering and so many awful sounds of
destruction.

Finally the shaking stops. Her elbow and knees are
bleeding. The baby is stirring. Her house is an odd shape. One
wall is badly cracked and the thatch is hanging down low on o[...]
side. It is creaking ominously. Dogs start to howl. Birds call
again. People are screaming and crying. She wonders where he[...]
children and other grandchildren are.

With numb fear in her guts she walks up to the top of t[...]
village. The stone lions outside the temple are cracked and
broken. The last houses have gone. The tap has gone. There is a[...]
orange scar where the Brahmins used to live. A big piece of lan[...]
has slid down the mountain towards the river. It is hard to mal[...]
out the missing houses. There is just a chaos of roof timbers,
rocks and sand. Neighbours are there with her at the edge

228

howling. People must be buried in there. Men and younger women are climbing down to see if they can help.

Her daughter appears and they hug. She takes her baby. The old woman walks in a trance. She returns to her house. It isn't the shape of a house any more. She looks inside. All the barley that was up in the roof has spilled. It is scattered in amongst the debris of their home. This was to feed them until the harvest. The drying cabbage leaves are buried under one wall of the house. Her expensive earthenware water pot is broken also.

She finds an old sack and goes inside. The mud floor that she replasters each morning is broken. Barley is strewn across it and much has fallen into the cracks. She squats down and starts picking up the grains one by one. She will be able to recover some of the barley but lots will be lost.

There is another awful wrenching sound. She looks up. There is a huge crash. The roof is falling. She starts a prayer. The world disappears.

Everything is black.

More than Mere Medicine
Jane Wilson-Howarth

When I first ventured overseas as a fresh young doctor, I thought
I could easily improve peoples' health. I knew so much. In
Indonesia, my brief was health education. I was to work on
Lombok with unsophisticated villagers with low levels of
literacy. I started my work with a house-to-house survey,
detailing – on several large sheets of paper for each household –
exactly each person's health problems. Staggering statistics
emerged: the most shocking was that up to 30% of the children
had died before the age of ten. This was a number that certainly
did not appear in government statistics, and perhaps confirmed
what my local friends said about the island being neglected by
central government since that assassination attempt decades
before.

Looking at my data, I was puzzled to find that polio and
measles were not mentioned at all in the list of diseases afflicting
the population. My Indonesian colleagues patiently explained,
'These are not diseases. People struck by polio or measles never
go to hospital. They are caused by a curse or Evil Eye; they are
cured in the Mosque.' I was astonished that a simple
straightforward question about what diseases were important
locally didn't earn me an accurate answer. I could speak
Indonesian but I understood little about the population with
whom I was trying to work. Perhaps I should also have thought
about the fact that in Indonesia, hospitals are known as *rumah
sakit* – literally houses of pain. They are places to go to die. I had
more letters after my name than in it but I was slow to realise
that to organise a successful community health programme, I
would need to understand more than epidemiology and
microbiology.

I tried hard to 'sell' my medically accurate ideas about bacteria and infection to my highly motivated local community workers. In their eyes my science was irrelevant. Even the fact that I had written books was unimpressive – because the only book worth reading is the Koran. They were patient with me though and finally my little team took my pontifications about microbes that couldn't be seen and turned the ideas I was passionate to communicate into useful information. We didn't attempt a formal programme of health education. We settled on simply giving out hand soap and a cheap little plastic soap box. Then through discussions at village water points or market places we imparted the gospel of hand washing after a visit to the loo. In four months, we achieved an 89% fall in the dysentery and diarrhoea rate immediately, and two years on there were still 75% fewer cases of gastroenteritis. We saved lives but I cannot claim much credit for that. The mothers of young children were crucial to the success of this project. They noticed their babies being less ill and growing fat since they'd started using soap; they became our health evangelists. Through them other villagers learned the value of hygiene in a way that I could never have communicated, because my scientific belief systems were so alien. I was beginning to appreciate the depths of my ignorance.

There was an impressive spirituality amongst the people with whom I worked, and if I was misguided enough to describe the unspiritual state of the British, my local friends either did not believe me, were bewildered, or felt great sadness that we should lack that important element to our lives. For them religion provided a structure for society, support systems, healing services, moral values – everything that a community needed.

Religion is inseparable from life in Nepal too. Here Hinduism dominates but there is also a strong Buddhist influence. In case of illness most Nepalis first resort to prayer and offerings at the temple, then the family might consult a *jankri* or some other kind of religious faith healer, and usually only if all else has failed they might go to the hospital. The hospital closest to our home in Kathmandu was a safe place. It had good government and overseas aid funding and a large staff of well-trained Nepalis supported by Western missionary doctors and nurses, and yet many Nepalis regard it with mistrust. It was less likely to help with family crises than the priests were.

Faith provides support but it can be socially handicapping and it can provide a burden of guilt. Hinduism is the religion that probably produces the greatest constraints to development and improvement. This is the religion that imposes a very strict caste system. Someone born into a high caste remains there however good or bad they are and a low caste person, however devout and kind and worthy can never elevate himself. In a region where resources can be severely limited, though, this is a force for passivity and stability that has – perhaps – avoided huge bloody uprisings. Yet from the outside it seems harsh. Despite attempts at reforms, the only escape for many is through conversion to Islam or Christianity.

During the horrendous bloody Partition of India in 1947, Muslims were supposed to move to the newly created West and East Pakistans, and Hindus were supposed to move into what is now India. Most of those Hindus who elected to stay in Pakistan converted to Christianity: this faith, like Islam, is a religion of 'The Book', the only book. Converts were mostly low caste Hindus who lived by cleaning up others' filth, and their families still perform that role today. When we lived in northern Sindh in Pakistan, our sewers and drains would often become blocked, and then David the 'sweeper' would be summoned. He was a stunted, unpleasant-looking character with a squint and a hunchback. He was small enough to be inserted into the sewer –

232

a living Dyno-rod. He was paid well for this disgusting work and was wealthy, though you'd never have guessed it to look at him. He'd become confident and was happy in the knowledge that his children would have a good chance to make something of themselves. With David's money, they were getting an education, and would have a good shot at improving their lot in life.

Spirituality is a tremendous force for social good, support for the ill and distraught and, especially in remote regions, may provide the only real system of health care available to villagers. And it is holistic. Even an agnostic like me can see that it is a force for good as well as providing fuel for religious racist attacks.

I Once Cycled through Syria
Sally Haiselden

I cycled through Syria once, as a traveller on a journey, not as a
tourist sightseeing. I was on my way home by bicycle after
teaching in Sudan for two years. I was travelling post 9/11, as a
single, British woman through Muslim Egypt, Jordan and now
into Syria. A Syria in 2002 with Bashar al-Assad as a relatively
new President, and a population in general hopeful he would
bring about good change after 30 years of rule by his father. As
pedalled through the country, again and again the people and
place contradicted the stark conclusion at the time that all
Muslim countries were dangerous for the likes of me, especially
as a woman. I was treated to unconditional hospitality and with
the utmost respect, if not with a little bit of confusion as to
exactly what I was and what I was doing.

I pedalled out of Damascus at first light just as people
were beginning to gather at road junctions to catch the first
buses. I had breakfast on a bench outside a barracks. There was
tap nearby for passers-by like me to use. I washed off the sticky
remains of the perfect locally made apricot jam and noted the
convenience of a tap compared to the earthenware zeers
thoughtfully placed on roadsides in Sudan and Egypt. These yo
had to dip a cup into. I was happy to be on the road again and
was exciting to be heading to a monastery founded by an
Ethiopian prince, run by Europeans, offering Arab hospitality s
on top of a cliff in the desert. I felt like a mixed up crusader.

Nabk was where the turn off to Mar Musa monastery
was. However the town failed to give me the usual warm
reception of, 'Welcome!', 'Itfaddalu', 'Drink tea', 'Come lady'.
The men hanging out on the street seemed a surly lot but I had
approach them. After 80km on the road already today I was no

keen to get my directions wrong at this stage. I explained I was going to Mar Musa. 'What is the road like?'

'Not difficult.'

'Is it possible by bike?'

'Possible.'

'Is there tarmac?'

'Yes, all the way.'

I was learning to be wary of the veracity of such information, usually given by people who did not cycle so had a very different experience of travelling the road than I would. I was justifiably unconvinced as the guidebook said getting there involved, 'some extremely stony terrain', and 'vehicles cannot go all the way and visitors must walk the last 1.5km along a winding path up a steep sided gully' with the need to, 'scramble over rocky outcrops'. What? With my panniers? I was also learning to be suspicious of information in guidebooks; it was often second hand and therefore not necessarily factual either.

'How long has there been tarmac?' I asked.

'One year.'

Another answer, 'Fifteen to sixteen years.'

A man who introduced himself as Mohammed seemed to know what he was talking about. He said it was 15 km and that would take me about two hours. That seemed realistic to me. A taxi driver with lovely green eyes, sitting nearby, did not try to persuade me to travel with him so I guessed the road was rideable.

An easy climb on smooth bitumen led me past the town rubbish tip and after shaking off flies, three dogs and a well-intentioned young man on a motorbike who wanted to show me the way, I crested the hill and the full desert ahead came into view. A desolate panorama of scrubby, rocky plain stretched to ridges on the horizon. Where was I headed I wondered?

I could hear the noise of an approaching motorbike. It was Mohammed transformed into Easy Rider with leather jacket scarf and an old Yamaha. 'I come to check you turn left not right so you do not disappear into the desert,' he explained. As the slight incline of the road began to pull he began the detailed questioning which seemed particular to Syria. Not content with knowing where I was travelling to and from he wanted to know about my family, the exact date I would be coming back to stay with his family and the address of my friend in Amman I had mentioned. Constant gear changes, thirst, aching knees, a barrage of Arabic, guessing the meaning and trying to give a comprehensible answer were all in a day's pedal here.

We reached a helter-skelter corkscrew descent which had me freewheeling faster than him. I shouted back to him that yes, would call him 'bukra' (tomorrow) adding the customary 'Inshallah' (God willing) to cover me in case I did not. I caught his words giving final instructions which included, '…not possible by bike', but I just decided at this stage it was easier to ignore them. As a sharp left turn shot me out onto a straight road reaching through the desert, I turned for a final wave then looked ahead. I scoured the far off hills. Where was this bloody monastery? I was cheered by a passing Skoda laden with passengers, everyone shouting, clapping, giving me the thumbs up.

At last I rounded a spur, and the road ended at a metal-fronted stone garage tucked up close to the mountain. I looked up, and there it was: the place some sixth century Ethiopian royal had fled to. And what a place he had chosen: 1230m above sea level, perched on a rock ledge over a steep ravine, Mar Musa looked like the kind of place the man in the Black Magic ads would scale to deliver those chocolates. This smelly cyclist could not at this stage climb up let alone with bike and panniers and

236

would need to eat the chocolates at the bottom for the energy to get to the top.

I chained the bike to the front of the garage, debating whether to take my panniers up now or later. I looked up again and decided I only wanted to do this ascent once. I could see three big, black dogs malevolently watching my progress from on high and wondered if any humans were also watching. I hoped that by the time I got up there someone might have called the dogs off. Abu Michael, who introduced himself as the monastery carpenter, was waiting for me at the top. Closer up the dogs transformed into attention seeking softies and were easily won over. Abu Michael led me through a low door set in a thick wall and we came out onto a cobbled threshold that led onto a terrace with a stunning panorama of the desert in the dusk.

Huda, another member of the community, found me a room, tucked round behind the First Aid cupboards, then rushed off before I could ask any questions. 'I've got to finish the accounts. Meditation at 7 and prayers at 8.' What about food I wanted to ask, but too late. I had found out from Abu Michael that I was the only guest if you did not count a troubled French lady who was on a locked in retreat in the annexe, reached by a narrow bridge over a ravine.

The community was established in the 1980s, in the monastery left ruined in the 19th century. Fr Paolo Dall' Oglio, a Jesuit priest and scholar of Arabic and Islam, had dedicated his life to Muslim-Christian dialogue and life in the monastery reflected his vision. Guests of either sex and any beliefs, were warmly welcomed as long as they respected the atmosphere and ethos of the place and did a few odd jobs. Abu Michael had told me that the community at present included a monk from

Germany, someone from nearby Nabk, a convert from Islam and someone nursing a broken heart.

There were four of us for meditation and I wondered who was who. A bulky figure in a black coat and cap burst in late, nodded at me and I guessed that must be Fr Paolo. Mediation started with morose chanting and a cycle of kneeling, touching forehead to the ground, then standing, performed perhaps 50 times. It certainly warmed me up. It did not seem like meditation to me, more like praying in the mosque. I had tried meditation before in Japan when the Zen monk had whacked me on the back with a stick because I had just wiggled my toes after two hours of sitting still and silent. I decided he would have been worked into a violent fit of fury by Mar Musa's working definition of meditation. With the fidgeting, itching, sniffing, nose blowing I could not concentrate on anything. However, the noise covered the crescendo of rumbles from my stomach which had had nothing since breakfast. The others, I decided, being monks, must have learnt techniques of blocking out all distractions and to have a powerful, focussed belief which I lacked.

Eyes stared at me from all directions. The almost intact figures of the frescoes dating from the 11th and 12th centuries were some of the most beautiful I had seen, vibrantly coloured, quirky depictions. On my left Mary, Abraham, Isaac and Jacob watched me. On the right, consorting with a red-tongued Devil were the sinners: impious nuns and corrupt priests writhing in the agony of Hell's fires. Other figures had symbols of their sins tied round their necks, followed by lines of chained and naked men and women with snakes entering their bodies. The message was obvious and after an hour in the cold gloom under the unblinking scrutiny, it began to work on me too. I started to pray 'God, I'm starving.' 'God, I'm freezing.' 'God, hurry up.' 'Please.'

238

Goatskins lay scattered over the stone floor of the chapel. A bible rested on a Koran stand. Worship was constantly interrupted. It all seemed in character with the eclectic vision of Fr Paolo. The heater ran out of fuel and had to be checked three times after refilling before heat and the service continued. Then the candles ran out. Someone dropped a book which blew out the new candles. The coughing and fumbling continued to interrupt the flow of the chanting. Finally, when all was settled, Fr Paolo then began to interrupt those reading the lessons.

I was pleased to return to my room. The February cold, enhanced by a clear desert sky and the altitude, overrode my hunger. I put on all my layers and got into my sleeping bag. The glass box on the wall which I thought contained stuffed pigeons, such was my random assumption in this eclectic place, turned out to be my window, home to a couple of living pigeons who cooed me to sleep.

Mar Musa was as chaotic in the morning. My observations were a little more measured than last night as the sun was up. It warming everything, including my mood which was also enhanced by a breakfast of tea and bread. The bread was a giant unleavened flat disk still warm. In the days prior to taking a detour here, I had imagined Mar Musa to be a quiet, isolated idyll. The reality was anything but. The stunning view across the browns, rusts, reds and ochres of the desert was spoilt by a botch job of cables, wires and hoses strung from rocky outcrop to rocky outcrop linking cave to ceil to building to stable. The bread arrived in a basket by aerial ropeway from the top of the mountain-motorbike delivery from town. Flies arrived independently, overspill from the nearby rubbish tip. Fr Paolo, perhaps true to his Italian background seemed to shout at everyone. As the monastery is on many levels everyone else seemed to communicate by yelling too, using the acoustics of the narrow ravine to amplify their messages and save walking up and down with them. The only semblance of peace and quiet to be had was in the chapel. Perhaps that's the whole point I thought. What brings people to come and live here, like this? Similar ones that had drawn me, temporarily? To try to understand a fascinating, old, complex country? Adventure? Something different? Even though I knew I did not have the religious or spiritual conviction of the community members, I could understand meaningfulness added to life by a return to ensuring the everyday necessities for everyone, of warmth, water, food, shelter and company in a trying location. That I realised is what community was about, everyone having a role play in ensuring these necessities were in place and then to con together at the end of the day to mark and reflect. There were n servants or hierarchy here and I liked that.

Rosemary arrived, an elderly English lady who looked like a posher version of my mum. She was a long-term visitor here, using it as a base to spend time with her archaeologist nie who was excavating a nearby monastery. She agreed with my opinion of the place. During worship that evening she sat reading her own book whilst the Psalms being intoned seemed me to describe a mean, nasty, vengeful thoroughly unpleasant God. I sat there wondering who were the people that wrote this to keep others in check through superstition and guilt. I had jus finished 'A History of God' by Karen Armstrong, herself a former Catholic sister. I had started it at St Catherine's monaste in Sinai, the place of Moses' burning bush. I found the symmetr of finishing it here rather poignant. The main message I had go from the book was the similarities between Islam, Christianity and Judaism, whether it was the fundamentalist or mystic end the spectrum you were considering. I asked Rosemary what sh had been reading in chapel. 'Oh I thought it should be somethi appropriate so I've chosen, 'The life of St Augustine'. I've left my more secular work in my room.' That was Byron.

The day I left, the community was to host a workshop on Ecotourism or 'Echotourism' as Jens, a monk of the community quipped. The Minister of Tourism was coming to open the new tarmac road that had brought me here. He would be watched by a host of tour operators none of whom would climb up to the monastery I was told. Soon, I imagined, coaches would arrive, parking in front of 'authentic' Bedouin tea tents and the monastery would be so overrun it would then become exclusive, travellers no longer able to stay for a small donation and willingness to cook and take part in community life. If this indeed did become the scenario, it would make me think hard about what I wanted for the place if I were a monk there. My eco-friendly departure by bike could be good publicity for the monastery and the Ministry I thought. I was glad to have seen Mar Musa when I had.

When I returned to Nabk, the same men who had given me contradictory advice were sitting outside the same teashop, chatting and smoking, joking. I stopped and shared a tea. They wanted to know about my stay. It occurred to me that they had probably never been there. What reason would they have?
***

One sunny afternoon I found myself on top of a green hill, eating my sticky mushabbak fritter. I was sitting on a lump of stone which had once been part of a façade along the Cardo of Apamea a city of grey granite founded in the third century BC. It had been renowned for its horses and war elephants. By the second century AD it had a huge population of 500,000 enough to entice Anthony and Cleopatra for a stopover. The long Cardo, the main thoroughfare of the city still has an intact colonnade which stretches for two kilometres over the hilltop. Close up the

241

paving of the Cardo shows chariot ruts, raised paved areas in front of the facades lining the street give a clear impression of shops and of how the centre of the large city must have looked. Even closer up the columns are decorated with fluting that twist upwards to still intricate carvings. Around the fallen stones spring flowers erupt in whites and yellows. I had been told to be careful; thick black snakes sunbathe on the warmed granite.

Licking the syrup from my fingers I wondered where to stay. There were no hotels, Apamea was no longer a large city. The young man in the ticket booth introduced me to the site warden, a grey haired bent old man who lived in a nearby wooden shed owned by Italian archaeologists who visited annually. After lots of gesturing and a simple explanation in a mix of broken English and Arabic he did not seem surprised I wanted to camp. I had a feeling word would spread that a foreigner was staying on the hill and he would receive a procession of visitors during the evening – it would be interesting.

The tent poles had barely hit the grass when an overcrowded moped bumped towards me. Three children were clinging on somehow, bracing themselves awkwardly for becoming airborne with each jarring bump, limbs askew as their father drove on at high speed. The impression was of an acrobatic troupe, albeit unsynchronised. After getting to know the family, I named them The Abdel Rahman Family Fliers. The moped barrelled on towards my tent poles, Abdel cruised past, kids now screaming with fear at falling off and fear at seeing a foreigner. He found time to say, 'You no stay here. Come with me,' and wobbled off. Why not? I jolted after him, giving my own solo flying performance over the outer walls of the ruined city disturbing various couples on their dusk strolls amongst the jumbled blocks.

242

I was led into a large lounge. It was difficult to work out who was related to whom. Everyone, neighbours, cousins, offspring, were sitting on the floor or sprawled on cushions drinking tea. My arrival did not faze Abdul's wife Abeer at all. I was welcomed and then taken by the hand, my polite protestations at not wanting to be any bother ignored. A huge pan of hot water signalled my first wash in days. Cheaper Syrian hotels do not have hot water and it had been too cold to brave a cold shower and anyway most of the communal bathrooms had very little privacy as few Syrian ladies stay unless with their husbands. I was shown into a room with a big double bed in it, which must have been my hosts' room and told to wash. Abeer was keen to get her hands on my clothes but only got away with my socks. I really could not inflict the washing of my bike shorts on such a kind stranger. The socks appeared the next morning, very white and dry. How had she managed that?

I ate with the men in the front lounge. Abdel Rahman had become less exuberant than on first arrival. Perhaps he had thought I spoke more Arabic or was disappointed with himself for not knowing more English. I did wonder whether behind the scenes Abeer had scolded him for bringing me home. Or was he uncertain how protocol in his culture indicated how to treat me?

Hassan his four year old was fascinated by me and me of him. He seemed older than his years, independent, engaged. Tugging at my sleeve he made it clear he wanted to know what the levers on my handlebars did and how my panniers stayed on the side of my bike. When I left, unasked and unaided, he put one on my bike for me.

News had spread fast and the best English speaker in town arrived. Abdel began to smile but he did not begin to quiz me through the interpreter as I imagined he might; where are you going? Why are you alone? Why does your husband let you

243

travel like this? Perhaps after all he had just been concerned about being a good host and including me.

'I learnt English from listening to the World Service,' my interpreter explained. This seemed a good chance to ask all those questions I had stored up in my head during my cycle north from the Jordanian border. 'What does the colour of a man's *keffiyeh* tell you?' 'What does a man not wearing one communicate?' I also wanted some information on Bashar's progress and what the regime was really like but knew it unlikely I would elicit any opinions if the secret police were as widespread as I had read about. Anyway, my interpreter was not listening to me. To him I was three books in one — dictionary, thesaurus and grammar. As he translated we did not get past me having to correct his mixed up idioms.

We moved onto a neighbour's house, Hassan leading me by the hand and fussing to ensure he could serve me tea first. Our new host Mahmoud was a locally renowned poet and singer. He brought out a selection of homemade string ouds, brutal constructions of cooking oil cans and pieces of wood and I realised why his following might not extend beyond Apamea. He scratched and wailed his way through interminable songs, indulged I think because there was not a lot else to do in the village of an evening and he was the only musician. We sat on cushions, leaning against the walls, eight men, Hassan and me. My translator began to make some of the lyrics more accessible to me, 'Your breasts glow in the moonlight', 'Your hair falls down, down your back to…' 'How you say Sally?' 'Bottom.'

'The first time I kissed you I became hot.' It didn't look as though my interpreter was 'becoming hot' and embarrassed. Abdel Rahman's smile was the same. There was no sleazy wink from the old chap opposite me, no mischievous grin from the singer. I wondered what Mahmoud's female relatives behind the

244

curtain in the next room were thinking. I know my male Sudanese friends would find the songs pornographic. Just before I had left Sudan a concerned European friend had addressed the question of sex and my safety obliquely. 'These men in Egypt and Syria they don't see their women. They will see you and maybe compare…' I wanted to laugh out loud now at the absurdity of my position – a lone female in a kind of no man's land, neither male nor female in this society, party to a serious performance celebrating the female form. 'You say in English, like melons?' my interpreter gestured.

I left the next morning the only thing glowing on me being my freshly laundered socks. Abdel asked me to stay longer. Abeer was apologetic that she had no food to give me for my lunch. Hassan was distraught. We all took tea outside overlooking the Orontes valley, rich and fertile supporting now as it had Apamea's residents in its heyday. Cousins, neighbours, grandparents joined, more and more plastic chairs appeared. The tea didn't run out. Abeer pushed a crying Hassan to the front of the crowd, her voice was joking but her face was serious. 'Take him with you. Take him to school in England. He will have a good life.' Younger than me but older in experience, less travelled but more knowing she understood her narrow reality.

***

My course through Syria was punctuated by constant generosity. Take for example the shopkeeper who much to my surprise refused to sell me bread and tomatoes for my lunch but instead ushered me behind the counter of his shop, lifted a curtain and there was his wife and child just about to serve a meal. I was taking quiet back roads to Aleppo *en route* to the Turkish border and knew my accommodation choices for the night might be limited. It was late afternoon and I found myself

245

100 km south of Aleppo intending to 'free camp'. This is what long distance cyclists refer to as finding a place to sleep under cover of dusk in the hope that the locals will not spot you and you can have a night off from their hospitality, inquisitive concern and not have to work hard to be entertained or be entertaining. This was going to be difficult as the unclaimed desert further had given way to orange soil scattered with sharp clumps of limestone; every area fenced off and planted with olives, apricots, plums or grazed by goats herded by women whose homes were never far away.

The road twisted and undulated through this landscape and into a small village where I stopped for a Pepsi whilst deciding what to do next. As usual the bought drink was followed by free tea: black, sweet and with a hint of sage. Friendly questioning followed. A small crowd began to gather. The shop owner said his sister was a teacher too and on cue she appeared. A short portly lady, clad in a full-length nylon burgundy dress stood in front of me. Heam spoke accurate English, a careful, capable translator I warmed to immediately. was probably the first full life English person she had ever spoken to but she was not taking advantage of me as a tool through which to improve her English but was genuinely enjoying her status as two-way mouthpiece. We had a mutual giggle as she explained with a certain amount of pride how she was three years older than her husband and had not married until 28. She went to work early and left her two toddlers to wake up whenever then climb up to grandma's flat for breakfast She struck me as a thoroughly modern young mum out here in small corner of rural Syria, far removed from a Westerner's ill conceived, ill-informed image of a typical Muslim wife.

Manoeuvred onto her balcony and served thick black Arabic coffee out of the best china, I realised I had now become

246

guest and knew I would not be camping. The crowd had grown but as I was now in her house they were all her family. I had never met such a large, interconnected extended family. Heam's uncle was her husband's father so she had in effect married her cousin. Her husband had three brothers and five sisters and Fatima, the 55 year old matriarch came downstairs to smile indulgently at me, her temporarily adopted daughter number six. Everyone laughed as trying to remember names, I gave mispronounced ones to the wrong people.

I spent two days in this small village amongst the spring blossom, its quiet routine and freely given hospitality. Arabic hospitality is an extension of Bedouin culture; as a traveller you are welcome for three days and nights, no questions asked, no payment expected. I helped milk the cows, learnt how to turn milk into yogurt, visited relatives in the afternoon and drank endless cups of tea. These were rural people, educated, self-sufficient, reasonably well off with an equality of the sexes many Westerners assume does not exist within a Muslim relationship. Each family member had chores to perform. Mohammed (the father) and a daughter looked after the cows, Fatima made the cheese, the youngest son drove the tractor, and Heam and husband brought in wages. Simple needs were met by a simple life; ownership of a little land, some cows, some olive trees, provided the scope for a very varied organic diet and the means for a comfortable life.

I watched them all in the evening sitting on the floor in the lounge everyone relaxing amidst the security of family and ease of familiar undemanding characters. It seemed harmonious to me. Nobody went off much to do their own thing except for the brothers perhaps who then just went to sit with another group of relatives downstairs in the family shop. I was not just an observer who could have felt lonely to watch all this, so far from my own

247

home. I was included and part of it. Not entertained. Not paraded around the neighbourhood but accepted, not judged, not suspected, not envied. They were all intrigued about my trip and the small size of my family but they seemed wise beyond their narrow experience of the world, far more accommodating and understanding than we would be of Syrians visiting England.

On the last evening I went for a walk with three generations of the family, Fatima, Heam and her daughter. We passed through their apricot and almond groves in the gentle light of the setting sun, between rows and rows of trees in delicate bloom, the petals soft shades of off white, subtle creams and oranges and pinks, fragile, tentative flowers with such potential to give. I envied Heam her sense of family, home, place and belonging. This was to become my abiding image of Syria.

***

In February 2002 I wrote this in my diary:

'Syria is perhaps the most accommodating country in the Middle East despite its range of different religious beliefs. This is because the recently deceased President Hafez al-Assad was himself part of a minority religion. He was an Alawite, an offshoot of Shia Islam. Assad came to power in 1971 and kept himself in power by forming alliances with Syria's many religious minorities. Christians make up between 10-13% of the population and many of Assad's advisors were Christians. Other minority religions include the Yazidis, a religion that now incorporates aspects of Christianity, Zoroastrianism and Islam. Assad's alliances have kept Sunni fundamentalism in check as of course, through intimidation, detention and disappearance of dissenters from any section of the population, has his Mukhabarat police. Assad is still everywhere in the country.

Assad always greets me at the edge of town where in the middle of a roundabout there is usually a large painting or statue of him. Smaller portraits hang in every shop, office and hotel reception. He looks like a quiet, kind uncle but I soon realised that you do not talk about him directly; you did not know who might be listening. As I cycle into villages I have been trying to guess in what role this uncle would welcome me: would he be portrayed as soldier, lounge suited 'man of the world', in Arab robes, as tribal leader, sportsman or academic with gown and mortar board. He is the same age in all the portraits, an indeterminate middle age like the Queen's profile on postage stamps. His son Bashar al-Assad was inaugurated as President in July 2000 a month after his father's death. Bashar was an ophthalmology student in the UK. I wonder if that is why he is portrayed wearing reflective sunglasses in his portraits, which are beginning to appear in public places. Is he protecting his eyes or has he not yet perfected the gaze that conveys the character he wants his subjects to think him to be?

An obvious change Bashar has made since coming to power is to provide access to the Internet. My guidebook was very out of date in this respect. I have had no problem finding internet cafes with speedy connections full of hijab clad, tight jeaned, smoking, tea drinking students logging onto porn sites and chat rooms. I know this because several times I have sat at a hastily vacated screen and found myself already logged on to Leila's vital statistics and images to prove them. Bashar also allows political discussion groups, whatever those could be. He has talked about peace with Israel and of reducing the number of Syrian troops in Lebanon. He wants to reform the economy too, for too long too state dominated with high unemployment. Both the rhetoric and situation observers have thought could make Syria a target of American aid or interference, depending on how you view that great nation. Some believe he was rather hoping this would happen but then 9/11 came along. With Syria on Bush's Axis of Evil, Bashar has refused to be bullied by the USA; Damascus remains the HQ of many terrorist groups. Syria along with Iran and Libya has received 0 US$ in aid from America in recent years. North Korea, however, also on the Axis of Evil, has reportedly; this funding is to support pro-democracy groups. The fact that the US has not identified any such groups to support in Syria is to me encouraging. The USA's brand of democracy seems very destabilising in other countries. Bashar and the Assad family, through whatever means, has a strong grip on power and so as a country can retain its independence and bargaining position. Syrian-made cola, which tastes good, will be drunk on the streets for a good while longer yet.'

***

Reading this now it is clear that Syria as a nation was never as simple as this traveller passing through assumed it to be. However, my observations then are pertinent to now. The al-Assad family came to power on the back of the ability to build alliances. The numerous factions fighting in the civil war now could be a product of this shifting sand style of ruling, whomever shouted the loudest or promised the most holding sway over others. Bashar did not live up to his rhetoric. The civil war started with anti-government graffiti scrawled on walls in the southern city of Daraa in March 2011, which criticised levels of unemployment, corruption and state oppression. And perhaps the current state of affairs is an unfortunate knock-on effect of 9/11? If 9/11 had not happened how might Bashar and the USA have built a relationship? Would it have meant Syria's identity lost through conditional US Aid? Perversely, even considering the enormous cost to Syrians in the present situation, I stand by my perhaps naive view that it is a good thing Bashar has remained in power this long. Regime change forced upon countries from outside, as in Libya and Iraq has not had a result any more stable than the regime change trying to be undertaken in Syria.

Mar Musa and Father Paolo's community have not escaped the civil war. During 2012-2013 An Nabk was on the front line. I wonder if those men I met drinking tea had to become more aware of the monastery, its work and its community when fate burst their calm lives, perhaps forcing them to think and act in ways to survive that did not reflect the Christian-Islam dialogue modelled by the monastery perched on their hill. During that time the monastery was searched for arms and money and there was a theft of goats, cattle feed and a tractor. Recent posts and articles though, in which Jens' and Huda's names appear, show that the community is still there, the church, its frescos and its vision still intact. As to Father Paolo, his fate is unclear. In 2011 he wrote an article calling for a peaceful transition to democracy in Syria. He followed this with an open letter to Kofi Annan at the UN. The Syrian government issued an expulsion order and Father Paolo left the country in June 2012. He joined another monastery in Iraqi Kurdistan. In July 2013 he entered Raqqa in eastern Syria. It is reported he entered the Islamic State headquarters to negotiate the release of hostages and to broker a truce with Kurdish militias. He has not been seen since 29 July 2013. No group has claimed his kidnap or murder; no group has asked for a ransom. His community at Mar Musa have helped to rebuild 70 homes in An Nabk. There are still only 330 steps separating the bottom of the valley to the monastery. Has the spiritual gap widened though and how long before the eco-tourism or the echo-tourism comes back?

Hassan is 18 now and a shepherd in the Orontes valley
hope he has a bicycle but most likely he has a moped like his
dad, which he zips around on running errands and keeping up
with the male community in his village. At least, this is how I li
to picture him. But did anyone predict that ten years after my
visit Hassan's country would be at war with itself and the hilly
countryside of Hassan's home a setting for fighting and looting
What part has he played in this, either through choice,
circumstance or both? Has he sold his sheep to provision the
garrison camped inside ancient Apamea? Has he tried to carry
his daily routine amongst gunfire and rockets? As the sharp,
feisty child I picture him to be, has that led him to take up arms
And on whose side?

Satellite pictures of Apamea taken by the UN and
interpreted by the University of Glasgow, show sections of the
north and south parts of the Cardo to be severely damaged. Th
little pictogram to signify 'severe damage' on UN documents
shows it to mean only the base of a column still standing. Other
pictures are covered in black dots. These are holes. These are
holes left behind when parts of Apamea are dug up. Apamea h
been and is being dug up by Syrians. Parts of Apamea have bee
seized by police in New York. We know anyone can make mon
out of war. Has Hassan also looted the history of his home? I
only hope it was for the right reasons, to survive, not gain. I ho
he is alive and will one day see Apamea again as the stunning
testimony to what man can create. That other tourists will come
and by accident of fate experience the warm hospitality of his
home. Inshallah.

Ihsem is in Idlib province, now a rebel held area in the
increasingly factionalised Syrian civil war. Alliances and powe
are constantly shifting in Idlib as outside influences from Turke
Saudi, Lebanon and others jostle to support and champion rebe

252

closest to their political aims or religious dogma. Living in Ihsem now, it must be impossible for Heam to know who to trust: who is in charge as the influence of any state institutions is long shattered. The only group with her interests at heart would be her family. The area suffered a chemical weapons attack in April 2017. Ihsem itself, which must have grown into a large town since I was there, has been under bombardment and its hospital hit. Would Heam stick around amidst such danger? What choices might she have? She will be about 45 years old now and her children in their late teens to early twenties. They would have been halfway through their schooling when war broke out. Was their education interrupted? Perhaps as a teacher would Heam have valued education for her own children so highly that they have left? To where? Many Syrian refugees from that part of the country have entered Turkey. Is she still doggedly following her vocation and teaching a population in exile? I can but guess and can by no means do so correctly nor imagine the choices made on emotions experienced.

Almost half of Syria's pre-war population, that is around 11 million people, have either been killed, are refugees outside the country or displaced inside Syria. Imagine the effect this has on community. Perhaps the saddest consequence of the war is the loss of such experiences as I had: to share, to learn from and about each other and to understand. A people regardless of religion or culture, so able to give freely has been removed and diluted across the globe. But perhaps in the diaspora there are small pockets of the same unconditional hospitality where the Heams, Father Paolos and Hassans welcome strangers into their homes. It is just harder for the likes of me to find it now. It will be a very long time before Heam and Fatima can tend their groves and harvest the fruit.

Waiting
Jane Wilson-Howarth

Life as a refugee is all about waiting. There are few distractions and scant opportunities for exercise. Some men and boys play football on scraps of uneven wasteland close to the tents. Most play in flipflops so we treat a lot of cuts, abrasions, scrapes and sprains. Another of my many tasks while I was helping provide healthcare to refugees in northern Greece is to write letters aimed at the local United Nations office. The hope of the requesting refugees is that such letters will fast-track their departure from the tented camp. The UNHCR help some people with disabilities who find it difficult to cope with the living conditions move more quickly to better accommodation. It is tough, especially for the elderly or those with small children as they sleep on camp beds, have a long walk to the loo and shower in cold water in a draughty Portacabin.

When a healthy young Syrian man strode into the clinic, I didn't expect I'd be able to write a letter that would help him. He wasn't old and crippled with arthritis. I was less than sympathetic, until – via the interpreter – I heard his story.

He'd been shot in the legs. A bullet had entered his right thigh bone and another into the flesh of his left leg. He had difficulty going to the toilet. I was puzzled. How did this stop him going to the toilet?

I looked at his legs. The right was a complete mess, with a wide scar running down most of the length of his thigh. He'd clearly received excellent emergency care. A surgeon had stopped the bleeding, stitched up what must have been a gaping wound and undoubtedly saved the man's life. There had, however, been absolutely no rehabilitation or further care in the intervening two years.

Now he was so weak that he had difficulty squatting. His legs trembled even on bending his knees just a little. I couldn't see how he'd mange to open his bowels over a basic outside toilet. He wasn't strong enough to join in with football either. His legs just weren't up to it. He was alone in the camp. Time dragged. His nights were tortured.

I tried to be up-beat. Quadriceps weakness should be reasonably easy to remedy. I showed him the necessary exercises which require no equipment and suggested he should try to do them once or twice a day.

I wrote his letter for the UN and told him to come back so that I could see if the exercises had helped improve his strength. I wondered he would be able to find the motivation to help himself. He looked depressed. And – like as many of the Syrians I treat – perhaps he hoped for a quick fix with medicines or a referral to a hospital. I know his salvation was through simple strengthening exercises.

I worked hard to persuade my patients to adopt simple self-help techniques. I had grown a little bossier in my consultation style. A young mother came to see me with her child and after I'd finished checking the patient, the mother asked for anti-inflammatory cream for her neck pain. I offered a consultation about her problem but my interpreter said that the mother wasn't interested in advice; she just wanted the cream. Feeling a little guilty I said, 'No advice, no cream!'

The woman – reluctantly, it seemed – agreed to talk to me about her pain. I showed her the soothing neck-stretch my physiotherapist son taught me for a similar pain that sometimes troubles me. At the end of the consultation there was quite a long exchange between the mother and the interpreter while I felt ever guiltier about having bullied the woman into listening to my advice. Finally, the interpreter translated the gist of the conversation. The woman liked consulting me because she always felt better afterwards. She invited me to take tea in her tent later. I got a lot of invitations to drink tea.

Phew – I'd got away with being overbearing this time....

Meanwhile, I wonder if I shall ever learn why she was reluctant at first to speak about her symptoms or why the man with weak quads never came back. Maybe he'd left the camp. Maybe he'd paid traffickers to smuggle him deeper into Europe. Maybe my letter helped. Maybe he'd crossed illegally into Albania. Maybe he'd travelled to another camp – there are many more near Athens – in search of friends and relatives. The refugee population is in constant flux.

I volunteered for two months with Médecins du Monde helping Syrian and Afghan refugees trapped in Greece. During these weeks the triaging nurse, interpreter and I saw around 60 patients a day, sometimes more. For me this was tantalising as I knew each refugee had stories I should hear. If I had time to listen I might better understand, but I only caught occasional fragments and glimpses of broken lives. Sometimes there were external signs, like the guy with a neat bullet wound in his left chest which must have missed his heart by a couple of centimetres. When I commented on his good fortune he agreed that yes, God is Great. For many others, the scars are invisible.

I came to know a cohort of cowed women, angry men and bereaved children. I grew to know very well several likable young men whose mental health was in tatters. Awful experiences and testosterone made the men's moods unpredictable and confusing. Many fight amongst themselves or seek oblivion with medicines or other drugs. Some get drunk then feel guilty about it. Often their frustrations boil over, and who can blame them? As their doctor, it can feel as if I am able to offer so very little in the way of comfort or healing. We have excellent psychologists in our team and a psychiatrist who comes to work in the camps once a week but sometimes the distress and traumas of these men get in the way of them accessing help. Women too can find it hard to talk to us about what they are experiencing. Sometimes they are just too busy as lone parents caring for their children or elderly relatives; sometimes a husband forbids them; sometimes they are just too shy or uncomfortable speaking to strangers. At least we are there for them throughout the week though, and I hope that knowing someone cares offers a degree of comfort.

The refugees' physical living conditions are tough and the camp in the decommissioned car factory at Oreokastro, although warmer than outside in the naked countryside north of Thessaloniki, is loud with sounds echoing around the vast stark building. They are townies, not used to camping or roughing it. Many used to live in air-conditioned apartments and houses. Some still have a little money; many are destitute. I can't see how anyone could rest in such a noisy environment even if they didn't have nightmares to disturb their sleep when it eventually comes. Their dreams are tortured because they've seen family members destroyed by bombs. They've suffered on their journeys to safety too. Nearest and dearest have died on these journeys. They've been separated from the loved-ones who have survived. If they've survived. Often they don't know.

One Sunday, there was a horrible accident. A car – probably speeding – was driving down the long straight road that passes the camp. It hit a refugee family. A mother and daughter died at the site. The whole camp was traumatised by the loss of their friends and subsequently I was inundated with people collapsing with anxiety attacks, patients overwhelmed by feelings of hopelessness, and many with a recrudescence of the symptoms of being out of control with post-traumatic stress disorder. Some days are just heart-breaking.

EUROPE

Les Clavettes
Françoise Hivernel

My house in France was called 'Les Clavettes'. This is a name for little brown lizards in Occitan.

I have to confess that I had reached the rather respectable age of 66, sometimes believing that I looked like an old clavette myself, before I re-discovered the art of sawing. Yes I said sawing – not sewing as you might have imagined better suited to a woman of my age. Coughing and wheezing I kept going at the log still covered in moss, which I had wedged between the first step of the outside staircase and a stone in the terrace. I looked at it and thought, 'I'll never have the strength to cut it. I only got out of bed yesterday after three days of illness… But it is still very cold and I need more wood for the wood burner and the remaining logs are too long'. There was no choice.

My first awkward movements were confounded by wanting to do too much, too quickly. Why? What was the rush? I had nothing to do, no meetings to attend, no patients to see, no one at all demanding attention. I was on holiday. 'Slow down woman,' I told myself and I started thinking that perhaps a peasant life had to be a slow one. Gathering and hunting are slow jobs and if you try and hurry them you spoil everything. Hum! Now that was a new thought. Why on earth did I want to get this done quickly? To do what afterwards?

I stared at the log and then started to look at it from a different perspective. I noticed that perhaps it would be easier to have a go at it diagonally rather than perpendicularly. The saw instead of bending and catching started sliding with less effort and I even produced some sawdust: the proof of the pudding. 'Okay well done old girl, keep going.' Soon I had made a mark all around the log and was trying to get the not-quite-joining cuts to meet… somewhere. They wouldn't meet in the middle of

259

course. Should they have done so? You must understand that I had not handled a saw in the previous 30 years of my life. A pen yes, many a time, but a saw no and you can't do with a pen what you do with a saw.

I decided to try speeding up the process by laying the log at a different angle. I stepped on it hoping to break it, having weakened it all around. Total refusal to cooperate, nature was not in the mood to help me. I blasted it with a 'stupid old log'. Returning to the toil with more ardour and determination powered by my anger at the strong resistance, 'Ouch, what's that hurting?' I looked at my hand. A blister had formed and, unaccustomed to these chores, a huge bit of my poor civilised hand was about to peel off. I started to feel sorry for myself. At the same time the cinema at the back of my mind started playing Damsel in Distress in black and white, and the fantasy that men were watching me and would eventually come to my rescue established itself into a virtual reality. I reinforced the image of my weakness with all sort of coughing and wheezing and moping of brow. I removed my fleece. But no one materialised. No knight in shining armour appeared, not even a farmer on his tractor or even on foot… poor little old me.

Then I got angry with myself: that will teach you, you old cow, to play at being able to survive all on your own in the middle of nowhere. Sweat was dripping off my forehead and then a miracle happened. During that entire internal monologue the log had shown signs of giving up the fight and I stepped on again and was victorious this time! What a pleasure, what a success and I had done it all on my own. I stopped for a cup of tea (Moroccan restorative herbal tea with spices) and then I tackled a second one with the cunning of hindsight and it submitted to my will in half of the time it took for the first one. Nothing needs to be said about the next four or five logs.

Now I am writing this *a posteriori*, sitting in front of the wood burner, watching my logs burn. I even managed to clean its glass door with the ashes of yesterday's fire. On the radio a Brahms concerto is playing. I have just been to close the shutters; a strangely menacing cloud formation is slithering across the sky in a horizontal way. 'Cold' and possibly 'Snow' it says. I spotted some snow this morning from the ridge above Salles Curan, adorning the Aubrac Mountains north of Rodez. But for today I have done my lot and I mentally purr as a cat in the warmth of the place.

A Memorable Welcome
Seeta Siriwardena

In the years past, if a doctor wanted to do postgraduate work in Paediatrics there was a recommended course of studies to follow prior to sitting the professional examinations. The large number of medical graduates from abroad who wish to follow this route attend a course in London recommended by the Postgraduate Institute. One of the most popular was at the Institute of Child Health, Great Ormond Street, London.

I attended this course shortly after arriving in England. I made friends with two doctors: a lady from Nigeria and a gentleman from Ghana. We two women attended the lectures in national dress, me in a sari, the lady from Nigeria in a long Nigerian dress with a lovely turban to match. Meanwhile the Ghanaian man wore a suit, the uniform of most British male doctors.

One day the three of us went to lunch at a fast food café on nearby Southampton Row. We were queuing up for our food when a woman who was already seated and had watched the three of us enter stood up and in a loud voice abused us for the colour of our skin and our clothes. She said she did not want us there.

In the pin drop silence that followed, a young white man pulled his chair back, got on to the chair and said how sorry he was for the insults and abuse we received from the woman and made a speech welcoming us.

Everybody in the café clapped, we thanked him and sat down. The Nigerian lady and Ghanaian gentleman ate while I wept copiously choking on my food. The woman in question walked out.

Many years later the gentleman became the minister of health in Ghana, the lady too obtained a professorial post in

Nigeria and I went back to the only children's hospital in Sri Lanka as a resident physician.

A Tourist in Budapest
Stephanie Green

An acquaintance telling me about her visit to Windsor complained that she didn't enjoy the experience because the town was crowded with tourists.

'But surely you were a tourist and were causing a problem for the others.' I said.

'I wasn't a tourist' she told me indignantly, 'I was a visitor.'

So why did she think it was better to be a visitor than a tourist? If I'd suggested that she was a holidaymaker would she have been even more indignant? Would she have been happier I'd called her a traveller? Everyone knows what a holidaymaker is; they're the ones that lounge on sunbeds drinking piña-colada or walk along promenades eating ice-cream. They're the ones enjoying themselves. But the tourist and the visitor are harder differentiate. Is the tourist the one with the itinerary, the guide book and the camera, the stereotype American doing Europe, 'if it's Tuesday this must be Belgium,' or the group of Japanese constantly photographing themselves in front of anything vaguely local? Is the visitor somebody who's there for a short time only or is in the tourist hot-spot for another reason: seeing friends, working nearby? What about the one higher in the pecking order, the adventurous one, the risk-taker, the traveller?

Last year when I donned a back-pack and took local buses and ate in local cafes around Ecuador I called myself a traveller. Although as I never went off the beaten track and simply stuck to the back-packers circuit the reality was that I was just a cheap-skate version of a tourist. Surely a traveller has to go by bike or canoe or foot, and keep away from the well-trodden routes of tour buses, especially the tour buses of the Adventure Package industry? A traveller should be travelling alone. A

264

traveller should not be clutching the Lonely Planet Guide because one thing is certain if he follows the recommendations in the guide he will be far from lonely. He will be accompanied, at each stopping point, on every local bus, by the same clutch of fellow travellers. A traveller should be travelling independently, off the beaten track and for a long period of time. A trip, however adventurous, that is only a few weeks' sabbatical from the accounts department isn't travelling it is escapism.

Yet before we get too disparaging about the tourists who clog the pavements in Windsor and Stratford-on-Avon we should remember that tourism is the life-blood of many economies. We have only to listen to the concern of Tunisia and Egypt when terrorism causes a threat to tourist numbers to understand the importance of the industry.

I'm flying with my daughter Clare, by EasyJet, for a four-day break in Budapest. I am most definitely not a traveller or a visitor or even a holidaymaker. I am a tourist. I will do the touristy tours. I will expect everybody to speak English. I will eat in tourist restaurants and buy postcards and take lots of photos of Clare standing in front of churches and on scenic steps. I will clutch my Lonely Planet Guide and visit the sights they recommend and go to the cafes they tell me are 'authentic'. I will ignore their advice to learn how to mix the perfect spritzer because by doing so I will be accepted as a local. I could never be accepted as a local in Budapest for one thing I can't get my tongue around the impossible Hungarian language, a language that bears a faint resemblance to Finnish but otherwise has no similarities to any other. I'm having difficulty with saying Hello and Thank You in Magyar. I'll never get any further forward than that. I am a tourist and I don't have any wish to be anything other than a tourist.

On the plane I sit next to a Hungarian lady, who gives me a brief but absorbing history of Hungary under the communist regime and carefully writes in my guide book addresses and directions for restaurants and cafes where local people eat. She even recommends a couple of places where we should just go for a coffee because the ornate Art Nouveau toilet are worth a visit. We are grateful for the information and decide that we will try and go off the beaten track where tourists seldom roam and mix with the local people and see the non-touristy sites. Then I manage to leave my book on the plane so without the names and addresses I've carefully written on the back page we are back to the using the itinerary prescribed in Clare's guidebook.

Our hotel is in old town Pest. It is modern and recommended by The Guardian so it must be trendy. I think it has been designed by a group of 'A' level art students; pink rope and pulleys decorate the foyer and large black, white and orange stylised paintings of faces and lips and fishes stretch across the white walls in the corridors and rooms. Breakfast is served in the stone-walled, black and white tessellated floored, downstairs room which looks out onto the courtyard. The renovated yellow walls and black balconies of the hotel are adjacent to an un-renovated building which is grey, derelict and has crumbling stone parapets hanging precariously over its own courtyard and the street alongside. The breakfast caters for the preferences of all nationalities. If you want to spot the nationality of your fellow breakfasters don't bother listening to accents or judging them by their clothes just look what they are eating for breakfast. Bacon and egg for the British, croissants for the French, salami and cheese for the Germans, Eastern Europeans seem to have a penchant for pickles. Breakfast is the meal where we are all the least adventurous. Clare, pregnant and queasy, has toast and

266

cereal I have eggs and a cream filled apple strudel. Cream cakes for breakfast? Well I'm a tourist; tourists can do that sort of thing.

The weather in late March is glorious and the sky is a cloudless, brilliant azure, and by the time we step out of the hotel the early morning chill is dissipating. Map and camera at the ready we start our tourist route in the Pest area of Budapest at St Stephen's Basilica. The Basilica is high, ornate and awe-inspiring. The sunlight filters through the high dome highlighting the colourful tiled floor and through stained glass windows in the chapel illuminating their treasured relic: the desiccated right hand of Stephen, the first king of Hungary. The huge gold organ high above the nave is impressive and as we are here on the day of the fortnightly organ and flute recital we book tickets. That evening, sitting in the chilly church we are disappointed that the organist doesn't play that impressive in-house organ but brings his own rather feeble electronic one. We are both moved to tears when the flautist plays a version of the Mozart Cello Concerto that we chose for the recent funeral of Clare's father.

Leaving the cathedral, we walk down to the banks of the Danube, the wide river flows fast, debris hurtles passed the tour boats and the large, river cruise boats. An amphibious vehicle takes tours around Budapest and then enters the river, so there is the incongruous sight of a yellow bus ploughing down the centre of the river in choppy waters. The route from the essential visit of the Basilica to the essential viewing of Parliament takes us through wide well-kept streets then unexpectedly passes a protest about a new statue being erected which suggests that the Hungarian removal of Jews to concentration camps during the Second World War was entirely the fault of the invading Germans. The collection of stones, photographs, shoes, suitcases and texts along the railings, in front of the offending statue, bring into focus not just Hungary's turbulent history but how little we both know of that history. We vow to visit the Hungary history museum the next day but somehow manage to buy tickets for the wrong building and end up wandering around the ancient Castle of Buda. It is a beautiful building, serene but not informative about the history of Budapest or Hungary. On the way to the Parliament we pass another impromptu pavement shrine around the walls of The House of Terror. This one commemorates some of the victims of the 1956 uprising of the Hungarian workers against the Communist regime. We vow to come back the next day to House of Terror to find out more about Hungary under the communists but we don't find the time so we remain in ignorance about that period of history as well.

Eventually reaching the Parliament building, a hugely impressive white structure on the banks of the Danube, the largest building in Hungary, we join a tour. Understandably a tour is the only option if you want to visit the Parliament as they won't want hordes of tourists wandering aimlessly around. We are led up red carpeted stairs, and more red carpeted stairs, and more and more stairs. At the top of the flights of stairs most of the party are too exhausted to absorb the incredible beauty of the decorative roofs and walls and tiled floors of this massive building. We too are busy concentrating on trying to get our breath back. The interior of the Parliament building is described as having Gothic revivalist décor, a plethora of gold leaf, statues, stained glass, turned wood. We are led along the endless corridors by a brisk guide, into chambers, down staircases, marvelling at the lamps and magnificent chandeliers, the marquetry, the carvings. Behind us two armed guards follow on rounding up the stragglers, making sure nobody lingers too long in any one place or gets left behind entirely. Like much of this part of Budapest the Parliament was built at the end of the 19th

268

Century, when the Austro-Hungarian Empire was at its height. Like the Basilica, The Opera House, many of the cafes and the toilets we were advised to visit but for which we have now lost the addresses, it owes much to the Art Nouveau style that was also being produced in Vienna and Prague.

The next day we cross the river to Buda and meander over the streets of the Buda hills. The houses date from the 13th Century and are painted brightly. The Citadel of Budapest sits at the top of the network of streets at a vantage point overlooking the Danube. Underneath it is a spider's web of caves. We read on a plaque that in the 16th century Vlad the Impaler was incarcerated for fourteen years in these caves. At that time Transylvania was part of Hungary; many years later it was handed to Romania as punishment for the Hungarians supporting Germany during the First World War. It is again a part of history I am ignorant about and an example of the fluid borders of Eastern Europe. We go down into the cold dankness of the labyrinth of caves with the intention of handing over our Hungarian Forints and visiting the cells. Above us at the entrance we hear a strident American voice, 'Hey guys, Dracula was a real dude!' The atmosphere of menace is dissipated by those damn tourists so we change our minds and go back out into sunlight that bounces off the white walls and statuary, where buskers play Hungarian folk songs, where a group dressed in medieval costumes hold hawks and where coachloads of tourists click away taking photos. Then it's back across the river to visit for a tour of the Opera House and afternoon tea and cakes at one of the traditional old cafes. It's hard work this tourist lark.

The following day we do mix a bit more with the locals. We go to the large, colourful Central Market, eat at one of the stalls and then cross the river to one of Budapest famous spa baths, the Gellert Spa. The ceilings are high and ornate and we

269

swim leisurely in the cooler pool and bask in the warmth of the hotter spa pools. I pay the equivalent of £10 deposit for the hire of a threadbare towel and it is removed from the bench I leave it on. I manage to purloin somebody else's towel so I don't lose the deposit. Clare is horrified at the hypocrisy of a mother who made her four-year-old daughter go back to a shop to return two fruit chews and apologise to the shop-keeper and yet can now deftly steal towels without a twinge of conscience.

In the evening we go to eat at the popular club and restaurant area a few streets away from our hotel. It's Saturday night and the stag parties are in town: loud and British carrying cans of beer through the streets and sporting wigs and Elvis costumes. The restaurants are full so we return to our quieter hotel district, eat venison stew at a small restaurant and have an early night.

The next day there is just time for breakfast before heading off to the airport. The novelty of salami, pickles, cream cakes and sparkling wine for breakfast has worn off and I simply have fruit and yoghurt before getting the taxi for the short journey back to the arms of EasyJet and home.

I loved Budapest; I loved the food, the wide-open streets the blue-eyed polite Hungarians and the decorative Art Nouveau architecture and interiors. I'll have to visit Budapest again to see the sites that the guide-books consider essential and we have missed. Next time I'll try to be better informed and learn something about the Austro-Hungarian Empire, the fluctuating borders and the turbulent history of Middle Europe. And you never know I might even venture off the established tourist route, I might find that back-street café with the memorable toilets and I might even travel beyond Budapest to the vast plain of Hungary. I could go on horseback in search of the Magyars. could become a traveller.

Bison in Poland
Jane Wilson-Howarth

Tomasz talked a lot about bison as we drove between various wildflower meadows in Białowieża in eastern Poland. 'We can go no closer than 50 metres,' he said. 'Cross that line and they will charge. Even 50 metres can be too close. You need to let them see you approach or that will upset them too.'

I'd dreamed of seeing free-ranging European bison since my nerdish wildlife-obsessed childhood. Now we'd come to their habitat but the light was fading and with it my hope of seeing them. Then, at the last meadow, Tomasz said, 'We have bison!' Even our undemonstrative guide seemed excited.

It was getting on for 10pm. We piled out of the mini-bus and scared a nightjar up off the ground. Tomasz had his binoculars trained across the meadow on a huge dark form. The half-light made it look gigantic, more like a rocky outcrop than any living thing. At first I'd presumed that the bison was on the other side of the rock but didn't pause to check with my binoculars. Tomasz had already set off across the meadow at an impressive pace and I was determined to keep up with him. Dew-covered meadow grasses and flowers were up to my neck. The ground was tusocky and uneven. All my concentration was on keeping close to our naturalist and on making it across the meadow. I'd soon lost sight of our quarry as I rushed on. I had no idea how close we might be to the bison.

We descended into a dip, where the plants were over my head, and then we began climbing. The long grasses even hid us from each other. I could hear Simon and the others behind me and knew Tomasz was a few paces ahead. I was following his trail of trampled grasses. Surely we were in danger of getting too close to the bison and spooking it? Then we'd be charged by a ton of angry testosterone-fuelled muscle. So far, though, all was quiet up ahead. Soon we were up on a piece of raised ground close to a copse of silver birch trees. The grass was shorter here. I looked across a slight dip to the unmistakable profile of a massive bison, less than 100 metres away. Its undercarriage announced this was bull. His skinny buttocks and bulky neck and shoulders made him look front-loaded, like a JCB. He was clearly one of the biggest bulls, nearly 2m at the shoulder. He was absorbed in grazing and didn't look up as we edged closer. Slowly though, as the light failed completely, he wandered in amongst some trees and we lost sight of him, leaving us celebrating and happy – if wet.

We were up again at 3.30am chasing around various likely meadows until we struck lucky again. Rain was tipping down. Approaching several dark forms through rain-soaked meadow grasses, we quickly became sodden but I didn't care. My enthusiasm made me feel waterproof. I had four browsing individuals in my steamed up bins, all bulls. The cows stay in dense forest during the summer where the calves are safest.

'It that the alpha male?' I asked Tomasz.

'No, he is just bigger, older. Bison reach adultery at four or five and maximum size at five or six.'

I watched mesmerised, vaguely aware of rain dribbling in through the neck of my jacket, as the foursome slowly grazed their way back into the forest where they'd spend the day. We'd only just got there in time. I was elated. I'd seen my bison roaming free.

For many hundreds of years, the European bison was protected as a high status game animal. Kings and Tsars liked to hunt it but turmoil beginning at the end of the nineteen century left poor people hungry enough to poach these animals. They were extinct in the wild by the end of the First World War. In 1923, though, the deputy director of the state zoo in Warsaw

272

suggested a breeding programme based on European bison that survived in captivity. In 1929 twelve animals were brought together and a captive breeding centre set up. The first bison were released into the wild in 1952 and species is recovering. There are now 546 roaming the Polish part of the Białowieża primeval forest, with other herds in the nearby Knyszyn forest and across the border in Belarus. It is a great conservation success story.

Eating out in Ponte-in-Valtellina
Stephanie Green

'Schiatt e pitzoccherie?' asks the unsmiling waitress.

This is more of a statement than a question because schiatt and pitzoccherie are the only dishes this restaurant serves We are in Ponte-in-Valtellina in the mountains of Italy in a local restaurant where the fluorescent light is harsh, the table-cloths are red gingham and the stone walls and tiled floors echo the clatter of cutlery and the chatter of customers. On a Tuesday evening in April the restaurant is full, not with tourists who don't frequent this village in high numbers or with the Milanese who visit their family and their holiday homes mainly at weekends, it is full with local people: local people who have come to eat the local dishes that are 'typico' of this area.

I have been coming to this region regularly for the last thirty years. I consider that I have a holiday home here because my sister lives in Ponte-in-Valtellina and I can come and stay whenever I want. Yet in all my visits I have somehow failed to come to this long established village trattoria and eat schiatt and pitzoccherie. I blame my sister of course, she isn't fond of the hearty fare of the mountains and doesn't suggest coming to these local places but today I have brought a friend over from England and we're exploring the area and we're partaking of the local food.

We order one dish of schiatt between the three of us, a portion of pitzoccherie each and a litre of wine.

A basket of bread and the litre carafe of wine arrive first. Earlier in the day we had visited a cantina in the nearby town of Sondrio, where the young wine grower was enthusiastic about his wines. The Grumello and Sassella grapes were long grown in this area but their quality had been neglected and he was determined to bring them back up to the standard of fine wines.

274

We tasted them and then tasted them again just to make sure we were right the first time. They were excellent and we could understand his enthusiasm. If we had anticipated a house wine of similar quality to be set before us in this local restaurant then we were out of luck. Valtellina may produce some excellent wines but this wasn't one of them. We poured a glass each, swigged and sucked in our cheeks and ran our tongues along our teeth to check that the enamel was still there.

The bowl of schiatt, accompanied by a chicory salad, followed shortly after the wine and bread. Schiatt is pieces of Casera, a medium, soft cheese rolled in buckwheat flour and then deep fried. The pitzoccherie, which arrives rather too promptly after we have eaten but not digested the schiatt, is a thick chunky pasta made from buckwheat which is layered with potatoes, cabbage and the same Casera cheese then smothered in garlic butter and baked. It is substantial food and the portions are generous, we decide it was a wise move to share the schiatt between us and wonder if we should have done the same and shared a portion of pitzoccherie. Yet, somehow, it doesn't take too much effort to clear the plates. The pitzoccherie, which doesn't look particularly appetising when it is plonked on the plates in front of us, is tasty, creamy and rather moreish. Of course the wine helps, its sharpness complements the buttery, cheesy pasta and when we order the second litre of wine we find it has become quite palatable.

Ponte-in-Valtellina is, as the name suggests, a village in the region of Valtellina. Valtellina is the area around the River Adda and its tributaries. The river starts above the Olympic ski resort and spa town of Bormio 1230 metres above sea level and flows down into Lake Como at 200metres above sea level. Switzerland is a few miles away on the other side of the mountains that form the northern rim of the deep valley. The terrain and many of the buildings are Alpine in appearance. Winters are cold and harsh, summers are hot and the rainfall is high.

People associate Italian food with tomatoes, olives, peppers and fresh ingredients but it is the last ingredient which is really the epitome of Italian food: the fresh ingredient. Here the mountains, climatically far from the Mediterranean coast, tomatoes, olives and peppers do not grow happily. What are grown locally are cabbages, potatoes, beans: vegetables more associated with northern climes than with the south of Europe because they have to survive the hard winters. An olive tree wouldn't last five minutes if it was planted here. Buckwheat is grown on the terraces along the valley of Valtellina. In the lower valley vines populate the terraces above the main road which threads its way up to Bormio, sharing its narrow space with the river and the railway line. The dun cattle have been raised here for centuries and in the summer they are taken high into the mountain pastures away from the summer heat of the valley, hence the prominence of cheese and milk in the food of the region. The cattle are also the source of bresaola, the air dried thinly sliced beef that is Valtellina's equivalent of Parma ham. Unlike the other dishes which stay firmly in the region, bresaola has travelled. I can buy Bresaola de Valtellina in my local Waitrose and Co-op.

Much of the lower grazing land has been replaced by swathes of apple, cherry and plum orchards and there are fewer cattle here than in times gone by. I comment that if bresaola is now being exported world-wide there doesn't seem to be enough cattle, here in Valtellina, to produce it all. 'Bresaola was an invention of a local butcher, sometime in the 50's or 60's,' my sister tells me, 'they use imported Argentinian beef and always have.'

The Italian tourist board disagrees; they cite the production of bresaola as beginning in the 15th century and exports to Switzerland starting in the 18th century. She might be right about the use of Argentinian cattle though because all information about Bresaola mentions the origin of the method but none mention the origin of the beef.

In the local markets baskets of mushrooms are on sale, fresh or dried. In the mountains they grow wild in the forests and the site of the most sought-after varieties are kept a closely guarded secret by the people who collect them each year, a secret often not shared with family members. The mushrooms are widely used in the risottos and pasta dishes of the region. Chestnuts are abundant and venom (and occasionally a shotgun) is directed at the Milanese when their cars are seen parked on lonely roads while their owners collect baskets of chestnuts to take home. Local food is considered to be for collecting by local people not just to be eaten by local people.

Honey is harvested according to season of flowering. The early acacia honey has an astringent flavour; the later chestnut honey is sweeter. Bilberries which once grew wild and are now cultivated are sold by the basketful in the local markets in June and July and are used to flavour a pasta which is eaten with a rich game sauce.

But it is still pitzoccherie that is the main dish of the area, the dish that is served in the local restaurants and at the fiestas. Although it is associated with Valtellina it is specifically the dish of Teglio. Tell an Italian you've been to Teglio and the first question is 'Did you eat Pitzoccherie?' Not 'Did you like the beautiful old town? Did you visit Palzzo Besta? Did you walk, ski, stand back and admire the snow-capped mountains looming above?' No, the only thing an Italian would expect you to do on visiting Teglio is to eat pitzoccherie.

Maybe in this country we are similar. If friends told us they visited Bakewell in Derbyshire the first question asked would be 'Did you try the Bakewell tart?' If it was a visit to the sea-side it would be 'Did you eat fish and chips?' Places are associated with food and that in itself is a good enough reason for visiting, especially if you are Italian.

We leave the restaurant as the church clock clanks the last strokes of midnight. Wood smoke from the cooling restaurant oven permeates the air. We walk in silence, the pitzoccherie is sitting heavily and we need all our concentration to digest it and to combat the effects of the wine. My sandals slap on the cobbles and the sound echoes down ancient stone passageways that snake off the main street. Some of the houses in this village date back to the 14th century, their walls made from the grey alpine rock. High windows protected by iron grilles and with closed wooden shutters make it difficult to tell if they are inhabited. Some with weed strewn surrounds and gaping black windows are definitely empty.

Our breathing is becoming laboured as we toil up the steep street. Below us in the main square a door slams and a moped stutters into life then whines its way down into the valley.

A cigarette glows from a dark doorway and a disembodied voice says, 'Buona Notte.'

'Buona Notte Senor.' In the bar behind him there is the click clack of dominoes being laid on a Formica table and muffled sounds of conversation and glasses clinking.

We plod on, the cobbles uncomfortable beneath the thin soles of our sandals. The roar of the river becomes louder and when we reach the bridge we pause to catch our breath and watch the tumble of snow melt hurtling downwards. The draught of cold air from the icy water is refreshing after the heat

278

and noise of the restaurant. From behind a high wall there is the smell of dung and straw and the sounds of the restless shuffle of cows impatient to be away to their summer pasture. In a few weeks the sound of cow bells will ring through the village as the herds start their journey upwards, a journey that hasn't changed in centuries.

We trudge on stopping often in essence to admire the crescent moon above the snow-capped peaks but in reality to take a rest and a deep breath before starting the slog up the vertical path to the stone house nestled in the stand of beech trees.

We must be starting to digest the schiatt and pitzoccherie because, as we lean against walls and look at the lights twinkling high up the mountains on the other side of the valley, we are already planning our next meal.

Tomorrow we will go to Val di Mello. We will walk up the narrow valley between the high granite walls, a mecca for rock climbers, and follow the route of the tumultuous stream as it tumbles down over the rocks. If we are feeling energetic enough we will walk up past the snow line and continue through rocky outcrops until we get to the point where we will need crampons if we are to go any further. Then we'll stop at the last mountain hut, sit at wooden benches and eat the big spicy sausages and ribs, which have been cooked on an open wood fire. We will accompany them with polenta cooked in a huge old black pot suspended over the flames. Polenta, which I think has the constituency of wall-paper paste and looks as appetising, can be made palatable when doused in melted cheese. If we're not feeling energetic we'll probably just stop at the first mountain hut and eat the sausages and ribs and polenta. We'll head back down as the sun is leaving the high valley and it's getting cold and we'll pause in the village and drink hot chocolate and eat cake

279

made with the chestnuts that grow in abundance on the trees in the woods on the mountainside.

We'll persuade ourselves that we have done enough exercise to be able to justify all those calories. After all you need fuel for walking in mountains and delicate Mediterranean salads just don't do the business in this terrain and this climate.

An Armchair's Story

Françoise Hivernel

'Are you sitting comfortably?' 'Good, now I can begin'.

Once upon a time, there was a good old armchair, which had had a good and long life, but like many old things, including humans I would say, it had started to sag. What else do you expect after all? Too many over padded posteriors had sat on it during its long life, and this careless selfish use of it had taken its toll. But I have a nasty feeling that in fact it was a less than well- endowed posterior which in the end created trouble for the good old sagging armchair. This person even had the audacity to complain that it was no longer comfortable enough. So, and of course it is entirely my imagination, because this armchair didn't tell me its story, that I believe something very sad happened to it. Perhaps it was discarded as are things which have become too old (sometimes it also happens to humans) or too worn out or broken or when people get bored.

On a beautiful summer day in 2008 in France, a young couple, very much in love, but with also a good eye for old things (as well as each other) saw a poor derelict armchair in a container skip at the dump. What a crime they exclaimed! How monstrous to cast away such a good old armchair. So they hauled it out of the skip and decided to make a present of it to their good old mother (a quite worn out old thing too!). The very much in love young couple managed to bring this old sagging armchair back to the good old mother's little cottage in France, because they felt that the good old mother needed a companion. Then they flew back to their far away land. When the old mother arrived for her holidays, she saw the good old armchair, tried it and fell in love with it. But because the mother didn't have a well-padded posterior she asked one of her friends in the village if she knew of someone who would be able to bring this good old armchair back to its former glory (half hoping that the same friend would be able to recommend a similar recipe for the good old mother herself). It is then that Magic came into play. The good old mother's village is a remote little community of thirteen people in the middle of "Deepest France", difficult to access and no one there versed in the art of upholstery and neither was the good old mother. But the nice friend told the old mother of people she knew in the big town far away, who were Magicians and would help. The good old mother was over the moon and the husband of the nice friend came in his pick-up truck, as the house of the good old mother could not be reached with a normal car, to take away the armchair and bring it to the big far away town, to be transformed by the Magicians. What happened to the husband the nice friend with his pick-up truck on the way to getting the good old armchair is another story for another time.

The old mother said good-bye to the good old armchair. Winter came and the good old mother returned to her far away winter land in the lingering mists of England. Snow fell, months went by and the spring came back and then the summer of 200 and it was time for the old mother to migrate back to her summer house in France. On a beautiful hot day, the good old mother's nice friend called her to say that her good old armchair was ready and to get ready for a surprise. So the good old mother found her puff again and ran all the way to the road to get into her car and drove as fast as the roads would allow her to her friend's house. And there, in the friends' house, hidden under a white sheet was the shape of the good old armchair. When the sheet was pulled away, the Magicians' spell was revealed, the good old armchair had morphed into a most handsome and noble "Voltaire". The good old mother was quite speechless at the transformation and gently and lovingly lowered herself into its inviting arms.

Now, the Magicians who transformed the good old armchair into this beautiful "Voltaire" armchair were patients of the Day Centre of the Local Psychiatric Hospital.

And the work and art they displayed is quite breath taking! This story is dedicated to them, to thank them for their magical skills, for their care and their love.

But the story doesn't end there. As soon as the beautiful new armchair was back in the good old mother's house (whose looks sadly hadn't magically improved as well!), the nice friend, her husband and the good old mother started to worry about its future.

The good old mother doesn't live in France very much and the main inhabitants of the house during the rest of the year are little mice and sometimes, bigger things too. The new upholstery of the beautiful Voltaire would of course have provided a choice place for the little creatures nesting there during the winter and that of course was out of the question. There were plenty of other places, which were allowed to the little creatures during the winter months. So it was decided to send the beautiful new armchair to the foreign land in which the good old mother lived. Again and as if by magic, it turned out that some friends of friends were going to drive back to England with their possessions and kindly offered to bring back the beautiful "Voltaire" to Cambridge where the good old mother lives.

And this is the end of a very happy story as the beautiful new "Voltaire" is now a prized possession and is the armchair from which I work in my consulting room.

Across the Fens
Stephanie Green

Crossing the Fens in a car you are conscious of endless earth and sky and telegraph poles; the dykes and drains and rivers are mostly hidden behind flood banks and buried amongst the greenery of the fields. When crossing the Fens by boat there comes the realisation that water, not earth or sky, is the natural element in this landscape. If it weren't for the intensive work of the Middle Level Commissioners who are responsible for Fen drainage in this part of East Anglia this dyke I am floating on would become a silted bog and the farmland would once more become waterlogged marshland. If global warming increases and water levels rise what is the future for this fertile, flat land? Will it eventually become uneconomical to drain and will the high yielding fields of wheat and vegetables once more revert to reed and will the wildfowl flourish, or will our climate then be warm enough for them to become paddy fields?

On this Saturday in September the Fens are dressed in their Sunday best: vast blue skies interspersed with big comfy, white sofa clouds. Black, ploughed fields march away to infinity. A road runs for miles alongside the drain, an old farmhouse askew on its foundations leans towards the water, a tumbledown bridge threatens to fall on passing boats, skew-whiff telegraph poles dot the horizon. On a grey day this landscape is depressing, today the openness and emptiness and the sheer volume of clouds and sky is uplifting. Skeins of geese honk overhead and balletic wind turbines churn in the light wind. I chug along happily, sometimes feeling the drag of the shallow water, passed reeds, bright flowers on the high banks, butterflies dragonflies and damsel flies, alone in the flat landscape, relieved that Brigate Bend is far behind me.

At Floods Ferry, the dyke picks up the course of the Old Nene and runs on into March, past pretty gardens falling down to the river where boats are moored. Smells of BBQs, sounds of children playing, the river is alive with noise and activity, mooring spaces are difficult to find. This riverside March bears little resemblance to the dour Fenland town that I've often driven through and which must be still lurking somewhere nearby.

As I leave March the following day a man standing on a metal bridge shouts at me as I move towards it. 'Is that your boat?'

'Yes,' I say.

He moves to the other side of the bridge as I pass under. 'Will you marry me?'

I laugh. I probably won't marry him but it was nice to be asked.

Then after straggling through the other side of March it's back to the wide, shallow drainage ditches and the wide skies. Signs direct us away from the wonderfully named Pophams Eau, which seems the most direct route and onto the narrow, shallow Well Creek. I wonder who Popham was and why his bit of ditch uses the pretentiously frenchified Eau and isn't named a Pophams Drain or Pophams Dyke or even Pophams Water.

Well Creek threads its way through the endless villages of Upwell and Outwell. The Middle Levels pamphlet warns boaters not to attempt to navigate Well Creek if ice is beginning to form because this makes the ice form unevenly and angers the locals who like to use the creek for ice-skating. At the first low bridge my tomato plant is knocked into the water, I'm so busy looking to see where it has fallen that my head nearly follows it, after that I get used to ducking down and steering the boat whilst squinting over the edge of the roof.

I have also been warned that it is a popular sport in Outwell for the locals to jump off one of the low bridges onto passing boats, run along the roof and haul themselves up at the next bridge. Today there are only a few elderly ladies walking alongside the river. I think I should be safe. They don't look the type to sling aside their shopping trolleys, sprint to the bridge and leapfrog over the parapet onto my roof. I could be wrong. Elderly ladies in these Fenland villages are somewhat unpredictable.

The mapmakers have forgotten to warn about the second sharpest dogleg in England. Coming out of Outwell there is an abrupt right hand bend. I negotiate it badly and end up flailing about in a willow tree, blinded, wondering what the front end of the boat is doing out of sight sixty feet ahead of where I'm struggling in foliage. I emerge, fortunate to still have both eyes intact, and find the bow heading towards a moored river cruiser. I take drastic evasive action, spin, hit the far bank and hear the scraping of paintwork at the front end and the clunk of the stern grounding. I pole off the mud and then check to see if anybody is watching. There are. Three grinning men, I can read their lips, 'Women drivers.' There wasn't a soul in sight when I completed a perfect corner at Brigate Bend but, of course, I always have an audience when I'm making a mess of things. Maybe I'm not as capable as I thought I was; maybe the learning curve is still steep.

I'd just been reading the book Waterlog by Richard Deakin about wild swimming. One of the places he'd swam was beneath the Mullicourt Aqueduct on Well Creek where he joined a group of local lads on a warm day in summer. Crossing the short aqueduct, I look over into the water of the Sixteen Foot Drain. Even on a warm day in autumn it doesn't look a very tempting place to swim, the water is flat and grey and the banks steep and muddy. Today there is no sign of life, nobody daringly

286

ignoring the Danger Deep Water signs or swimming lazily under the No Swimming signs.

I'm booked to go through Salters Lode Lock onto the short tidal stretch of the Great Ouse, at 3.30pm, the tide should have turned at 3.18pm but it's being awkward. There is a narrow boat lurched on the mud at the far entrance to the lock waiting for the water to rise. I sit chatting with the lock-keeper, looking over glistening mud banks. Lapwings pee-wit in the fields behind us and across the river a spume of slurry rises from a hidden tractor. As we wait for the water to arrive, I learn about both the predictability and the vagaries of tides, about spring tides and neap tides and how winds affect them and how a cruiser grounded under a bridge on the Old Bedford waiting for the tide to lift him may be waiting a long time. We're twenty miles from the sea at King's Lynn and this weak neap tide is taking its time getting here. Eventually it comes crawling in, edging over the mud flats, making a ripple on the glassy smoothness of the channel bringing with it the scent of the sea.

Leaving the lock, I start to turn left and behind me hear a shout, 'Are you planning on going to Sweden?' I do a handbrake turn and go to the right, to Denver Lock and then onto the wide expanses of the Great Ouse where I can wave good-bye to The Fellow Traveller and head towards my winter home.

Extract from *Wide Woman on a Narrow Boat, 2016.*

Hearing Voices
Seeta Siriwardena

Poverty and deprivation manifest themselves in different forms
in different parts of the world. The Oxford Dictionary defines
deprivation as 'the damaging lack of material benefits consider
to be basic necessities in a society.' The key word is damaging.
People have mental health problems the world over.
Schizophrenia is as common in Asia as in Europe but sufferers
are better supported and still loved in my native Sri Lanka. The
may be few state benefits, nor are there housing allowances, bu
there are plenty of relatives who will care for others. For those
without relatives there are always Buddhist temples, Hindu
Kovils, and Christian churches to help. These give food and
shelter. The abundance of bright sunshine also plays a part in
one's sense of well-being.

These thoughts were uppermost in my mind when, in
my role as GP in middle England, I was asked to visit a
distressed young woman one Saturday morning in early
December. Two weeks earlier, this patient had been discharged
from our local psychiatric hospital. I remembered the discharge
letter, which said that she had had electro-convulsive therapy 1
times while in hospital. This is a lot.

I trudged up to the eighth floor of the high rise block o
flats in which Angela lived. (I do not like lifts since I got stuck i
one some time ago). There were four or five of these high rise
flats – ugly monsters rearing their heads from the background
noise and squalor. I knocked on the door, the key turned and
Angela let me in. Not only did see look untidy and wild but the
furniture was in total disarray. She was unkempt and her eyes
were staring. I wondered who the duty psychiatrist for the
weekend was.

I wished her good day and asked what I could do for her. She said she could hear voices coming through the walls, from the floor and the flat above. She hadn't taken her tablets since she had been discharged from hospital. She said they didn't suit her. To cut a long story short she refused hospital admission but agreed to see a psychiatrist.

I closed my bag, said I would arrange for a psychiatrist to visit her over the weekend, and turned to leave. Quick as a flash, she rushed past me and locked the front door of the flat. Perhaps the voices in her head had told her to keep me here. I walked calmly to the door and asked her politely to open the door. She smiled sweetly, said, 'Yes certainly,' and turned the key in the lock. It wouldn't open. She tried several times. Then I tried. The key wasn't catching in the lock. To my horror, I realised that one of the teeth had broken and jammed the lock.

There was nothing to do but to find other means of getting out of the flat. We were on the eighth floor. I went to the window but Angela pulled me back begging me not to let anyone see. I found a balcony with a window opening on to it. As Angela would not let me go near it I suggested she tried the front door while I sat down.

As soon as she was out of the room I managed to get to the window. I climbed onto the balcony, which overlooked the central area of several of these tower-block monsters. I tried to attract the attention of two or three people going past, but my high-pitched voice carried away. At last man looked up, but when I waved and tried to explain, he waved back at me and went on his way. Angela begged me to come in and I thought it best to comply.

She was looking wild and menacing. By now my whole mind and body had turned to jelly. With super human effort I walked to the front door of the flat and banged the door with my fists, my knees and my case.

After a few minutes – which seemed like an eternity – I heard a door open. I knelt down and opened the letter box and spoke to a half dressed sleepy women. I explained the situation and she said she would get dressed and go down to get the caretaker.

About 10 minutes later the caretaker appeared and tried to open the door with his bundle of keys, but the broken key tooth had jammed the lock. I told him I had been in the flat for over an hour, I had urgent visits to do and would he please call the police.

After a long wait a women constable came to the door. The WPC tried the door and then said she would get a couple of her male colleagues to come and break it open. At this point Angela went berserk, shouting that she didn't want the door broken open and asking who would pay for the damage. Then she stood in front of the door blocking my only means of exit. The police wouldn't break the door in fear of harming Angela.

Angela was bigger than me and younger than me. I looked at her from the corner of my eye, grabbed her by the arm and dragged her into the bedroom and literally sat on her, at the same time giving the go-ahead to the police to break the door. They obligingly did so. My shaking legs wouldn't make the stairs, so I took the lift down, fell into my car and drove away.

Living alone in a soulless high-rise block of flats isn't good for the health and must played a part in Angela's illness. She had adequate material benefits but she lacked human contact which one gets living in the overcrowded noisy towns and villages of Sri Lanka.

The most upsetting thing in this whole traumatic incident for me personally, was that when I came home and opened the front door my family, who were watching television, asked me straight away, 'What is there for lunch?'

The voice in my head said, 'Shoot them now'. But did I do it?

Links
Sally Haiselden

As a primary school teacher, I am always trying to make my pupils see the link between what they are learning in the classroom and the real life outside it: to get their answers to, 'Why are we learning this?' to move away from, 'So that we do well in our exams and get a good job.' Where is the joy in that? Where is the love of learning, of discovering for yourself, of finding meaning for yourself?

I travel to escape the 'good job' and in a way to become better at it. I travel to discover, to learn, to understand, because I am inquisitive and because I like to launch myself, bicycle and tent into the unknown of a landscape, its history and weather. In doing so I am left wondering how does what I know, what I have read help me to understand what I am seeing.

On a recent cycle tour of the Orkneys I had one of those moments, an epiphany, when I recognised links to places I myself had visited and so was able to understand more deeply the significance of what was in front of me and to bring life, briefly, to the people involved in the story. The story links Japan, Sudan and Egypt only because of me and where I have travelled and what I have read. Therefore this is a unique story, never told before and never would have been if I had not visited Orkney. It is a personal story that tries to relate a moment to you, that happens to all of us but not often enough, when life pulls you up short and you think, 'WOW!'

The story starts in Scapa Flow, Orkney, an iconic name, conjuring up all that bad weather can make a sea do, naval vessels, submerged wrecks and uniformed be-whiskered captains. What you see when you get there is all that, minus the bearded uniforms. During World War One and Two Scapa Flow was a strategic thoroughfare for shipping routes through to the

Baltic and a relatively sheltered haven for ships to lay at anchor. Enter the first character of this story, Sir John Jellicoe, Admiral of the Royal Navy's Grand Fleet, who set forth from Scapa Flow in May 1916 to the Battle of Jutland. At the museum at Lyness, on the island of Hoy in the Orkneys, displays list the staggering numbers of ships and men lost. In effect, there was no clear outcome to the battle but our history books record that we won, just, because after that the German sailors mutinied at conditions on board ship and so for the remainder of the war the German navy was an impotent force. Jellicoe wallowed back to Scapa Flow, with over 6000 seamen lost and 14 ships fewer than he set out with. Churchill, the second character in this story, a Liberal MP at the time and former first Lord of the Admiralty, said of him, he is, 'the only man on either side who could lose the war in an afternoon'.

A couple of days after the battle our third character enters the story: Kitchener, Secretary of State for War and that hatted, moustached figure pointing at you from the poster, 'Your Country Needs You'. He came to lend Jellicoe moral support, a 'well done' slap on the back, regardless of remarks like Churchill's. There is a photo of Kitchener just about to leave the base at Scapa Flow after lunch. He was on his way for a good will visit to Russia. We know, looking at it, that he only had a few more hours to live; he did not. As ever, the weather was atrocious and unpredictable so it was decided that the HMS Hampshire he was travelling on would go round the west of the islands and not follow the route that had already been swept for mines. The inevitable happened: off Marwick Head on mainland Orkney, the ship hit a mine. Only twelve sailors survived. So our man, demanding you serve your country, did not himself see the war out.

293

Why does Kitchener so intrigue this storyteller? Becaus
I did not know he died then. I know Kitchener as the avenger o
Gordon of Khartoum, arriving 12 years after his death. Even
though staggeringly tardy, Kitchener did right the shame of th
relief expedition that arrived two days after besieged Khartour
was overrun and Gordon murdered. Kitchener sailed up the N
to defeat the remnants of the Mahdi's followers and to stamp
Britain's authority on The Sudan again. Churchill was with hin
on this campaign, as an officer in the Hussars. The remains of
Kitchener's boat now forms part of the dock at the Blue Nile
Sailing Club in Khartoum. The mud ramparts build by the
Mahdi's followers to protect Omdurman, a suburb of Khartour
can still be seen as you walk to the souk there. But how you ma
ask do I now link Scapa, Kitchener, Churchill and Sudan to Eg
and Japan, as I have mentioned?

Let's go to Egypt and remain with our second characte
Churchill. It is now World War Two and he is Prime Minister.
The entire British fleet is anchored in Scapa Flow. Anti-
submarine nets are laid across the navigable entrances into the
Flow. Even so we continue to lose ships. In 1939 HMS Oak is
torpedoed by a U-boat, more than 800 lives are lost. The breach
of Scapa Flow's defences prompts Churchill to order barriers t
be built along the eastern edge of Scapa, four causeways joinin
four islands with the mainland. Work began in 1940 and was
completed in 1944; 66,000 five and ten ton sized concrete block
were needed. The Orcadian work force did not have the capaci
so 1300 Italian POWs captured in the Western desert of norther
Egypt were sent over.

I have visited the Italian war memorial near El Alamei
in northern Egypt where 5000 graves are swept by warm wind
brushed by white sand, sited by the most beguiling crystal blue
sea. Inside the tower are small headstones set in the wall. Some

294

have names, dates, ages on them, many just have 'Incognito' written on them. Their comrades who survived were shipped to Scapa Flow and encamped on a very small island called Little Holm at the end of the first Churchill barrier. When I cycled across the barriers, even though it was sunny, a brutal wind was blowing. There was absolutely no shelter from it. I stood and tried to imagine how the Italian POWs, used to being warmed by the sun and eating tomatoes and olive oil produced by its heat and light, coped with being incarcerated on a wind torn, rain-soaked blob of rock between the Atlantic and the North Sea. How did they deal with being in the heat of the Egyptian Sahara fighting to the death to then arrive in the midge-infested isles of green but damp Orkney? They did by first striking. They claimed that as POWs they should not be involved in acts of war and building these barriers were for the war. Churchill responded by saying the barriers were to improve the infrastructure for the people of Orkney, and they have. So the Italians responded by building a thing of beauty on Little Holm. As you crest the hill with a view of the barriers unfolded in front of you, its white walls reflect the sun. The POWs converted two Nissan huts into a chapel complete with light holders made out of corned beef tins and a font from a panel beaten car exhaust.

The final part of this story continues to head east from Scapa Flow to Sudan, to Egypt and beyond to Japan: to what happened in Japan on 6th August 1945.

At the end of World War One, the German fleet, that of the Battle of Jutland, was taken to Scapa Flow and guarded whilst the terms of peace were discussed at Versailles. Skeleton German crews manned the ships and waited and waited. Eventually, fearing that ships would be divided up amongst the Allied powers, the German commander decided to scuttle the fleet. 52 vessels sank in Scapa Flow. Little did he know he was creating an invaluable commodity.

Fast forward from 1919 to August 1945. Hiroshima was wiped out by an atom bomb. The war ended. Churchill gave his victory speech. The Italians could go home. But Scapa Flow remains significant still. The hulls of the sunken German fleet contain steel made before man released radioactive isotopes into the Earth's atmosphere. I have visited Hiroshima and watched Japanese school children leave garlands of origami cranes, symbols of peace, in the gardens around the haunting skeleton of the Hiroshima Prefectural Industrial Promotion Hall, that iconic picture of Hiroshima recognised worldwide. What happened to 166,000 people that day in August was irreversible but I had not realised that the actions of the USA unleashed another irreversible effect. We cannot produce steel anymore that is not slightly radioactive. The low-background steel preserved by that German commander in 1919 is crucial to Geiger counters, medical, scientific and space equipment which require optimal sensitivity to radiation levels.

That is the end of my story. If Kitchener had not acquitted himself admirably in Sudan he may not have become Secretary of State for War. His death was a wakeup call to the vulnerability of ships in Scapa Flow. Churchill recognised this and as luck would have it found a labour force of Italians from Egypt to come and build his protective barriers. And from Hiroshima, Japan, even though the air flowing over Scapa is contaminated, what remains below the surface is a valuable, crucial resource for all nations, for everyone. If I had not travelled to Sudan, Egypt and Japan this story would not have been told. What a story I have to tell my new class.

Reverse Culture Shock
Jane Wilson-Howarth

Nepali pilots try to avoid flying through cloud because there are mountains in them. The himals are so vast that you often have to crane your neck and look above the cloud to enjoy the stunning scenes of snow-caps with their trailing spindrift scarves against an azure sky.

When we returned to East Anglia after six years in Nepal the greenness of our home seemed deliciously, extravagantly lush but we missed contours terribly. At weekends we sought hills and views and early on told our oldest son we'd visit the Bronze Age fort at Wandlebury. We didn't tell him that although this was a Cambridgeshire highpoint, the altitude we'd ascend to was 75m. As we approached the hill we asked him what he thought of Cambridge's Everest. He did the Nepali thing of looking towards where we pointed and, seeing no more than a pimple on the landscape, looked up above the clouds. He was appalled that Wandlebury had even earned the title of hill. And he was also mightily unimpressed that our region boasts the UK's lowest point: Holme Fen at 2.75m below sea level.

For me coming home was invigorating; I was seeing everything as if for the first time – noticing delightful detail, resolving to try new things and explore new places. The Chinese say there is no scenery in your home town. They're right; you don't see it. But being away in another place allows you to see again. It heightens the senses, makes you more observant, allows you to enjoy more, take delight in small things; it makes life richer. Not only does travel make you feel more alive, less cocooned, but the home-coming is poignant too.

Continuing the quest for contours, we found the Devil's Dyke. Walking the seven-and-a-half-mile length of it you can appreciate that it must have been an effective barrier to invasion.

My son's imagination was piqued by the fact that such an impressive wall could have been built by ancient people. It is up to 11m high and in places it is too steep to scale. What impressed him most though was that there had once existed a civilisation so lofty as to build their own mountains. And this – he suggested – was what we needed to do to solve the difficulty of surviving the flatness of East Anglia. We needed to construct our own mountain range. If unsophisticated Iron Age peoples or Saxon warlords had managed it without earth-moving equipment, then why couldn't we – in our tiny back garden?

Home?
Sally Haiselden

*A homecoming poem written after returning from three and a half years
of working as an education specialist in rural Uganda and South
Sudan.*

I don't want to be here
But I am
Unpacking…A friend Cassie says
'It's a bit like Christmas
complete with ridiculous items that you will never use and
wonder why you have them.'
They're now in bin bags, down Mill Road
To the Sally Army
This Sally army, just me
Trying to get my life in order
Things in their allotted place
'Where did I used to fit those baking trays?'
A rectangular shape in too small a space
Me, cliché,
Square peg in round space
This space – Cromwell Road, Cambridge, the education system,
teaching
Another rectangular space-the classroom
But as I have always thought
And believed for pupils
There's a life outside the classroom, that rectangle
I gaze out from my four walls
Trying to concentrate on a job application or writing
Like this
Beyond the back garden, a tree

A tall, pendulous acacia
Branching, majestic
Transported, in my mind
From Makinyde Hill, Kampala
I am back there, searching
Searching each bulbous pendula for….
A blue turaco
Here, I see…
A magpie
Uniquely singular but not described as..
'A psychedelic flying turkey',
Now where?
Nowhere.
A magpie, smart, black and white, as good as you can get
Home? Where?
At the moment,
As good as you can get.

(October 20

ABOUT THE AUTHORS

Stephanie Green

When family commitments lessened, Stephanie travelled to Australia to visit a friend. From the plane she saw a green volcanic island surrounded by an azure sea and determined to visit it. Since then she's visited Asia, South America and Africa and has travelled around England on a narrow boat. She has just launched a memoir called *Wide Woman on a Narrow Boat* on learning, loving and hating the life aboard and observing the life on the canal and riverbanks. She hasn't found her island yet but is still looking for it.

She has contributed pieces to the anthology on what it is to be a tourist, a guest, an ex-pat and a traveller.

Sally Haiselden

Sally likes nothing better than to pack her tent on the back of her bicycle and head off with the minimal of plans. Travelling by bike means she is immersed in the environment and the moment. She has had several 'moments' on her bike including cycling home to Cambridge from Khartoum (http://www.cambridge-news.co.uk/Teachers-cycle-ride-globe/story-22461965-detail/story.html) and touring in Uganda, South Sudan, Iceland and most recently the Outer Hebrides,

Orkney and Shetland. In other moments she tries to instil in her current class of primary school kids an understanding of life outside the classroom. She uses the school holidays to support initiatives to improve the quality of education in northern Uganda and war-torn South Sudan.

Françoise Hivernel

Françoise arrived on English shores from France in the 1970s. After a full life beginning with Archaeology leading slowly to Psychoanalysis and then retirement (www.en.wikipedia.org/wiki/Francoise_Hivernel), she is now considering what to do. She spent over 15 years working as an archaeologist in Ethiopia, Lebanon, Kenya and Jordan, researching her PhD and writing a number of academic articles. After that she slowly slithered towards a career in psychoanalysis and, with colleagues, wrote the first book on Françoise Dolto in English: *Theory and Practice in Child Psychoanalysis.* She then, with a colleague, translated into English Françoise Dolto's seminal work, *Psychoanalysis and Paediatrics.* Most recently Françoise published a travel narrative, *Safartu: travels with my children,* which describes her work and extensive travels in Africa and the Middle East before and then with her children.

Seeta Siriwardena

Seeta fled Sri Lanka when she and her husband feared for their lives. The family arrived in England by ship in 1971 from Colombo. She is a doctor and worked in a hospital as a paediatric registrar, then as a School Medical Officer and a tutor in mental handicap at the Children's Hospital in Birmingham and became a General Practitioner in 1976.

She brought up three children while working and they are now all in medicine. Her professional life has been shaped by following her husband's medical career and trying to have a family life at the same time. Her almost lifelong contact with sick children prompted her to write an adventure story for children called *Maya and the Dragon* which was published in 2016. This has been followed by *The Lonely Cat* in 2017.

She has contributed five pieces on her various adventures in India, Egypt and London and the serendipitous events that have occurred in her life. Seeta's writes poignantly about her pilgrimage to India, reminding us that – even to someone raised in Sri Lanka – it was a foreign and challenging country to visit. She was even nervous of eating the local food and took the precaution of travelling with a large supply of biscuits in her suitcase.

Jane Wilson-Howarth

Jane has been fascinated by wildlife for as long as she can remember and has always had a hankering after adventure. In her teens she discovered that cave exploration was one way of being intrepid without leaving Britain and then that caving in the tropics held even more excitement. She worked as a doctor in various remote corners of Asia for 11 years and in the autumn of 2017 moved back to the Kathmandu Valley where she is currently working with PHASE Nepal.

She is passionate about natural history and wild places and aspires to become a better linguist so she can eaves-drop more successfully. Eight of her books (all of which have appeared in multiple editions) have been published so far; these are detailed at www.wilson-howarth.com where there is also a blog. Her Instagram account is @wilson.howarth. She has compiled nearly 200 thousand-word health features for *Wanderlust* magazine and writes on occasion for other magazines and national newspapers.

Her contributions to this anthology reflect her delight in the natural world and her passion for supporting the underdog.

Travel Books by the Authors

Green, Stephanie 2016. *Wide Woman on a Narrow Boat.* FeedaRead

Hivernel, Françoise 2015. *Safartu: travels with my children.* FeedaRead.

Siriwardena, Seeta 2016. *Maya and the Dragon.* Vijitha Yapa Publications.

Siriwardena, Seeta 2017. *The Lonely Cat.* Melrose Books.

Wilson, Jane 1990, 1995. *Lemurs of the Lost World.* Impact Books.

Wilson-Howarth, Jane 2007, 2012, 2015. *A Glimpse of Eternal Snows.* Bradt Travel Guides & Speaking Tiger.

Wilson-Howarth, Jane 2017. *Snowfed Waters.* Speaking Tiger Books.

Awaiting Publication:

Green, Stephanie. *A Wiser Woman on a Narrow Boat.*

Haiselden, Sally. *Khartoum to Cambridge on a Bike.*

Haiselden, Sally. *'Mwono Bye!' A Teacher's Guide to volunteering in northern Uganda.*

Lightning Source UK Ltd.
Milton Keynes UK
UKHW042118060219
336867UK00001B/23/P

9 781788 764285